Voices of
Alberta

People, Places, and Possibilities

PEARSON

Education
Canada

Toronto

Dedicated to the Grade 4 students of Alberta whose inquiring minds have inspired this resource.

ISBN 0-13-173744-9

Grade 4 Project Team
Publisher: Susan Cox
Product Manager: Patti Henderson
Executive Editor: Elynor Kagan
Coordinating Editor: Rosalyn Steiner
Development Team: Susie Berg, Sheila Fletcher, Patrick Gallagher, Susan Hughes, Cara James, Judith Scott
Production Editorial Team: Allana Barron, Ann Echlin, Susan Ginsberg, Anita Levin, Rebecca Vogan
Production Coordinator: Helen Luxton
Design and Composition: Word & Image Design Studio Inc.
Maps: Crowle Art Group
Illustrators: Diane Dawson Hearn, Clive Dobson, Stephen MacEachern, Paul McCusker, Allan Moon
Research: Darcy Dobell, Catherine Rondina, Norman Sacuta
Photo Researchers and Permissions: Christina Beamish, Lisa Brant, Sandy Cooke, Glen Herbert, Karen Hunter, Amanda McCormick, Lynn McIntyre, Terri Rothman

Pearson Education Canada gratefully acknowledges Alberta Education's support in the resource-development process and the support of the many teachers/educators who have provided advice and feedback for Alberta Education over the course of the development of *Voices of Alberta: People, Places, and Possibilities*.

Printed and bound in the U.S.A.
1 2 3 4 5 QC 10 09 08 07 06

ACKNOWLEDGEMENTS

Student Resource Author Team

Leanne Baugh-Peterson
Susie Berg
Lynn Bryan
Andrea Cartwright
Alisa Dewald
Louise Finlaison
Sheila Fletcher
Susan Hughes

Carolyn Hunter
Sonya Irvine
Fiona Kramer
Jenifer Ludbrook
Elizabeth MacLeod
Sharlene McGowan
Edie Reichardt
Deborah Seed

Program Advisors and Reviewers

Pearson Education Canada thanks its Program Advisors and Reviewers, who helped shape *Voices of Alberta: People, Places, and Possibilities* through discussions and reviews of prototype materials and manuscript.

Program Advisors

Melina Akins
Dana Antaya-Moore
Lynn Arnold
Jim Barritt
Andrea Cartwright
Elizabeth Cressman
Bev den Ouden

Anne Gafiuk
David Harvey
Kay Haslett
Bob Hesketh
Carolyn Hunter
Fiona Kramer
Renee Mikkelson

Edie Reichardt
Dr. Alan Sears
Tom Smith
Michelle Sutton

Subject Specialist Reviewers

Lynn Anderson
Lynn Arnold
Bob Beal
Louise Breland
Leith Campbell
Dean Cunningham
Darcy Dobell
Ken Ealey
Leo Fox

Glenbow Museum Staff
    Dr. Gerald Conaty, Sandra
    Crazy Bull, Michale Lang,
    Holly Schmidt
Diane Gregson
Victor Fines
Angela Hall
Carrol Jaques
Dr. France Levasseur-Ouimet

Mark McCallum
Carole-Sophie Mitchell
Robert Morrow
Ben Moses
Anne Mulgrew
Fern Reirson
Jim Scott
Cliff Whitford
Colin Woelfle

Grade 4 Field-Test Teachers

Pearson Education would like to thank the reviewers and the teachers and students who field-tested *Voices of Alberta* prior to publication. Their feedback and constructive recommendations have been most valuable in helping to develop quality social studies resources.

Karen Anderson, Sunalta Elementary, Calgary Board of Education

Lynn Arnold, Jackson Heights School, Edmonton SD

Vaughn Atkinson, Nicholas Sheran, Lethbridge SD

Desiree Baratta, Good Shepherd School, Edmonton Catholic SD

Ann Baty, Caladonia Park School, Black Gold SD

Stephanie Cardinal, Holy Family, Red Deer Catholic SD

Jodi Carlson, Carseland Elementary, Golden Hills SD

Nicole Carney, Roland Michener Elementary School, Calgary Board of Education

CherylAnne Coon-Senchuk, Good Shepherd School, Edmonton Catholic SD

Elizabeth Cressy, Parkdale Elementary, Edmonton SD

Sue Crocker, Our Lady of Peace School, Calgary Catholic SD

Shelley Davis Forman, Vulcan Prairieview Elementary, Palliser SD

Cheryl Dawes, Blueberry School, Parkland SD

David Dempsey, St. Joseph Catholic Elementary School, Evergreen SD

Wayne Durksen, Robert Rundle School, St. Albert SD

Joe Gillis, Father Doucet School, Calgary Catholic SD

Mike Goldmintz, Edgemont School, Calgary Board of Education

Sandra Greenslade, Ministik School, Elk Island SD

Gina Hanevich, St. Mary Elementary, Edmonton Catholic SD

Pamela Lazowski, Stratford School, Edmonton SD

Katie Little, Jackson Heights School, Edmonton SD

Celeste I. Lorenzen, École Elizabeth Barrett School, Rockyview SD

Cindy Macauley, Midnapore Elementary, Calgary Board of Education

Jeff Miller, St. Joseph Catholic School, Evergreen SD

Kevin Newman, Percy Pegler School, FSD 38

Dianne Nykolyshyn, Our Lady of Victories Elementary School, Edmonton Catholic SD

Natalie Oliphant, Elm Street School, SD 76

Bela Paleja, Grant McEwan Elementary, Calgary Board of Education

Carol Perry, École Elizabeth Barrett School, Rockyview SD

Michael Pollack, Viking Colony School, Battle River SD

Oriana Profiri, St. Bernadette School, Edmonton Catholic SD

Kathy Rachmistruk, Dunluce School, Edmonton SD

Sandra Raposo, St. Gabriel the Archangel School, Calgary Catholic SD

Deirdre Richardson, Sunalta Elementary, Calgary Board of Education

Sue Scott, Norwood School, Edmonton SD

Renee Shevalier-Lavin, Good Shepherd School, Edmonton Catholic SD

Kevin Shilling, Grandview Elementary School, Red Deer Public SD

Dale Todd Sikorski, Sifton School, Battle River SD

Dory Smyth, Holy Cross School. Calgary Catholic SD

Joyce Stretch, St. Rita School, Calgary Catholic SD

Wayne Teske, St. Ambrose Elementary, Calgary Catholic SD

Miss Lori White, C.P. Blakely School, Chinook's Edge SD

Jean Wishloff, Westboro School, Elk Island SD

Grade 4 Teacher Reviewers

Lynsay Atchison, Lamont Elementary School, Elk Island SD

Teresa Behl, Eugene Coste Elementary, Calgary Board of Education

Anne Butner, Colchester School, Elk Island SD

Meghan Calder, St. Patrick Fine Arts Elementary School, Holy Spirit SD

Shauna Dunning, Jack Stuart School, Battle River SD #31

Jefferey Girard, Our Lady of the Prairies Elementary School, Edmonton Catholic SD

Mary Grant, Vanier Community Catholic School, Living Waters SD

Penny Holst, Enchant Colony School, Horizon SD #67

Brenda Lochtie, Glen Allan Elementary School, Elk Island SD

Tammy Marks, J.C. Charyk, Prairieland School Division #25

Linda Nicholson, St. Thomas More, Grande Prairie Catholic SD #28

Barb O'Connor, Acadia Elementary School, Calgary Board of Education

Russanne Perry, Beacon Heights, Edmonton SD

Geraldine Plumb, H.A. Kostash School, Aspenview SD

Lauren Podlubny, St. Gabriel Elementary School, Edmonton Catholic SD

Marlo Price, Camilla School, Sturgeon School Division

Tiffany Smith, Chief Justice Milvain School, Calgary Board of Education

Bonnie Wawrykow, St. Maria Goretti, Edmonton Catholic SD

K. Janet Wilkinson, Westhaven School, Grande Yellowhead Regional Division

Linda Wnuk, Rosalind School, Battle River SD

CONTENTS

Getting Started

Alberta: Then and Now

I sometimes imagine I can see
The way Alberta used to be—
Blackfoot and Plains Cree, hunting buffalo,
Then Canadiens trading furs where the rivers flow.

Métis carts on the prairie wide,
Then farms and towns in the countryside,
As British, Ukrainians, and others too
Settled the land and Alberta grew.

Today there are cities and industries,
But still there's rangeland, crops, and trees.
When I think of it all, it's wonderful how
Alberta's past is part of now.

Alberta: Many Places, Many People

I magine you have been asked to create a time capsule that would tell people in the future about your community. What would you put in it? Photographs? Newspapers? Clothing? Toys? Think hard and ask yourself, "What would people learn about my community's history and culture? What would they learn from these objects about who we are?"

Something like this has already happened. To celebrate Alberta's Centennial, the 100th birthday of the province, communities all over the province made their own time capsules. They collected all sorts of items to tell people of the future about Alberta today. All these capsules were gathered together and put in an Alberta Centennial Time Capsule. In 100 years, Albertans will open the capsule and find out about all the places and people who make up Alberta today.

January 26, 2006

Alberta Centennial Time Capsule Touches Down at Royal Alberta Museum

Edmonton – Alberta's Centennial Time Capsule, loaded with Albertans' memories and mementos, will spend the next 100 years at the Royal Alberta Museum.

Celebrating 100 YEARS

2005 Alberta Centennial

Outside the Alberta Centennial Time Capsule

Alberta's Story

This book tells the story of Alberta. As you will discover, the story of Alberta is not really just one story. It is made up of many different stories, just like Alberta's Centennial Time Capsule. These stories tell about many places and many times—even times before it was called Alberta. They also tell about many different people who have lived here in the past, and who live here now. All these stories helped make Alberta what it is today.

You have a story, too. Your story is part of what Alberta is today, and what it will be in the future.

words matter!

Quality of life refers to a person's or community's sense of safety, comfort, security, health, and happiness.

? Inquiring Minds

Inquiring minds are questioning minds, searching minds. Your inquiring mind will guide you when you explore the land, history, and stories of Alberta. Throughout your Alberta exploration, think about the following questions:

- How do the land and its natural resources affect **quality of life** for people in Alberta?
- How do stories, history, and culture give people in Alberta a sense of identity and belonging?
- How do people and events help to change Alberta over time?

All year, you'll be gathering information to help answer these questions. You'll return to them in Wrapping Up at the end of the book. Then you will see how much you have learned!

Partners in Inquiry

An **inquiry** is an investigation into a topic, especially by asking questions.

Meet the ten companions who will join you on your Alberta exploration. They will be your Partners in **Inquiry**. Like you, they will be exploring the land, history, and stories of Alberta. You will find their thoughts and questions throughout the book.

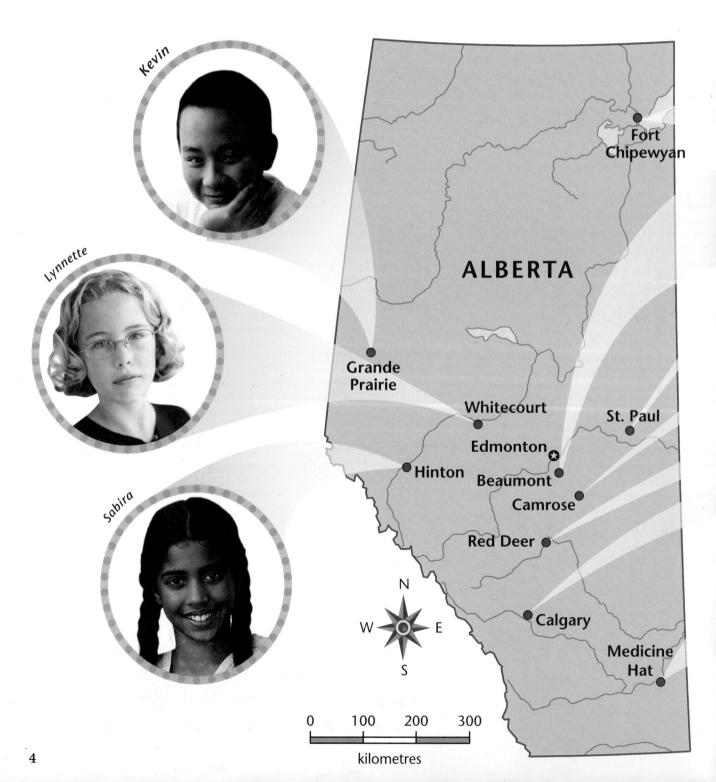

Kevin

Lynnette

Sabira

ALBERTA

Fort Chipewyan

Grande Prairie

Whitecourt

St. Paul

Edmonton

Hinton

Beaumont

Camrose

Red Deer

Calgary

Medicine Hat

N
W E
S

0   100   200   300

kilometres

Anita

Carlos

Natasha

Giselle

Marc

Omar

Justin

Where would your community be on the map? Which of the Partners in Inquiry lives closest to you? Look at the scale at the bottom of the map. It helps you tell the distance between places.

5

What Is in This Book?

Take a look through the book. Check out the main headings and photos—they'll give you an idea of what the book is about.

Now take a closer look. You'll spot your Partners in Inquiry, of course. You'll also see features that help you understand what you are reading and guide your inquiry. Let's learn about a few of those features.

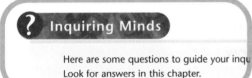

Inquiring Minds: See an example on page 3.

- The inquiry questions you read on page 3 are the ones you will think about all year.
- There are other inquiry questions on the second page of each chapter. They will provide you with a purpose for reading and exploration. Your Partners in Inquiry will be thinking about these questions, too.

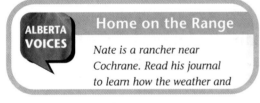

Alberta Voices: See an example on page 79.

This is where people tell a personal story about something in the chapter.

Viewpoints: See an example on pages 72–73.

On these pages, you will look at different opinions or viewpoints about something important. You will also get a chance to give your own viewpoint.

Now do some of your own exploring. With a partner, pick a chapter to look through and find these other features: **Words Matter!**, **Skill Smart**, **Skill Power**, **Then and Now**, **Thinking It Through**, **Set Your Skills in Motion**, **Alberta Adventure**, **Imagine This!**, and **Alberta Treasure Chest**. Talk about why these might be in the book and how you will use them.

How Can I Begin My Inquiry?

Alberta is here for you to discover. You will enjoy finding out about Alberta more if you first decide what you'd like to explore. As the diagram on pages 8 and 9 shows, the first step in an inquiry is to ask questions. Then search for answers. Once you find out what you want to know, you might discover that you have even more questions. There's always more to explore!

This book can guide you in your exploration. It will help you learn how to find information and how to gather what you need for your inquiry. It will help you understand the information you find. It will show you how to share your information with others.

Enjoy your adventure!

The Information Quest

There are many places to look for information as part of your inquiry. Look at the list below. Where else can you find information?

• Books	• Maps
• Magazines	• Paintings
• Newspapers	• People who know
• Letters	• Museums
• Diaries	• The Internet
• Television	•
• Photos	•

When I came to Alberta, my aunt gave me a pin with a pink rose on it. She said it is one of Alberta's provincial symbols. I wonder why.

This diagram shows some questions you can ask as you explore the land, history, and stories of Alberta.

I'm enjoying making a poster to show what I've found. It helps me sort my information and then share it with the class.

Evaluating

What can I learn from this inquiry that will help with my next inquiry?

Do I need to take action based on my information?

Sharing

Am I going to share what I've found?

If so, how will I share it?

I'll start by planning my inquiry.

Planning ❯

Retrieving

What questions do I need to ask?

How will I find the information?

Reflecting

Thinking About Your Inquiry

How will I record my information?

Is my information accurate and reliable?

There's so much information. It's hard to know what to use! My plan should help.

How will I organize my information?

Do I need to ask other questions?

Processing

Creating ❮

Turn the page to see how Natasha used this model.

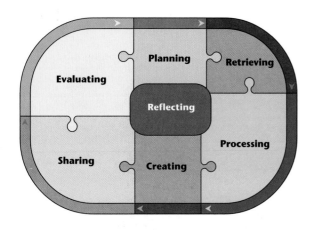

What Might an Inquiry Look Like?

To start her Alberta Adventure, Natasha had something she was wondering about. See how she followed the Inquiring Minds model to find the answer.

PLANNING: Asking a question

"Why is the wild rose one of Alberta's symbols?"

RETRIEVING: Searching for information

"I could research with a friend and look on the Internet."

PROCESSING: Writing, checking, and wondering

"I've checked information on three Web sites and in a book—that should do it."

"I'd like to find more places where the symbol is used."

Information about the Alberta wild rose	Where can I see the symbol?
- bush with pink flowers - grows wild almost everywhere in Alberta -	- pink colour in Alberta tartan - Coat of arms -

CREATING: Putting it together

"Now I'll pick out the important points."

SHARING: Telling others

"I think I'll make a computer slide show."

Alberta's Provincial Flower

Alberta is called "Wild Rose Country." Do you know why?

EVALUATING: Thinking about your inquiry

- "I could have used a web instead of boxes."
- "The wild rose was chosen because it grows wild almost all over Alberta. People see it and they think *Alberta*!"

Where Is Alberta Located in Canada?

Before we continue exploring Alberta, it would be a good idea to look at a few more things. First, what do you know about where Alberta is located in Canada?

Look at the map below. It shows all of Canada's provinces and territories, and the capital city of each one. The capital city is where the government of each province or territory meets to make its decisions. The capital city of Canada is Ottawa, Ontario.

- Which provinces and territories are Alberta's neighbours?
- How would you describe Alberta's geographic location—that is, its location in relation to its neighbours?

Using Direction to Locate Places on a Map

Cardinal Directions

Intermediate Directions

How did you describe Alberta's geographic location in Canada? It can be difficult to describe the geographic location of a place unless you use a compass rose.

You probably already know the cardinal directions of a compass rose: north, south, west, and east. When we want to give more exact directions, we can also use intermediate directions: northwest, northeast, southwest, and southeast. Look at the compass rose showing intermediate directions. What do the letters stand for?

Practise the Skill

Use the compass rose and the map of Canada to answer these questions:

1. Which province is west of Alberta?
2. Which territories are north of Alberta?
3. In which direction do you go from Alberta to reach Manitoba?
4. Which territory is northwest of Alberta?
5. Which provincial capital city is southwest of Edmonton?
6. Describe Edmonton's location relative to a) Whitehorse, b) Iqaluit, and c) Ottawa.
7. What compass direction is halfway between south and east?

Now try again to answer the question on the previous page: How would you describe the location of Alberta in Canada using the compass rose?

What Will I Do on My Inquiry?

Now let's look at what you will do on your Alberta inquiry. You will

- learn about the people, places, and challenges that make up Alberta's story
- explore your part in Alberta's story
- be involved in inquiries, projects, and activities

Alberta Treasure Chest

You may want to save many items from your year-long exploration. They will show that there is much to treasure about Alberta—much that makes it a unique place you can be proud of.

- You could keep your work in a file folder or a shoebox. You could even make a special "treasure chest." Each time you view your treasures, you'll have a chance to reflect on what makes Alberta unique.
- You can share your work with others so they can appreciate all of Alberta's treasures.

Look at the pictures on this page. Which ones do you want to learn more about?

Set Your Skills in Motion

Make a Compass Rose

Use craft sticks and glue to make a compass rose.
Label each stick with its direction.

- Find out which way is north. Now use your
  compass rose to play "I spy" with a partner.
  Choose an object and give your partner cardinal
  and intermediate directions. You should each have
  at least two turns.

Look What You Know Already!

Review the inquiry questions for the year:

- How do the land and its natural resources affect quality of life for
  people in Alberta?
- How do stories, history, and culture give people in Alberta a sense
  of identity and belonging?
- How do people and events help to change Alberta over time?

Make a chart similar to the one below.

Land, Natural Resources, and Quality of Life
-
-
Sense of Identity and Belonging
-
-
Change Alberta
-

Under each heading, briefly jot down what you know or think.
Exchange lists with someone. Ask questions to help you understand
some points on each other's lists.

Perhaps you could save your chart as an Alberta
Treasure. It could tell quite a story as you fill it in.

Explore the Land

Imagine walking through a grassy field in the foothills of southern Alberta. In the distance, you can see the Rocky Mountains. Suddenly you spot something up ahead. As you walk closer, it gets bigger and bigger. It looms over you, as big as a three-storey building. It's a rock—a *big* rock! What is a huge rock doing in the middle of an empty field? Where could it have come from? Why is it here?

What you see is "Big Rock," outside the town of Okotoks. Big Rock is unlike any of the rocks around it. It is made of quartzite, a type of rock found in the mountains. In fact, it has travelled hundreds of kilometres to get where it is now!

Alberta's Story

You must be wondering how Big Rock got to where it is now. In this chapter, you'll find out about Big Rock and other stories of the land in Alberta. You'll learn that, millions of years ago, the land did not look like it does now. It changed over time, and was shaped in a way that makes Alberta unique. You'll also explore the different parts or regions of Alberta as they are today.

? Inquiring Minds

Here are some inquiry questions to keep in mind while exploring this chapter:

- How have the unique land features of Alberta been shaped over time?
- What is it like living in each of the regions of Alberta?

Look for answers in this chapter.

Mount Columbia is the highest mountain in Alberta. Why does Alberta have mountains?

Alberta has sand dunes! They are at Lake Athabasca. I wonder where this sand came from.

The area near High Level is good for growing crops. I wonder why.

What Does Alberta Look Like?

The next six pages will show you some different parts of Alberta. Think about unique features that make them different from one another. Which place is similar to where you live?

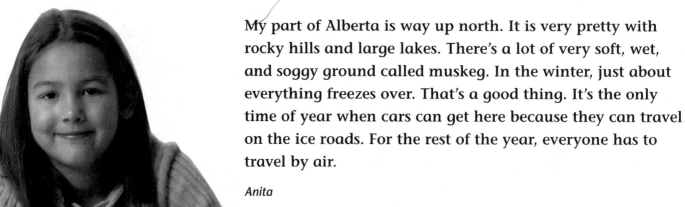

My part of Alberta is way up north. It is very pretty with rocky hills and large lakes. There's a lot of very soft, wet, and soggy ground called muskeg. In the winter, just about everything freezes over. That's a good thing. It's the only time of year when cars can get here because they can travel on the ice roads. For the rest of the year, everyone has to travel by air.

Anita

Thinking
It Through

Compare the pictures on these two pages.

■ How are these two parts of Alberta different?

■ How are they similar?

Where I live, there are lakes and rivers, but mostly thick forests. There are also wet muddy marshes with tall grasses growing in them. There must be something just right about our marshes and lakes because in April the very rare trumpeter swans come to nest. We also have some farmland. The swans often stop and rest in the farmers' fields—especially when the rain has flooded them.

Kevin

19

We live in a place where two big rivers meet. We're close enough to the mountains to have lots of rolling hills and forests—and snow, too. In the summer we can go hiking and bike riding along trails. The trails go through our town and into the hills, past the ranches, and through the trees. In the winter, we have lots of fun cross-country skiing on the trails.

Lynnette

Thinking
It Through

People come from all over the world to see the Rocky Mountains. Why do you think they come?

To me, Alberta is jagged, snow-capped mountains. We live right at the foot of one. I love the smell of the pine trees when I hike up mountain paths with my uncle and cousins. Pinecones and wildflowers are everywhere. We usually look for a spot by a clear mountain stream to have a picnic. We often go on drives in the mountains to see snowy peaks and waterfalls.

Sabira

There's a lot of farmland where I live. I help my dad on the farm, but there's also time for fun. In the spring, I hunt for frog eggs along the ditches. In summer, the timothy grass grows so tall that I can disappear by walking into the field. In fall, I make forts in the broken hay bales. In winter, I ride across the snowdrifts with friends from the other farms.

Natasha

Thinking
It Through

Look back at the pages about parts of Alberta (pages 18–23).

■ Which part seems most like where you live? In what ways?

■ Which part of Alberta would you like to visit? What would you do there?

Do you like to be HOT in the summer? If you do, then my part of Alberta is the place for you. The land can be dry here, and we don't have many trees, but there are lots of farms and ranches. The farms grow crops like wheat, barley, and oats. I like the farms that grow my favourites—corn and tomatoes. My mom buys them fresh at the farmers' market. De-li-cious!

Justin

What Is the Story of the Land?

Geologists study land and rocks, and how they are formed.

Glaciers are very thick sheets of ice and snow that move slowly across the land.

Landscape is the natural scenery of a very large area.

Landforms are the different features of the land, such as mountains, hills, or plains.

These events helped shape and change Alberta. That'll help me answer one of our inquiry questions for the year.

The land of Alberta has quite a story! **Geologists** tell us that changes in the land have been going on for millions of years.

First, what is now Alberta was covered with rock. Then, huge oceans formed and covered the rock with water. Later, the rock pushed upwards and became the Rocky Mountains. Then, the oceans drained away, leaving the mountains towering above the land. Geologists also tell us there were earthquakes and volcanoes, and that for thousands of years **glaciers** covered the land.

All of this has given Alberta unique **landscapes** and **landforms**.

Today, the Rocky Mountains are part of Alberta's unique landscape. At one time, there were no mountains here.

How Is Big Rock Part of the Story?

As the glaciers melted, they created unique landforms. One of these is Big Rock.

Huge rocks fell onto a glacier from a mountain near Jasper. The ice slowly moved, carrying the rocks out of the mountains. When the ice melted, the rocks were left along the foothills. The largest one is Big Rock.

What Are Some Big Rock Stories?

Okotoks is famous because of Big Rock. For thousands of years, the First Nations used Big Rock as a landmark to guide them when they travelled. People today still look for it as a sign that they are nearing Okotoks.

Big Rock: A Blackfoot Story

This story is about Big Rock, but it also tells of important values. What can you learn about generosity and honesty from this story?

Napi was out with Fox on a very hot day. When they came to a large rock, Napi took off his robe and threw it over the rock, saying, "Here, I make you a present of this robe." Napi went on, but saw a rain cloud coming up. He sent Fox back to get the robe. "No," said the Rock. "He gave it to me as a present. If you give anything to a Rock, you cannot take it back."

Fox returned to Napi and told him what the Rock had said. Napi was angry. So he ran up to the Rock and took the robe. Then Napi started on, but suddenly heard a great noise behind him. When Napi looked back, he saw the Rock coming. It was rolling along.

So Napi and Fox ran, but all the time the Rock was getting closer. Finally, Napi called for help from some Meadow Larks. The Meadow Larks stopped the Rock and broke it into pieces that we still see today.

Niitsitapiisinni: Our Way of Life (Glenbow Museum Exhibit)

A Part of Life

When we get visitors, we always take them out to Big Rock. We stand in the middle of our flat prairie grass and look up at this huge rock. As we drive out of town, we pass the Big Rock Inn, Big Rock Towing, and Big Rock School. People who live in Okotoks use the name "Big Rock" every day. It's part of our way of life.

Pat Shultz
Okotoks resident

The name "Okotoks" comes from the Siksika or Blackfoot word for "rock."

Life by the River

I love living near the river. My dad takes me fishing. We catch northern pike and walleye. If we're lucky, we get a trout or goldeye. We also skip stones across the water. We look for the flattest, smoothest stones, and flick them across the surface to see how many times they skip. I once had a stone skip eight times before it sank! When I'm older, we're going to go whitewater rafting on the river. Lots of people come to raft around here. I can't wait!

Laura Hohn
Red Deer

How Did Glaciers Create Lakes and Rivers?

Is your community beside a river or a lake? If so, then it's likely you can see evidence of Alberta's icy past. When the glaciers melted, they made Alberta a place with many rivers.

Glaciers still provide some of the water for Alberta's rivers. Some rivers, like the North Saskatchewan River and the Athabasca River, begin in the glaciers of the Columbia Icefield, near Jasper.

River Communities

Throughout the story of Alberta, rivers have been important to people. The First Nations people fished the rivers and also used them for travel. Paddling in their canoes, they could cover great distances. When the first Europeans came, they also used the rivers as highways. They built forts beside the rivers. Their forts were their homes, their stores, and their warehouses. Later, many more settlements grew by rivers.

Why do you think people choose to settle near rivers and lakes? Give at least four reasons.

The Athabasca River is the longest river that begins and ends in Alberta. It winds from the Columbia Icefield in the Rocky Mountains to Lake Athabasca, in northeastern Alberta.

Major Lakes and Rivers

Map of Alberta showing major lakes and rivers, with compass rose (N, W, E, S) and scale (0, 100, 200, 300 kilometres).

Labels on the map:
- Hay River
- Slave River
- Peace River
- Lake Claire
- Lake Athabasca
- Fort McMurray
- Peace River
- ALBERTA
- Lesser Slave Lake
- Grande Prairie
- Lac La Biche
- Cold Lake
- Athabasca River
- ROCKY MOUNTAINS
- Edmonton
- North Saskatchewan River
- Jasper
- Red Deer
- Red Deer River
- Calgary
- Bow River
- Medicine Hat
- South Saskatchewan River
- Oldman River
- Lethbridge
- Milk River

Thinking It Through

What part do you think rivers and lakes play in the location of cities and towns?

THEN ◆ AND ◆ NOW

In Edmonton in 1909, Fred Marshall got a rowboat to take people across the North Saskatchewan River. He charged 5 cents a trip! Now, there are bridges that cross the river. Many people can cross the river at one time.

27

How Were Other Features Shaped?

As the glaciers melted, other features were formed. Read about some of them below.

As the glaciers melted, lakes formed in many places. Today, we still have some mountain lakes that are fed by melting water from glaciers. They are called glacial lakes. They are often a beautiful light blue colour, as you can see in the photograph of Bow Lake shown here.

The Canadian Shield is in the northeast corner of Alberta. Here, rocks from many millions of years ago still cover much of the land. Long ago, the rocks were ground down by glaciers. Now, they are shaped by wind and water.

Hoodoos are also shaped by wind and water. The soft stones of the bottom layers have been worn away, but not the hard top ones. This gives the hoodoos their unique shape. Hoodoos are found in several places in Alberta, including the badlands near Drumheller, and in the mountains near Banff.

Skill Smart

Look on the Internet or in books to find out more about the Canadian Shield in Alberta. Keep track of where you get your information.

My Visit to a Glacier

ALBERTA

Edmonton
Jasper
Columbia Icefield
Banff
Calgary

You've seen how glaciers shaped Alberta's land, but would you like a unique glacier experience? That's what I had when my family visited the Columbia Icefield. It's a huge field of ice and snow not far from Jasper. Eight glaciers slope down from the icefield like gigantic tongues. You can get right onto one of them—the Athabasca Glacier.

We took a tour on an Ice Explorer, a big bus with massive wheels. It drove us onto the glacier so we could walk around and take a closer look.

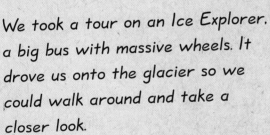

The surface of the glacier is amazing. It's covered with tiny cracks and streamlets running with pure icy water. There are also deep crevasses in the ice, so you have to be careful. If you don't watch out, you could fall in!

What Are Alberta's Natural Regions?

words matter!

A **natural region** is an area with its own natural vegetation, climate, and landforms.

Earlier in this chapter, you learned that Alberta has a varied landscape. There are several areas of the province, each one different from the other. We call these areas **natural regions**. Alberta has six natural regions, as shown in the map below. The combination of all the regions gives Alberta its unique character.

Skill Smart

Look at the map.

- Which natural region covers the biggest area?

- Look back to the parts of Alberta you explored on pages 18–23. Match them to the regions shown on these two pages.

Alberta's Natural Regions

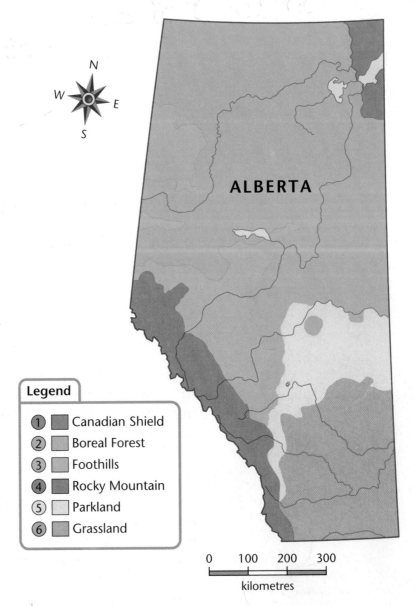

Legend

1. Canadian Shield
2. Boreal Forest
3. Foothills
4. Rocky Mountain
5. Parkland
6. Grassland

0   100   200   300

kilometres

1 Canadian Shield

This rocky region in the north has many lakes and marshes. There is little soil in this region, and only certain types of plants can grow here. Some of these plants only grow in this part of Alberta.

2 Boreal Forest

This region takes up most of the northern part of Alberta. It is almost entirely covered with trees. These trees are used in the forest industries. The region has rolling hills and plains. There are also many rivers and wetlands.

3 Foothills

This region is made up of hills that lead to the Rocky Mountains. In the far south, grasslands cover the foothills. This is a ranching area. As you go farther north, the area is covered with trees.

4 Rocky Mountain

The Rocky Mountain region is the highest area in Alberta. There are deep valleys and rugged peaks. There are still some glaciers here. Trees grow in some areas. Other small plants grow in the rocky soil.

5 Parkland

The Parkland was once an area of grass and trees. Much of this vegetation was cleared so farms could be developed. This area has rich soil and gently rolling hills. This region is sometimes called the parkland prairie.

6 Grassland

It can be very dry in this southern region. Rivers cut deeply into the land. The grasslands are used for farming but also have large areas of grass, with some trees growing near rivers. This region is sometimes called the grassland prairie.

My group has to gather information about the Boreal Forest region. I'll start by gathering some photos off the Internet and this CD-ROM. I can learn a lot from photos.

What Makes a Natural Region?

To understand why parts of Alberta are in a particular region, we need to think about three things:

- **natural vegetation**—the plants that grow there naturally
- **climate**—how hot or cold it gets, and how much it rains or snows
- **landforms**—the features of the land, such as mountains, hills, and plains

Skill Smart

Look at the map.

- Which natural region of Alberta is your community in? (You may need to check an atlas or a road map.)
- Which region has the fewest large communities? Why do you think this is so?
- Use cardinal and intermediate directions to describe the location of each natural region in Alberta.

Alberta's Natural Regions

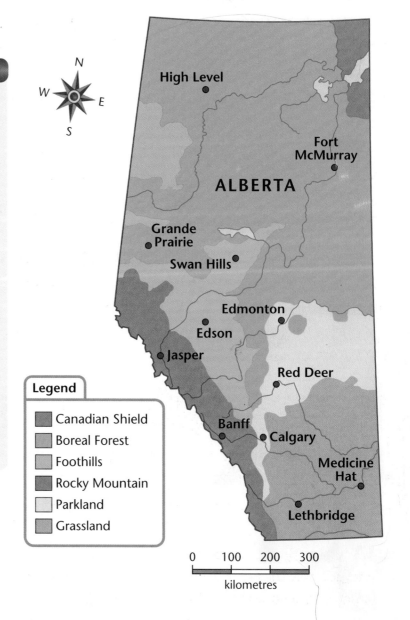

Legend

- Canadian Shield
- Boreal Forest
- Foothills
- Rocky Mountain
- Parkland
- Grassland

0   100   200   300
kilometres

Do Regions Change Over Time?

The regions give Alberta its character, but what happens when a region changes?

Imagine this! You are visiting the prairie grasslands 200 years ago. Herds of bison, deer, and pronghorn antelope graze freely. Hundreds of birds live on lakes and waterways, and burrowing owls nest in the ground. You might even see a wolf or a prairie grizzly bear!

The land is covered in native grasses—plants that grow here naturally. There is june grass, spear grass, and western porcupine grass. In the spring and summer, hundreds of flowers bloom. There might be some Siksika [sik-sik-AH] or Piikani [pee-KAH-nee] people camped near a lake with their horses, but there would not be a lot of people. ◆

What Are the Changes?

Today, many people live in the Grassland region. There are roads, railways, cities, towns, and farm buildings. There are crops growing in fields, instead of the native plants. There are fenced-in pastures where cattle graze. Here and there, you will see oil pumps in the fields. Many of the birds are gone. So are the grizzly bears and most of the wolves.

I wonder how changes like this affect quality of life. That's something I need to really think about.

The pronghorn antelope and songbirds like the western meadowlark are still found on the grassland prairie, but there are not as many as there once were.

Thinking *It Through*

- How can you find out more about the native plants and animals of your region?
- Why do you think some plants and animals are disappearing?
- Some people try, as good citizens, to protect plants and animals that are native to an area. Do you think it is important to do this? Why or why not?

Viewpoints

Should City Grasslands Be Protected?

Rough fescue grass is the provincial grass of Alberta.

Nose Hill Park is a large park in Calgary. Many people use the park for recreation. It has over 300 km of trails that are used by cyclists and walkers. Yet the park has other purposes as well.

Protecting the Past

Nose Hill Park is home to about 200 wildlife species—animals and plants. One of the plants that grows here is rough fescue grass. Rough fescue grassland used to cover the Prairies. Today, it exists only in small areas. Nose Hill Park is one of these areas. In addition, many teepee rings have been found in the park. These are stone circles left by people who lived here thousands of years ago. Some parts of the park are also sacred areas for the Piikani First Nation.

The Trail Question

To protect sacred areas and the grasslands, the city of Calgary made a plan to keep people out of more than half of the park. The number of trails would be cut back. Some trails would be paved, instead of being covered with gravel. Many people agreed with the plan, but some did not. Look at some of the arguments on the next page.

Paved paths will be better for people in wheelchairs and people with strollers.

The trails that are left will be crowded. And cyclists will go too fast on paved paths.

The trails will allow people to see the teepee rings without damaging them. Trails will allow the park to close off the sacred areas, except for special ceremonies.

Nose Hill Park is one of the largest city parks in Canada.

Fewer trails will protect a greater area of the park, especially the grassland.

I'm a mountain biker. I wouldn't use paved paths. I like to ride through natural areas.

Over to YOU!

1. Form a small group. Take different points of view, as shown above, and discuss what should be done with the trails in Nose Hill Park.

2. Is there a park in your community? What does the park give to the community? What does the park give to you? As a good citizen, what can you do to protect the park?

Exploring Points of View

Should people try to save plants and animals that are native to an area? When you consider a question like this, it's important to understand the points of view that different people might have. It helps to sort out opinions on a chart like this one.

What is the question or issue?	
Who are the people giving their opinions?	• • •
What are the different opinions?	• • •
Which opinions do you agree with, and why?	
Which opinions do you disagree with, and why?	
What is your opinion? Why?	

Practise the Skill

Copy this organizer onto paper, or use a computer to make a copy.
Then use it to explore the viewpoints on the previous two pages.
How does the chart help you explore the viewpoints?

How Does Climate Affect Quality of Life?

Have you ever noticed how often people talk about the weather? That's because the **weather** and **climate** help to shape the way we live. Some communities are even named after them—like Cold Lake, Spring Coulee, Sunnybrook, and Windfall. What do the names say about these places?

Why Does Climate Vary?

Climate includes

- temperature: how hot or cold a place gets
- precipitation: the amount of rain or snow

Factors that affect climate include

- latitude: how far north or south a region is
- elevation: whether the region is in the high mountains or the low plains

Some of Alberta's regions are warmer and drier than others. Some are farther north or higher up, and get more snow. Factors like these affect what grows in the regions and what the land looks like.

words matter!

Weather tells us about conditions such as temperature, rain, and sunshine on a single day. **Climate** is the kind of weather that is common in an area over a long period of time.

Where can I get this information for my region? My dad suggested that I look in the *Farmers' Almanac*.

ALBERTA VOICES — Nature's Weather Report

When we walked with my *Musum* (grandfather) in the forest, he would show us many signs that nature gives us. He showed us how the bees would build a nest late in the summer. If it was low to the ground, the winter would be mild, and the snow would not be high. If the nest was high in the trees, then the winter would be cold and long, with lots of snow. He would often remind us that it could be different somewhere else in the country.

Darrell Willier
Sucker Creek First Nation

Thinking It Through

- Why do people check the weather?
- What is the climate like in your community?

Is There a North/South Difference?

The tables below show temperatures for two communities in different parts of Alberta: High Level and Lethbridge. Check the map on page 32 to find the location of these communities. What do you notice?

High Level (northern Alberta)

	Jan	Feb	Mar	Apr	May	Jun	Jul	Aug	Sept	Oct	Nov	Dec
°C	−20	−17	−9	2	10	14	16	14	8	0	−12	−19

Lethbridge (southern Alberta)

	Jan	Feb	Mar	Apr	May	Jun	Jul	Aug	Sept	Oct	Nov	Dec
°C	−18	−4	0	6	11	16	18	17	12	7	0	−6

The farther north you go in Alberta, the cooler it becomes. Also, winter days are much shorter in the north. Summer days are much longer in the north. All the same, the effects of climate in these areas might not be what you expect.

This is farmland near High Level. How might colder temperatures affect crops in this area?

Skill Smart

- Use technology to make a line graph showing the information in the tables above.

- Use the Internet to research the temperatures in your community. Add the information to your graph. How is your community similar or different? Why? Explain.

ALBERTA VOICES

North and South

We have a short growing season here in High Level, but the summer days are long and warm. Even when I get up early, the sun has been up for hours! The sun shines for nearly 18 hours every day, allowing the crops to grow quickly. Sometimes I think I can see them growing before my eyes!

Paul Champagne

Lethbridge summers are very hot and dry. Even so, the temperature can fall quickly at night. We can get frost at night, any month of the year. We always have to be ready to cover the vegetables in our gardens to protect them from the frost!

Kim Webber

What Happens As You Climb?

You don't need to go north in Alberta to find cooler weather. You can just go up! There are places where the trees stop growing, and grass becomes bare rock. This is because the higher you climb, the cooler it becomes. That's another reason Alberta's climate changes from one region to another.

How Do Winds Make a Difference?

Alberta is famous for its **chinook** winds. In the Siksika language, chinook means "snow eater." In the winter, that is exactly what a chinook does. It is a dry, warm west wind that comes down from the mountains. It has been known to raise temperatures by 25°C within a few hours. The chinook is felt in the southeast more often than in the north. It comes in all seasons. In the summer, it brings very hot, dry weather.

Other winds also affect Alberta's climate. For example, cold winds blowing in from the Arctic can make winter temperatures drop quickly. The foothills and the grasslands often get hot, dry winds.

Plants that grow at the top of the Rocky Mountains are much like those that grow in the far north.

Skill Smart

Make a chart, like the one below, showing three factors that cause climate to change in Alberta and the effect of each.

Cause	Effect

ALBERTA VOICES — The Chinook

In 1988, Alberta hosted the Winter Olympics. I was really looking forward to watching the bobsleigh event at Canada Olympic Park in Calgary. Everyone knows that Alberta has lots of snow and is cold in the winter. Right? Not always! During the Olympics, a chinook wind came down from the mountains. It was warm and dry. Ice melted, so the bobsleigh and luge races were delayed. We all had to wait for the cold winter weather to come back!

Frances Chan

How Does Climate Affect Us?

Think about what you wear, what you do, and how you get from place to place each day. How does that change with each season—or does it? Here are some ways climate affects Albertans.

Activities

Outdoor activities in Alberta change with the season and sometimes with the region. What outdoor activities do you do each season? What activity would you like to do in a different region?

Summer is fun in Edmonton!

Work

The jobs of many people are affected by climate. Imagine how the seasons bring different challenges to farmers and ranchers. If spring is too cold, crops might not be planted on time. In the summer, very wet conditions can affect the harvest. Hailstorms can cause a lot of damage to crops.

Very cold temperatures can be hard on livestock in the foothills.

Travel

This air ambulance helps people in Fort Chipewyan and other northern communities.

In summer, the only way to get to northern places like Fort Chipewyan is by air because the ground is soft and wet, and it is hard to build roads. Air ambulances take very sick people to hospitals in Fort McMurray or Edmonton. In winter, people travel on special winter roads and on ice roads. If the weather is unusually warm, the ground thaws. Then people need to rely on airplanes again.

Thinking *It Through*

Talk with a partner about how climate affects quality of life. Use information on this page and the next to get you started.

Stormy Weather!

Tornado Hits Edmonton

On July 31, 1987, a severe storm struck the Edmonton area. Then, at 3:00 p.m., a black funnel cloud touched the ground. It swept through the east side of the city, roaring like a freight train. It was one of the biggest tornadoes in Canadian history, carving a path of destruction that was 37 km long! Twenty-seven people died, and 600 were injured.

EARLY SNOWSTORM IN CALGARY

On September 16, 2003, people in Calgary woke up to a snowstorm, even though it was still officially summer! West of Calgary, Jasper and Banff got the most snow—up to 25 cm. But there was good news: this summer snowfall helped to cool the Lost Creek fire in Crowsnest Pass.

WILD WEATHER

April 14, 2002, was a wild weather day in Alberta! On the same day, there was snow in Edmonton, while grass fires burned near Calgary. Near Medicine Hat, a 10-vehicle accident was caused when strong winds blew dust clouds across fields and roads.

What Is Alberta's Climate?

Look at the climate map below. The legend tells you what the climate is like in different parts of Alberta. The numbers on the map match the numbers on the photographs on the opposite page. Look at the photographs to see the effects of climate and weather in these places.

How do the climates match up with the natural regions? I can look back to the map on page 32 to see.

How do the climates match up with the natural regions? I can look back to the map on page 32 to see.

Skill Smart

- Use the map to locate the places with extreme weather described on the opposite page.

- Make a chart to show what the climate is in each region and explain how climate would affect life there.

Alberta's Climate Areas

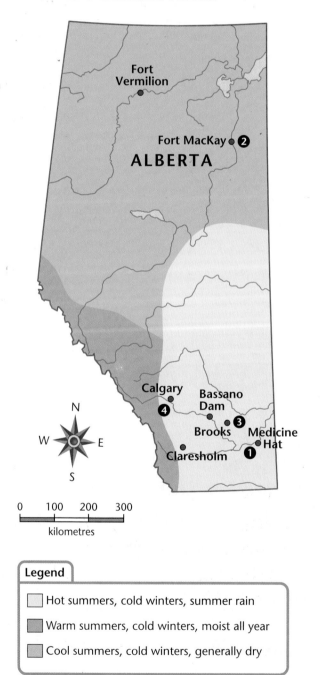

Legend

- Hot summers, cold winters, summer rain
- Warm summers, cold winters, moist all year
- Cool summers, cold winters, generally dry

What Are Some Weather Extremes?

Alberta's weather has many surprises, like the extremes shown here. How do you think these extremes help give Alberta a character of its own? How do you think these extremes affect quality of life?

- Many parts of Alberta are very cold in winter, but Alberta is the sunniest province in Canada.

- Alberta is famous for its dry, warm chinook wind. It raises temperatures very rapidly. The **Alberta clipper** is a fierce, cold wind that starts near the Rocky Mountains. It quickly blows out of the province.

- The coldest day ever recorded in Alberta was in January 1911, in Fort Vermilion. The temperature was –61.1°C. Yet in December 1999, it was over 20°C in Claresholm. It was so warm that grass fires broke out in the area, and trees sprouted leaves.

- It has been known to snow in parts of Alberta even in summer months, but look at the temperature on the warmest day ever recorded in the province. It was 43.3°C at Bassano Dam on July 21, 1931.

- Alberta can get a lot of rain and snow, but parts of the province can get very dry, making forest fires a hazard.

- The foothills and eastern slopes of the Rockies are areas in Canada most likely to be hit by lightning. They get about half a million strikes each year!

Set Your Skills in Motion

Explore Points of View

- Whitecourt is known as the "snowmobile capital of Alberta." Its rolling hills, forests, and snow make it a great place for snowmobiling in the winter. How do you think people in Whitecourt feel about this? With a partner discuss what the points of view might be.
- Each of you should take on the role of a person with a different viewpoint. Express your thoughts. Use the organizer from the Skill Power on page 36 to record your views.

Use a Map Scale

Big Rock travelled, roughly, from Jasper to Okotoks. Use the scale on a map of Alberta to measure the distance Big Rock travelled.

Create a News Article

- Ask people in your community, check at the library, or search the Internet to find out about a severe storm or unusual weather event in your area. Look for stories about how people helped one another during this weather disaster.
- Create a newspaper or e-news article about the weather event. Include photos or diagrams.

Compare Regions

Compare the region in which you live with another region in Alberta. Record your comparisons in a Venn diagram or use a chart with the following headings: Natural Vegetation, Landforms, Climate. Gather your information from this chapter or other sources. List your sources below your diagram or chart.

Write a paragraph telling more about the unique features in your region that make it different from the other region.

Look What You Have Learned!

In this chapter, you explored how Alberta's land has been shaped and changed over time. You've learned how these changes have created the landscape and landforms of today. You've found out about the regions of Alberta—where they are and how they are different from one another. You've looked into climate and weather and how they affect people's lives.

Review the inquiry questions for this chapter:

- How have the unique land features of Alberta been shaped over time?
- What is it like living in each of the regions of Alberta?

Pick a region other than your own. Gather information to inform people about it. Use this book and other sources. Be sure to keep a list of your sources.

- Make jot notes about important aspects of the landscape, interesting landforms, the weather and climate, the region, and things people can do outside.
- At the end, list important points about what it would be like to live there.

Present your information as a page for a magazine or Web site. Include a title, headings, and photos with captions. Finish with a summary of what it would be like to live there.

Take Time to Reflect

- What steps did you take to help you read this chapter?
- What did you learn that will help in the next chapter?

 Choose something from this chapter to save for your Alberta Treasure Chest.

Alberta's Fossil Heritage

Wendy Sloboda is a dinosaur hunter! In 1987, when she was just 19 years old, Wendy made a very special find. This is her story.

"I've always loved looking for fossils. While I was growing up in Warner, near the Milk River, my parents and I went for walks to look for them. Then one day, when I was older, I was walking near Devil's Coulee. On the dry, sandy soil, I found what I thought might be bits of dinosaur eggs. Soon scientists from the Tyrrell Museum came to investigate.

"In a few days we made a special find on a nearby hillside. We found nests that had whole fossilized eggs and baby dinosaurs! We were so excited. It was a unique find. Something like this could only happen in Alberta!"

Alberta's Story

In the last chapter, you learned how the land helps to give Alberta its identity. In this chapter, you will find out how Alberta's **fossils** also help to make the province unique. You will learn what fossils can tell about Alberta's past. You will find out why fossils are important today and how they are protected. You will discover why fossils are an important part of our heritage—a part of the past that we still value because it helps make us what we are today.

This is a fossil of a baby dinosaur.

? Inquiring Minds

Here are some questions to guide your inquiry for this chapter:

- Why are fossils important to Alberta?
- How are fossils part of Alberta's identity?

Look for answers in this chapter. If you'd like to know more, look for information in other sources.

I wonder how fossils make Alberta unique. To find out more, I will
- ask questions as I read
- use the question words Who, What, When, Where, Why, How, and If

What Do Fossils Tell About Alberta?

Skill Smart

Look at the fossils below. What clues do they give about Alberta's past? With a partner, write a paragraph to share your ideas.

Fossils are remains of the past. They give us hints about what Alberta was like millions of years ago. Some fossils are pieces of an ancient plant or animal that have turned to stone over a very long time. Others show the shapes of plants or animals that have been pressed into mud and hardened over time. Fossils tell us stories. We can study them to learn about the plants and animals that no longer exist on Earth.

These fossils are now rock. What were they before?

What Are Other Clues to the Past?

Imagine this! Dinosaurs are walking through huge swamps and ponds with sandy shores. In the distance, there are forests with hundreds of dinosaurs guarding their nests. The nests have eggs in them, each one about the size of a volleyball. Some eggs nearby have just hatched. The babies are over half a metre long. They can't walk yet, and they don't have crests on their heads as their parents do. ◆

How do we know that this scene could once have happened in Alberta? If you said that fossils help to tell us, you were right. Remember when Wendy found the fossil eggshells? Dinosaur fossils like the ones Wendy found are another clue to Alberta's past. They tell us where the dinosaurs lived. They tell us what types of dinosaurs lived here. They tell us how big the dinosaurs were. Fossils can also give clues about what the land might have been like millions of years ago.

I wonder what kinds of dinosaurs lived in Alberta. I will check the Internet to find out more.

This is what an artist thinks some of the dinosaurs in Alberta looked like millions of years ago. Today, we call these dinosaurs *Hypacrosaurus* (hi-PAC-row-SAW-rus).

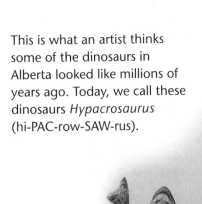

Thinking *It Through*

Think about the land around your community. How is it different from Alberta long ago, as it is described on this page?

Why Do We Find Fossils in Alberta?

Scientists who study fossils to learn about very old forms of life are called **paleontologists** (pay-lee-on-TOL-o-jists).

One of the most famous **paleontologists** in the world is Dr. Phil Currie, professor at the University of Alberta.

These paleontologists are digging for fossils in the badlands, near the Red Deer River. What can you tell about the land from this photograph? What makes the land perfect for finding fossils?

Fossils do not form very often. Millions of animals die and leave no traces. Alberta is unique because so many fossils are found here. There are very few other places in the world with as many fossils. Why does Alberta have so many fossils?

Fossils are found in Alberta because of the way the land formed. In Chapter 1, you learned that the land changed over time. In some places, there were earthquakes and volcanoes. Plants and animals were covered over and preserved. They became fossils buried below layers of dry soil and rock.

Over millions of years, water and Alberta's strong winds carried away the soil and rock. In parts of Alberta's hot and dry grasslands, many fossils were uncovered. This was the area known as the badlands, but these lands aren't "bad" for fossils. They are perfect!

Finding Information on the Internet

What do you know about Alberta's badlands? You can use the Internet to find out more. But beware! There are thousands of sites, and not all of them have accurate information. Follow these guidelines:

- Ask your teacher or a librarian to help you choose a "search engine." A search engine is a way to find sites.

- You will need to type in a topic. Choose a few keywords. Find out how to use the words *and* or *not* to find sites that are more likely to have the information you need.

- Look at the sites on your list. Identify museums or universities. They are likely to have reliable information.

Practise the Skill

1. **Searching:** Use the Internet to find answers to these questions.

   a) Where are the badlands?

   b) How far are the badlands from your community?

   c) What plants and animals can you find in the badlands?

2. **Sorting:** How many sites did you visit? What made you skip some sites and not others? Which ones were most useful?

3. **Selecting:** Now share your answers to these questions.

   a) Did you all use the same search engine?

   b) Did you use the same Web sites?

   c) Did you all have similar answers? If not, how can you check which information is accurate?

Where Are Fossils Found in Alberta?

What other fossils can be found in Alberta? I'll ask a librarian to help me find out more from books and CDs.

Petrified wood is also a fossil. It is wood that has turned to stone. Petrified wood is the provincial stone of Alberta. Why do you think it was chosen?

Skill Smart

- What would you do if you found a fossil?
- Post your ideas on the bulletin board.
- Read what other students think.

Most of Alberta's fossils are found in the badlands, but they are also found in other parts of the province. The map below shows some of the places in Alberta where fossils have been found. Match the numbers on the map with the photographs on the opposite page to see which fossils have been found in these locations. You can see that many different types of fossils have been uncovered. Not many other places in the world have such a variety of fossils.

Alberta's Fossil Finds

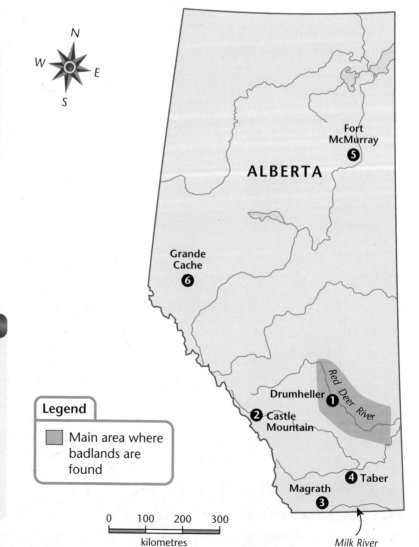

Legend

Main area where badlands are found

0 100 200 300

kilometres

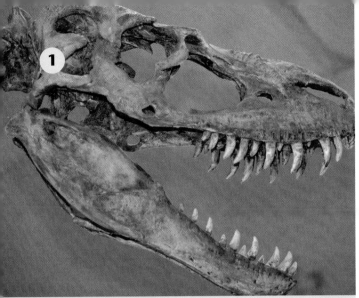

1 Many different types of fossils have been found near Drumheller, in the badlands.

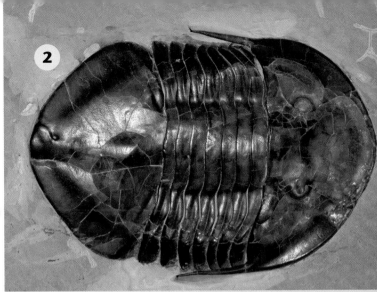

2 Fossils of small sea creatures have been found at Castle Mountain, near Banff.

3 Ammonite, a fossilized shell, has been found at Magrath, near Lethbridge.

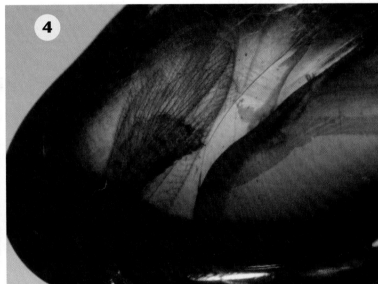

4 Amber, a fossil made from ancient tree sap, has been found at the coal mines near Taber.

5 Sea reptile remains have been found in the tar sands near Fort McMurray.

6 Dinosaur tracks can be seen at Grande Cache, near Jasper National Park.

How Did Alberta Become Known for Fossils?

The *iinisskimm* [in-nis-kim] are special stones with great spiritual importance. Some, but not all of them, are fossils.

From the earliest times, the First Nations of Alberta knew that there were fossils in the land. The Blackfoot called some of the fossils they found **iinisskimm**, or "buffalo stones." They knew that these fossils came from animals from the past. They called the animals "grandfather of the buffalo." These *iinisskimm* are still considered sacred.

This Piikani pouch was used to store *iinisskimm*. It belonged to Charlie Crow Eagle, who lived near Lethbridge.

This is a model of *Albertosaurus*. Tyrrell took the bones to Calgary, but they were so big, he could not get them all into his wagon!

Tyrrell's Find

In 1884, a fossil find made Alberta famous around the world. Joseph Tyrrell was looking for coal. He was also mapping the land between the Oldman River and the Red Deer River. With his crew, he camped in the badlands, close to where Drumheller is now.

Tyrrell soon made an exciting discovery. He found the bones of a huge, meat-eating dinosaur. It would later be called *Albertosaurus*, after the province where it was found.

What Happened to Alberta's Fossils?

Tyrrell reported his discovery, and before long, collectors began coming to Alberta to look for fossils. The badlands became known as the most important fossil field in Canada. Soon there was a rush to find fossils! Many more people came to Alberta, eager to see what they could uncover.

In 1909, a collector named Barnum Brown came to the Red Deer Valley. Brown worked for an American museum. He found so many fossils that he was known as "Mr. Bones." Brown sent thousands of fossils back to the United States.

Then people began to wonder why the fossils were being taken out of Canada. In 1912, the Canadian government hired its own fossil hunters. The fossils they found are now displayed at the Canadian Museum of Nature in Ottawa and at the Royal Ontario Museum in Toronto.

Over the years, many thousands of fossils were discovered and shipped away from Alberta.

Thinking
It Through

Why do you think people felt it was important to keep the fossils in Canada?

Barnum Brown spent five years searching for fossils in Alberta.

Viewpoints

Should Alberta's Fossils Be Protected?

Brianna Hunt lives near Lethbridge. One day, she was walking with her dad next to a river. She saw an interesting rock and picked it up. It was a fossil. What do you think Brianna should have done with this fossil? What would you do?

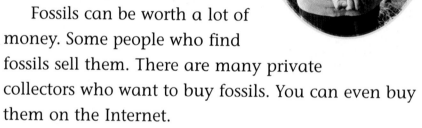

Fossils can be worth a lot of money. Some people who find fossils sell them. There are many private collectors who want to buy fossils. You can even buy them on the Internet.

There are some people in Alberta who dig up fossils to sell or keep. Should they be allowed to do so? Read the following views to learn more about what different people think about this issue.

Thousands of fossils get washed away by the rain. There is no way paleontologists can get them all, so collectors should be able to have some.

I love the dinosaur tooth I bought! I can imagine the animal that had that tooth. Fossils help bring the past alive for me!

People who collect fossils could be taking remains of an animal we know nothing about. An expert has to look at the fossils.

Alberta has so many fossil remains. What difference does it make if I have a few teeth and anklebones?

These pieces of jewellery are made from ammonite, a kind of fossilized snail. Some companies have permission to find ammonite and use it in jewellery.

Fossils are a valuable resource. We'd be upset if people went into a park and started cutting flowers or trees. We should be just as upset when they take fossils.

Over to YOU!

1. As a group, discuss each of the viewpoints. Which opinion do you agree with the most? Why? Did your opinion change after reading these viewpoints?

2. How do you think Alberta's fossils should be protected? Brainstorm some ideas in your group.

If fossils were not protected, how would I learn about Alberta's past?

Sharing a Discovery

[We] want to share this discovery with the rest of the world and agree to have the remains of this creature removed from our lands. [We] have a great respect for our Mother Earth through our culture and spiritual beliefs. Through this agreement, we are contributing in a positive way.

Chief Chris Shade
Kainai First Nation

How Do We Protect Our Fossils?

Until 1978, anyone could collect fossils in Alberta. People who found fossils could keep them or sell them. No one recorded who collected the fossils or where they were kept.

In 1978, that changed. Alberta passed a law to protect its fossil heritage.

- The province now owns all fossils that are found in Alberta. People are allowed to collect fossils that are lying on the ground, but they must report anything they find.

- In some areas where many fossils are found, no one can pick them up. Only paleontologists are allowed to dig for fossils, and they need a special permit to do so. The fossils they find are sent to museums, where they are preserved and studied.

Brianna Hunt and her dad reported their find to the Royal Tyrrell Museum. A scientist at the museum told them that it was a fossil of a squid. Brianna was happy to hear that she could keep the fossil because she found it on the surface of the ground, outside a protected area.

Rick Tailfeathers, of the Kainai First Nation, is presenting a curator at the Royal Tyrrell Museum with a *mosasaur* fossil found on Kainai land. This is only the second *mosasaur* found in Alberta.

Why Was Dinosaur Provincial Park Created?

In the early 1900s, one Albertan was worried about the number of fossils being taken away. This person was George Anderson. In 1914, he started a campaign to protect the fossils. To keep people from taking the fossils away, he wanted to turn the Red Deer Valley into a protected area. Anderson wrote about his idea in the local newspaper. He sent letters to the Canadian government and to the Alberta government. For years, nothing happened.

Anderson did not give up. Slowly, more people became interested in his idea. Newspapers began to show their support. Finally, in 1955, Dinosaur Provincial Park was created.

In 1979, Dinosaur Provincial Park became a World Heritage Site. World Heritage Sites are places that are important to the whole world. The park has the world's richest collection of fossils from 75 million years ago. Fossils of dinosaurs, crocodiles, fish, insects, and plants have been found there.

These are fossil bones in the ground at Dinosaur Provincial Park.

Skill Smart

Prepare a short speech to explain why you think Dinosaur Provincial Park is important. You could record your speech.

Paleontologists come to Dinosaur Provincial Park to study the fossils. On the hillsides, visitors can see layers of rock and tour the dinosaur "bone beds."

Dinosaur Provincial Park

I had a great time when I visited Dinosaur Provincial Park, near Drumheller. The park is in the badlands. You can go on hikes through the park with a guide. My guide taught me lots about the dinosaurs, plants, and animals that lived here millions of years ago. I learned that large rivers used to flow through the area. Now, there are just creeks. I also found out that cacti grow in the badlands.

ALBERTA

Dinosaur
Provincial
Park

Drumheller

Medicine Hat

Lethbridge

The best thing about the park was seeing fossils right in the ground. I felt just like a paleontologist!

I'm happy I live in Alberta. No other province has a Dinosaur Provincial Park!

Why Is the Royal Tyrrell Museum So Important?

The Tyrrell Museum opened in 1985. It was named after Joseph Tyrrell. The museum was built in Drumheller, close to Dinosaur Provincial Park and close to where Tyrrell found *Albertosaurus* in 1884.

Because of the museum, Alberta's fossils can remain in the province. Paleontologists in Alberta now have a place to study their finds, and people living in the province can see the fossils on display. Visitors and scientists come from all over Canada and the world to learn about life in Alberta millions of years ago.

I want to know more about *Albertosaurus*. Did it only live in Alberta?

Skill Smart

Think of three things you would like to find out about the Royal Tyrrell Museum. Look in books or on the Internet. Report your findings in a photo essay, picture essay, or PowerPoint presentation.

In 1990, the Tyrrell Museum was renamed the Royal Tyrrell Museum. What do you think the name "Royal" says about the importance of the museum?

What Are Fossil Fuels?

I wonder how fossil fuels help to give Alberta its identity.

In this chapter, you have seen how Alberta's fossils help to give the province its sense of identity. But do you know another way that ancient plants and animals are important to Alberta?

Some of the plants and animals that were buried long ago did not turn into fossils. Over a long time and under the weight of the rock that covered them, they turned into coal, oil, and gas. We call these resources **fossil fuels** because they come from ancient plants and animals.

Alberta is rich in fossil fuels, just as it is in fossils. Fossil fuels are very important to Alberta today. Many people work in the coal, oil, and gas industries. Coal, oil, and gas from Alberta are sent to other provinces and other countries. They can be used to heat homes or provide power for items like computers and ovens. Gasoline from fossil fuels is used to run cars and other machines.

Thinking *It Through*

Some fossils have turned into fuels that people can use to produce power and energy. How might your life be different if you did not have power for your favourite machines? Explain.

The dark area in this photo is a coal seam, which is a layer of coal underneath different kinds of rock. Coal seams like this one are found in many places where fossils are also found.

OCEAN
300–400 million years ago

It's hard to believe, but at one time, much of Alberta was covered by ocean. Over time, millions of tiny plants and animals that lived in the ocean died. Slowly they were covered by layers of silt and sand.

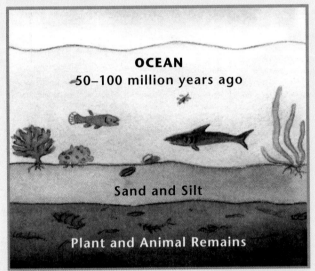

OCEAN
50–100 million years ago

Sand and Silt

Plant and Animal Remains

Over millions of years, the oceans began to disappear. The remains of plants and animals were buried deeper and deeper. Heat and pressure of the silt and sand turned them into oil, gas, and coal.

ALBERTA
Today

Sand and Silt

Rock

Oil, Gas, and Coal Deposits

Today, we remove the oil, gas, and coal from the ground by using many different methods. You will learn more about this in the next chapter.

Set Your Skills in Motion

Ask Your Own Questions

With a partner, brainstorm some questions you would like to ask about Alberta's fossil heritage. Use the Internet to try to find answers to your questions. Look back at the steps on page 51 for hints.

Create a Web

Print the words *fossil heritage* in the centre of a page. Show how fossils are protected. How are they part of Alberta's identity? Use photos, drawings, or words.

Make a Chart

How did the land look millions of years ago? How does it look today? What has stayed the same? Look through the text, visit the library, or check the Internet for information. You could use technology to make your chart.

Plan a Tour

In a small group, plan a tour in Dinosaur Provincial Park. Plan what you will tell visitors about Alberta's fossil heritage as you go on a hike. What might they see, hear, or smell? What will you do at the park? Now role-play your tour by showing another group around the park.

Give Your Opinion

Look back at the Skill Smart on page 52. What was your opinion then? What is your opinion now? Ask your teacher to help you make a flow chart. Show what you would do if you found a fossil today.

Look What You Have Learned!

Alberta's fossil heritage helps to make the province unique. Very few other places have as many fossils. We protect our fossil heritage in several different ways. We have laws that prevent people from taking fossils away, and special areas like Dinosaur Provincial Park are protected. The Royal Tyrrell Museum preserves and displays fossils for all Albertans. Fossils and fossil fuels are also important to Alberta today. They are part of Alberta's identity.

Review the inquiry questions for this chapter:
- Why are fossils important to Alberta?
- How are fossils part of Alberta's identity?

Tell about what you have learned by writing a short report. Think about the types of plants and animals that were in Alberta millions of years ago. What did they leave behind? How do they help to make Alberta what it is today? Add pictures to your report and share with a younger student.

Take Time to Reflect

Before you go on to the next chapter, think about what you have learned in this one.
- How did you use technology to find information?
- Which words can you use to ask questions?
- What did you learn that will help you the next time you use technology to find information?

 Choose something from this chapter to save for your Alberta Treasure Chest.

CHAPTER 3

Natural Resources in Your Life

With a roar, oil gushed out of the new well at Leduc, near Edmonton. Five hundred people were watching. They roared back in excitement. They had come out on a bitterly cold day to see the opening of the well. It was February 1947. For many years the search had been on to find large deposits of oil in Western Canada, but without luck. Then the oil crews came to Leduc. They drilled for 10 weeks but found nothing. They were about to give up when, suddenly, one of the crew noticed a thick liquid oozing from the well. Success at last! Newspapers in Alberta and across Canada announced the discovery with headlines. There was a huge oil reserve in Alberta!

Leduc Blows In!

Découverte de pétrole à Leduc!

Big New Oil Field Near Leduc

Alberta's Story

Alberta is rich in **natural resources**. These resources are important in many ways to people in the province. In this chapter, you will find out how natural resources meet people's needs and help communities grow. You will learn how natural resources have helped build Alberta's identity.

? Inquiring Minds

Here are some questions to guide your inquiry for this chapter:

- How do we use natural resources?
- How have natural resources helped communities in Alberta grow?

Now try to add some questions of your own about natural resources in Alberta. Look for the answers in this chapter. If you can't find them here, explore more!

How can I organize the information I find?
I will
- make a two-column chart
- print each question as a heading
- make jot notes

Why Was the Leduc Discovery Important?

words **matter!**

Energy is power, or the ability to do work. We call oil and gas "energy" because they allow us to do our work, usually by giving power to the machines that help us.

Oil and gas were discovered in Alberta before 1947. However, the Leduc oil fields were the largest the province had seen. Many other natural gas reserves were found, and oil and gas companies grew quickly. They provided many jobs for people in Alberta. Alberta soon became known as an **energy** province.

ALBERTA VOICES — Big Changes in Our World

Karen Bower was five years old when her parents took her out one night in 1947 to watch the flares from the Leduc oil field.

"Look at that!" my mother said…. It looked like the sky was on fire….

"Those are flares," my father said. He said men put big pipes into the ground to get at the oil….

"Why are they burning up the ground?" I asked.

"It looks that way, but they are really burning the part they can't use," he explained. "They set it on fire to get rid of it."

He said the oil could be made into other things like gas to make cars go, and someday it would heat houses all over Canada. I thought about that. The winter before, my blanket had frozen to the wall of my room because our house was so cold….

"There's probably enough oil in the ground, Karen, to keep every house in Canada warm in the coldest winter…," he said. "This is going to make big changes in our world."

Thinking It Through

- How do you think people in Alberta use oil and gas? List some ideas and then read on to check if you were right.
- Why do you think oil and gas created jobs?

Oil rig workers at Leduc in 1947

How Do You Use Energy Resources?

Did you turn on the light this morning? Did you travel to school by car or bus? If so, you used energy resources. Energy produces **electricity** for heat and light, and it runs machines. Most of the energy resources we use in Alberta are fossil fuels. Do you remember why, from Chapter 2? Alberta has far more fossil fuels than any other province in Canada. The chart below shows some uses of fossil fuels.

I'll add this information to my chart about how we use energy resources.

Fossil Fuel	How We Use It
Oil	• To make gasoline, motor oil, plastics • To generate electricity
Coal	• To generate electricity
Natural gas	• To heat homes • To generate electricity

This oil field is near Brooks in southern Alberta. These machines are called pumpjacks. They pump the oil out of the ground.

Siksika Oil Reserves

The oil and gas industry in Alberta has benefited many communities. For example, oil and gas were found on lands of the Siksika First Nation. Now the Siksika work with companies to drill for oil.

This sample of oil sands contains bitumen, which is a sticky black substance. Scientists had to find a way to separate it from the sand.

Working on the Oil Sands

Thousands of people in Alberta work in jobs related to oil and gas. Many work on the Athabasca Oil Sands near Fort McMurray. The **oil sands** are a mixture of sand, clay, and rock. They also contain **bitumen**, a thick, sticky tar made of oil.

The oil sands in Athabasca are the largest oil reserve in the world. Look at the steps below to see how workers remove oil from the oil sands.

How Oil Is Taken from the Oil Sands

1. Before mining begins, all the trees in the area must be cleared away. The topsoil, sand, clay, and gravel are also removed.

2. The oil sand is dug up by huge vehicles called shovels. Massive trucks take the sand to the crusher, which breaks up the lumps and removes the rocks.

3. The oil sand is mixed with hot water. The bitumen separates from the sand.

4. The bitumen is cleaned in several stages. Then it can be made into different products such as gasoline, heating oil, and motor oil.

5. It is time to restore the land to its natural state where possible. Clean sand replaces the oil sand, and topsoil is added. Shrubs and trees are planted on the topsoil.

Discovering the Oil Sands

We visited my uncle in Fort McMurray. While we were there, we spent a day at the Oil Sands Discovery Centre. The centre was built to tell people all about the Athabasca Oil Sands. The exhibits show how the oil sands formed and how the oil is removed. I saw some of the biggest machines on Earth!

Fort McMurray

ALBERTA

Oil Sands Discovery Centre

Edmonton

Calgary

The shovels can scoop up about 100 tonnes of oil sand at a time. Our guide said that's about the same weight as 58 elephants!

Then the shovels dump the sand onto the back of a heavy hauler truck. The tires of the truck alone are about three metres high. That's about twice my size! The biggest piece of equipment was the bucket wheel excavator. It's as tall as a seven-storey building!

Ask the Pipeline a Question

What products are moved in pipelines?

How do pipelines work?

How fast does synthetic crude or diluted bitumen move in a pipeline?

How big are modern pipelines?

Viewpoints

What Are Some Oil Sands Challenges?

Mining the Athabasca Oil Sands

People in Alberta have different opinions about the way the oil sands are used and mined. Let's look at what they have to say.

Alana Ingram: I am an environmentalist. I work with others to care for and protect the land in Alberta. The oil sands industry is tearing up the boreal forest. The oil companies have dug deep craters wider than football fields. Animals have to find new homes.

Philip Marceau: I am a trapper. A new oil sands project near where I trap has changed the land. There are no moose, no rabbits, or squirrels anymore. The land is dead.

Myrtle Calahaisn: I am a Cree Elder. People have lost respect for Mother Earth. We take oil and gas out of the ground, but we do not offer anything back. Whatever you take, you have to put back. Even a tree. If you take a tree for firewood or shelter, you must replace what you took.

The Athabasca Oil Sands

Jim Miller: I drive large trucks at the Athabasca Oil Sands. Oil companies reclaim land after it has been dug up. This means they put down new soil and plant trees to replace the ones they took from the earth. They also bring wood buffalo to land that has been reclaimed.

The oil companies replace the trees they cut down.

A hauler truck at the Athabasca Oil Sands

Kahlil Jiwa: I work at the Athabasca Oil Sands. Before my company plans a new dig in the Athabasca area, I meet with Cree and Chipewyan First Nations. We work together to protect areas that are important to these Nations.

Anna Itto: I drive a minivan. I use it to take my children to school, to get to work, and to run errands. My van runs on gas. Mining and drilling for oil may affect the land, but we cannot go back to the days of the horse and carriage!

Over to YOU!

1. What are some oil sands challenges? How are these challenges being met?
2. How do you think the oil sands challenges might affect you?

Energy from Coal

Coal is another fossil fuel found in Alberta. It is found in **seams**, or long layers of coal below Earth's surface. Coal is mined in communities such as Grande Cache, Hinton, and Wabamun. Some of the coal is used to make electricity in plants like the one at Sheerness, near Hanna. Some of the coal is sold in other parts of Canada and the world.

Using coal can bring some challenges. Coal mining disturbs the land. Burning coal to make electricity can also harm the environment. What can mining companies do? They are reclaiming some of the land they mine. They are also looking for new ways to burn coal without polluting the air.

People in Alberta also mine for salt, limestone, gravel, and sandstone. This old city hall building in Calgary is made of sandstone.

Coal mining at Wabamun, just west of Edmonton. Alberta generates most of its electricity from coal.

How Can We Meet Some Energy Challenges?

Some people believe we should reduce our use of fossil fuels. Burning fossil fuels produces gases that pollute the air. These gases smell and can make people ill. Also, fossil fuels are **non-renewable resources**. This means they cannot be replaced. As you saw in Chapter 2, fossil fuels take millions of years to form. It will take a long time to use up all of our fossil fuels. All the same, once they are gone, they will be gone forever. None will be left for future generations. What are some of the things we can do?

Conservation

If you said we can try not to waste energy, you are on the right track. We can all help to **conserve** our resources. This means we can use them carefully, so that they last longer. **Conservation** will help to protect our resources for the future.

words matter!

Non-renewable resources are resources that cannot be replaced or renewed.

Conservation means using our natural resources carefully, so that they will not run out.

I see that we can work together to discuss problems, find solutions, and save our resources. That's a great way to improve quality of life!

HOW CAN YOU CONSERVE ENERGY?

Home	School	Both
Hang clothes out to dry.	Write on both sides of the paper.	Turn off lights and computers when not in use.

Skill Smart

Look at the chart to the left. Identify two other ways you can conserve energy. Make a flyer or poster to encourage people to save energy in these ways. Use a paint and draw program on the computer, if you can.

How are these students conserving energy?

What Are Other Sources of Energy?

If you said we can save fossil fuels by using other sources of energy, that's another good idea. Scientists have been using wind, sun, and even animal or plant waste to make electricity! These **resources** are all **renewable**. They won't run out.

Super Sunshine

Energy from the sun can be collected in solar panels that sit on the roofs of buildings. Then the sun's energy can be turned into electricity to be used inside the building. Solar power is useful in sunny areas. Which parts of Alberta do you think would be ideal?

I wonder if we use solar power in my community. I'll ask some people who might know.

New solar panels on the roof of Cochrane High School

Pig Power

The Iron Creek Hutterite Community, on the Prairies south of Viking, uses pig manure to make electricity. The manure is closed in a concrete container, where it gives off methane gas. This gas is then used to produce electricity.

Wind Power

Modern Windmills

Lethbridge is known for its windy days. I remember the fun I had as a child, playing with the wind. I took my coat off and held it over my head. My coat filled up with air, just like a parachute. The wind pulled me along the field. I imagined I was flying!

Who would have thought all this wind would someday come in handy? Around Lethbridge we have some unusual farms. We call them wind farms. Driving along the highway you can't miss the tall, metal windmills called turbines. These turbines produce electricity. Stronger winds produce more power!

Nicole Mills
Lethbridge resident

Most of Alberta's wind farms are south, in the foothills where the winds sweep down from the Rockies. Wind power provides only a small amount of the energy used in Alberta, but it is becoming more important. Why do you think this is so?

This doesn't mean that wind is the perfect source of energy. Some people think that wind turbines are ugly. The blades make a noise as they turn, and sometimes birds get caught in them. Other people like the way the turbines look. What do you think?

ALBERTA VOICES

Land of the Piikani

It's good to get up in the morning and see the turbines and know they're working to make our lives better.

William Big Bull—in charge of installing a wind turbine on the land of the Piikani First Nation, 16 km west of Fort Macleod

Why Is Agriculture Important?

ALBERTA VOICES

Life on a Ranch

As a child, I gathered eggs, and I saw the cow grazing in the field behind my house become the roast beef on our dinner table. I ate fresh vegetables from our garden and waited every year to taste fresh grain seeds plucked from... a shaft of barley. I had no idea that most people only bought their milk in bags or cartons and never saw the actual source.

Gina Lorinda Yagos

Alberta's land is rich in fossil fuels, but some of the land in the province is also good for **agriculture**. Nearly one third of Alberta is farmland, and the province has about 59 000 farms and ranches! Look at the map of natural regions on page 30. Which regions do you think have the most agricultural land?

How Do We Use Agricultural Products?

Where do you get your food? People who live on ranches and farms might produce some of their own food, but most Albertans buy their food from a store or market. All the same, a lot of the food we eat comes from the ranches and farms across the province. Look at the table below. What other examples can you add?

FOOD FROM ALBERTA

Dairy cattle	Milk, cheese, yogurt, ice cream
Beef cattle, pigs, sheep, buffalo, chickens, bees	Meat for steaks, hamburgers, roasts; eggs, honey
Grains such as wheat, oats, barley	Bread, cereals, crackers, muffins
Canola	Cooking or salad oil
Vegetables, fruits	Corn, sugar beets (to make sugar), potatoes, blueberries, strawberries

This is a canola field in Hairy Hill. When canola plants flower, the fields turn bright yellow. Canola is used to make cooking and salad oil. In fact, its name comes from "Canadian oil."

Why Is Ranching Important?

Alberta is sometimes called "Cowboy Country." That's because ranchers in Alberta raise more beef cattle than any other province. Almost half of Canada's beef is produced in Alberta. Some cattle graze on the rich grasslands. Others are raised in pens and are given food at feedlots. Some ranchers also raise sheep, buffalo, llamas, and even emus.

ALBERTA VOICES

Home on the Range

Nate is a rancher near Cochrane. Read his journal to learn how the weather and land affect his work.

Ranching near Cochrane

5:00 a.m.   Time to get up! I grab a bowl of cereal before I step outside into the crisp morning air. The cattle stay outside all year, even in the winter. They can find shelter in the coulees. The chinook winds also help keep the cattle warm. We bring the pregnant cows into the barn in case they have trouble giving birth.

8:00 a.m.   I check the weather reports on the computer and phone the veterinarian about a young calf I am concerned about.

9:00 a.m.   Every morning, I ride my all-terrain vehicle and do chores. I pass a large oil derrick on my way to check on the cattle. I make sure the cattle have enough water. Fences okay? Any signs of coyotes? Our ranch has almost 13 000 hectares. Sound like a lot? Alberta has almost 7 million hectares of rangeland!

1:00 p.m.   In the afternoon, I go to meetings, make phone calls, and plan which cattle I will buy and sell.

7:00 p.m.   Guess what we had for dinner tonight? Beef! Nothing tastes better.

9:30 p.m.   The Web site on Alberta agriculture had interesting information about reducing the number of calves born at night. Simple! You feed the cattle in the evening.

Why Is Wheat Important?

Have you ever noticed the picture of wheat on Alberta's flag? Take a look at page 310. Wheat is included on the flag and on Alberta's coat of arms because it is part of Alberta's identity. Wheat grows well in Alberta and is a very important crop. Page 81 shows some examples of products made from wheat.

ALBERTA VOICES

Growing Wheat

My grandpa tells me how his family has been farming wheat since they settled near Hanna in 1911. His eyes always dance when he talks about working on the farm. He tells how he loved the smell of the moist earth in the spring because it made him feel that the earth was coming to life again after the winter. He says he is proud to be a farmer because it is so satisfying to watch the crop coming in and to know he had a part in making that happen.

My best time of the year is harvest time. Grandma and I always load up the back of the car with a hot meal and coffee and juice to take to Grandpa and the other workers in the field. I love hitting all those bumps and rocks as we make our way across the dusty field to

Harvesting wheat near Hanna

Products from wheat

where Grandpa is working. We spread the blanket out over the stubble and get everything ready for when the workers stop to eat. They don't like to take much time to eat, so I try to talk to Grandpa as much as I can while we're together. Harvest is very busy, so I don't see him much unless I get to go with Grandma to the field! Grandpa often tells us about the animals he spots while he's making his rounds in the field. I especially love to hear about the antelope!

Sometimes Grandpa lets me climb up on his combine and go for a ride around the field. The smell of wheat fills the air. My mom says that the dusty, sweet smell tells us "prairie kids" that fall is coming. Grandpa usually sneaks a few wheat kernels for me to chew on during my ride. He tells me if I chew long enough, it will turn to gum, but I usually lose patience. I love sitting on his knee, gazing out at the harvest moon and the stars through the big window. I'm having fun while most of my friends are at home getting ready for bed!

Harvest doesn't end when Grandpa gets his crop off. Often he'll take his machinery and help his neighbours get their crops off, too. Grandpa says that helping each other is an example of good citizenship.

Elisabeth Grace Marks

Thinking *It Through*

In what ways do the weather, land, and resources affect the jobs and activities Elisabeth and her grandparents do?

How Is Dry Land a Challenge?

Periods of drought and dry land make farming and ranching more challenging. Yet, people still use the grasslands for agriculture.

How can farmers grow crops where the soil is so dry? The answer is **irrigation**. Farmers build channels or use pipes and sprinklers to bring water from nearby rivers or dams to their fields.

The people of Kainai [KI-NI] (Blood) First Nation live southwest of Lethbridge. They worked with the government to overcome the challenge of dry land. They built a large irrigation system. Now about 10 000 hectares of land can be used for farming.

ALBERTA VOICES

Irrigation in Action

Campbell Eaglechild is the general manager of the Blood Tribe Agricultural Project. He talks about the project in an interview.

What crops do you grow?

Barley, canola, wheat, and more. We also grow timothy grass for cattle feed and as hay for horses. The timothy grass is shipped as far away as Japan, Korea, and Taiwan.

What is the best thing the project has accomplished?

It has become one of North America's largest irrigation systems! The project has also created lots of jobs. It makes us self-sufficient [able to support ourselves]. That's really important. The project is a challenge every year, and we're meeting the challenge.

The Kainai irrigation project. Identify the dam that has been built for water, the fields that have been irrigated, and the land that has not been irrigated.

Using a Concept Map to Organize Information

What do you know about agriculture? In this chapter, you read about agriculture, but how can you sort the information so you can answer this question? A concept map might help.

First, put your question in the centre of the concept map. Put the important topics around the question. Use simple phrases or single words to write your answers under each heading.

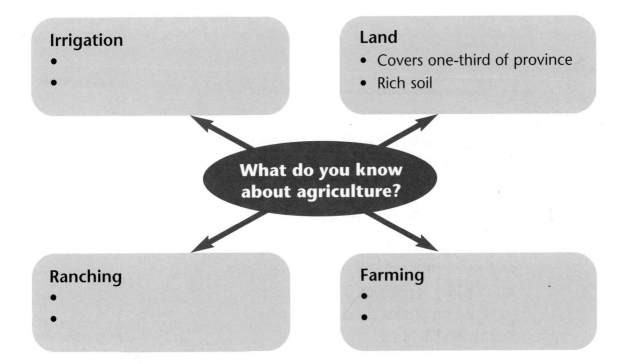

Irrigation
-
-

Land
- Covers one-third of province
- Rich soil

What do you know about agriculture?

Ranching
-
-

Farming
-
-

Practise the Skill

Copy the concept map above into your notebook. Now complete it by adding in the missing details. Then make a similar concept map to organize information for the following topic: What do you know about fossil fuels? Look back at pages 62–63 and 69–77 for information.

Now use the information you have organized. Choose one of your concept maps, and use it to write a short essay on the topic.

Alberta's Forests

Skill Smart

What do people value the forest most for? Oxygen, wood, or recreation?

- Survey at least 10 people.
- Use tally marks to record responses.
- Share your findings.

Forests cover half of Alberta. Their roots hold the soil together. Their branches and leaves give us shade. They are home to thousands of birds and animals. Forests provide wood that we use in many ways. We also enjoy hiking and camping in the forests.

Forests are called the lungs of the Earth because they produce much of the oxygen we breathe. They give us beauty and peace, too. Forests are one of our most valuable resources. They are part of Alberta's identity.

A forest in Spray Valley Provincial Park in Kananaskis country

How Do We Use Forest Products?

What is the paper in this book made of? What about the pencil you use to make notes? How about some of the chairs you use at home or at school? Or the power and telephone poles carrying the cables that bring important services to your home? All of these products came from wood.

Alberta's wood products come from trees that are logged, or chopped down, by forestry companies. Most of the **logging** takes place in two regions of the province: the boreal forest in Alberta's north and the foothills at the base of the Rocky Mountains. In many cases, the **lumber** is shipped to other provinces and countries, where it is made into the products we use. Then these products are shipped back to Alberta.

words **matter!**

Logging means cutting down trees and taking the logs to mills. There the logs are cut into boards or wood chips.

Lumber is wood that has been cut into boards. These boards are used to make various products.

This is a lumber mill in Grande Prairie.

Some of the wood in Alberta is turned into OSB (oriented strand board). OSB is made from fibres, or strands, taken from trees. The fibres are pressed together to make boards that are so strong they can carry more weight than concrete! The boards are used for many purposes, including building structures and making furniture and shelving.

I'll ask three people how they think we should use the forests.

Thinking
It Through

What can you do to protect the forest? Share your ideas with a friend.

How Should We Use the Forest?

People have different opinions on how the forest should be used. Consider the following points of view:

- Forests are a renewable resource. If we cut them down, they grow again.
- We can't replace the really big, old trees that have taken many decades to grow.
- Forest companies plan for the future. They replant or reseed to replace trees that have been cut. They also put limits on how many trees they can cut.
- New ways of making wood boards, like OSB, use small, young trees that can be replaced quickly.
- Logging can harm places that are sacred to First Nations people.
- Logging companies are working with First Nations groups, who explain which areas should be avoided.

To get to lumbering areas, companies often have to cut logging roads through the forest. Do you think this is a problem? Why or why not?

How Can We Meet Some of Forestry's Challenges?

Read about the following forestry workers. How does each one help make Alberta's forests a **sustainable resource**?

words matter!

A **sustainable resource** is one that is used only as much as it can be replaced, so that it lasts for the future.

Replanting

I am a student, and every summer I get a job planting trees for the forestry company. I enjoy working outside. I also learn about different species of birds, plants, and wildlife that live in the boreal forest.

Protecting

I am a forestry officer near Hinton. Tourists often visit the area. Every season, my job is to patrol the forest and keep it safe for wildlife. I love the fresh smell of the forest just after it rains. The leaves sparkle with raindrops.

Educating

I am a park ranger at Cross Lake Provincial Park. I teach visitors different ways to protect and use the forests. Campers enjoy hiking, listening to the birds, and cross-country skiing on trails.

ALBERTA VOICES

Mapping the Land

Rita Loonskin is a mapping technician for Little Red River Forestry. The forestry company is owned and operated by the Little Red River Cree Nation.

Before we prepare a logging plan, people in our field services department collect information about what is on the land. We map out the land and resources, such as the trees, streams, and areas that are important to wildlife. We also map sites that are important to the community, such as historic cabins and medicinal plant sites.

How Do Communities Form?

Many of Alberta's communities have grown because of natural resources. Look at the diagram to find out how.

HOW TOWNS GROW

Towns start near places where natural resources (e.g., rich soil for agriculture, forests, coal, and oil) are found.

People come to the area to find work.

Workers need homes, so houses are built.

Workers need services, so banks, stores, hospitals, and schools are built.

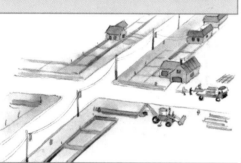

More workers such as builders, store and bank clerks, doctors, nurses, and teachers come to provide services.

They settle, start families, and need more homes and services.

Towns grow larger.

Where Are Alberta's Natural Resources Found?

Look at the map below to find out where the natural resources you read about in this chapter are found. What link can you make between the natural resources and the natural regions? Look back to Chapter 1 for clues. Then read on to visit some communities that have developed around natural resources.

I'll check an atlas to find my community. I wonder how the land has helped my community to develop.

Natural Regions and Resources

High Level

Fort McMurray

ALBERTA

Grande Prairie

Bonnyville

Edmonton

Leduc

Jasper

Red Deer

Cochrane

Calgary

Banff

Medicine Hat

Lethbridge

N W E S

| 0 | 100 | 200 | 300 |

kilometres

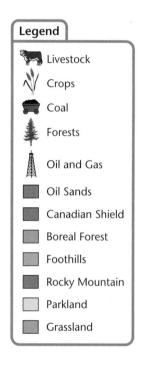

Legend

- 🐄 Livestock
- 🌾 Crops
- 🛒 Coal
- 🌲 Forests
- 🗼 Oil and Gas
- ▨ Oil Sands
- ▨ Canadian Shield
- ▨ Boreal Forest
- ▨ Foothills
- ▨ Rocky Mountain
- ▨ Parkland
- ▨ Grassland

Skill Smart

Try using your computer to make a chart similar to the one below. Fill in the two columns with information from the map and from Chapter 1.

Region	Resources
Boreal Forest	oil sands

Some Communities Built Around Natural Resources

Locate these communities on the map on page 89. Predict which natural resources helped each one grow. Then read the text below to check your predictions.

Medicine Hat

"Medicine Hat is in southeastern Alberta along the South Saskatchewan River. It is Canada's sunniest city. The weather and land are perfect for growing crops. I'm a gas pipeline operator. We have so much natural gas that Medicine Hat is known as 'Gas City.' The city uses gas for heat and electricity. I'm proud that my job helps the community meet its needs."

Tom Ealey

Red Deer

"I live in the province's third-largest city. It is built along the banks of the Red Deer River in central Alberta. The area near Red Deer has rich soil for farming, and oil and gas. It's a great place to live. We have good hospitals and schools. We also have beautiful parks and trails. In winter, we skate on outdoor rinks."

Joan Chin

Bonnyville

"My community borders the Athabasca Oil Sands, but it's also next to Jessie Lake in northeast Alberta. Bonnyville has farmlands and natural gas. But I think our most important natural resources are the wetlands, lakes, and wildlife. Residents and tourists like to fish in the lakes, walk along the wetlands trails, or bird watch. I'm glad not all the land is used for farms or natural gas."

Chantal Mitchell

Grande Prairie

"Grande Prairie has rolling plains and forests. A Francophone missionary called the area *la grande prairie*, which means 'the big prairie,' and that's how we got our name. When my grandparents were younger, many people were farmers. Then a large pulp mill was set up. That's where logs are chopped up so they can be used to make paper products. My mom, and lots of other people, went to work there. My dad still works on our farm. Later, oil and gas were discovered. My cousin is a mechanic in an oil company."

Joe Breland

Fort McMurray

"I moved to Fort McMurray to work at the Athabasca oil sands. I love the scenery, fishing, and hiking trails. My job pays better than my old one did. But so many people are moving here that houses are hard to find, and they're expensive. My wife and daughters stayed behind until I found a house. It took months! The hospitals and schools are overcrowded, too. Other services haven't kept up with the population boom either. But as long as there is work at the oil sands, the community will keep growing!

"One thing that interests me about Fort McMurray is that it's a new city with an old history. The Cree lived along the Athabasca River near here. They knew the land was rich in bitumen, and they used it to waterproof their canoes. Fur traders once lived here too, and later there were fish plants. It's hard to believe how much has changed."

Terry Papadakis

Set Your Skills in Motion

Create a Concept Map

How can responsible citizens protect or conserve natural resources? Consider energy resources, agricultural resources, and the forests. Make a concept map to organize your ideas.

Research Natural Resources in Your Community

Look in the library or interview people to find out how your community is connected to natural resources. How do natural resources and the land help your community grow? Keep track of where you find your information. Make a PowerPoint presentation or give a speech to share what you know.

Talk About a Current Event

In a small group, brainstorm a list of natural resources you read about in this chapter. Discuss some of the challenges of using one of these resources today. Look in the newspaper, listen to the radio, watch television, or search the Internet to find different views about the way we use natural resources. Post some of your information on the class bulletin board.

Make a Chart

With a partner, pick a community from page 90 or 91. Make a chart to show how the land, weather, and natural resources in the community affect the jobs and activities people do.

Look What You Have Learned!

Natural resources have helped Alberta become the province you live in today. Many towns and cities started near natural resources. Fossil fuels provide gasoline, heat, and electricity. Farms and ranches provide food such as grains, fruit, vegetables, eggs, dairy products, and meat. Forests provide oxygen, lumber, and places for recreation. Energy resources, agricultural resources, and forests provide goods and jobs. They are all part of the province's identity.

Review the inquiry questions for this chapter:
- How do we use natural resources?
- How have natural resources helped communities in Alberta grow?

Show what you have learned in the form of a collage. Think about where natural resources are found in Alberta. Which communities have started or continue to grow around natural resources? Include ways people use resources. Draw pictures, cut out photos from old magazines or calendars, or print images from electronic sources.

Take Time to Reflect

Before you go on to the next chapter, think about what you have done in this one. What did you learn that might help you in future activities? How might you improve the way you did your work?

 Choose something from this chapter to save for your Alberta Treasure Chest.

Looking Back: Chapters 1, 2, and 3

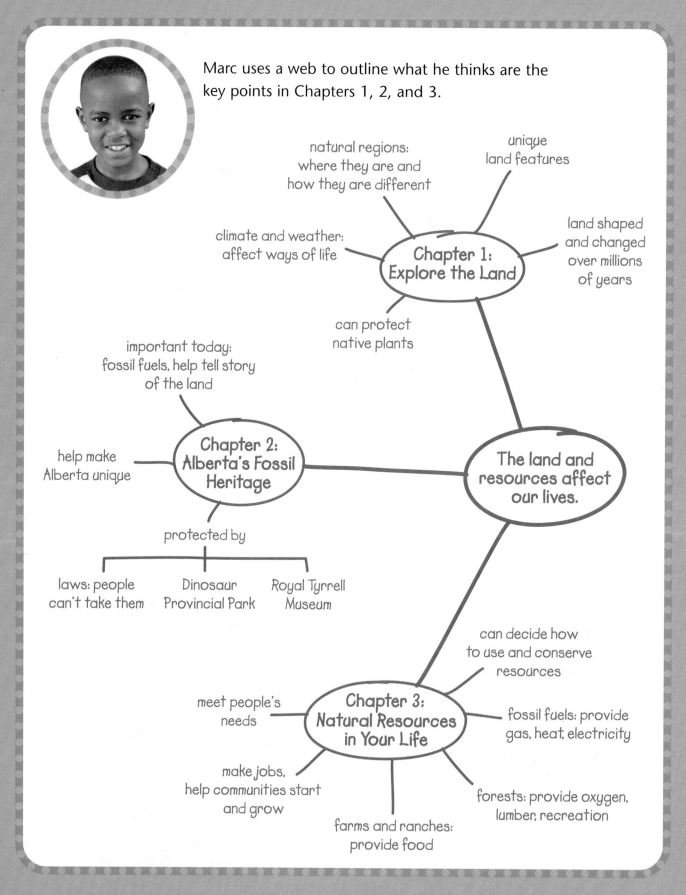

Marc uses a web to outline what he thinks are the key points in Chapters 1, 2, and 3.

natural regions: where they are and how they are different

unique land features

climate and weather: affect ways of life

Chapter 1: Explore the Land

land shaped and changed over millions of years

can protect native plants

important today: fossil fuels, help tell story of the land

Chapter 2: Alberta's Fossil Heritage

help make Alberta unique

The land and resources affect our lives.

protected by

laws: people can't take them

Dinosaur Provincial Park

Royal Tyrrell Museum

can decide how to use and conserve resources

meet people's needs

Chapter 3: Natural Resources in Your Life

fossil fuels: provide gas, heat, electricity

make jobs, help communities start and grow

forests: provide oxygen, lumber, recreation

farms and ranches: provide food

Share What You Know

? Inquiring Minds

Study the web that Marc made. Then skim through Chapters 1, 2, and 3 to help you recall what you learned. Now turn to page 3 in Getting Started. Which one of the overall inquiry questions for the book is the main focus of these chapters? Why do you think that?

Work in a group to give an Alberta Treasure virtual tour of one of the regions in Alberta.

Plan to include information about
- where the region is in Alberta
- the landscape and any interesting landforms
- natural resources and how they are used
- the climate and how it affects the lives of people

You could have different group members work on each point, and then put the information together.

Retrieve, or recall, what you've learned about the region from this book. Check your projects and activities, too.

Process, or think about, your information. Select what fits with the four points you are to include.

Create your virtual tour by organizing your information. Combine captions, written or spoken information, and images.

Share your virtual tour by presenting it as a slide show, or as a series of images on a mural or in a scrapbook. Present this region as one of the many things to treasure about Alberta.

Evaluate how well you worked in each of these steps. Then ask yourself: Am I pleased with my tour? Did others seem to like it? Is there something I would do differently next time?

Living with the Land

"We believe in telling stories," says Marge Friedel. She is a Métis Elder and teacher at the Amiskwaciy [a-misk-wa-chee] Academy in Edmonton. *Amiskwaciy* is the Cree word for Beaver Hills. Beaver Hills House is what the Cree called Edmonton. At this school, students of many First Nations learn about their cultures. They learn in modern and traditional ways, including listening to stories told by Elders.

Marge Friedel helps the students understand the importance of the land and everything it has to offer. She says, "Everything from Mother Earth must be used for a purpose." That includes plants. She tells the students, "Most plants are considered a medicine.... Each of the plants is a teacher in itself—not just in what the plant can do, but in what each teaches us about life. These are teachings you should not read about; you should have an Elder tell you about them in person."

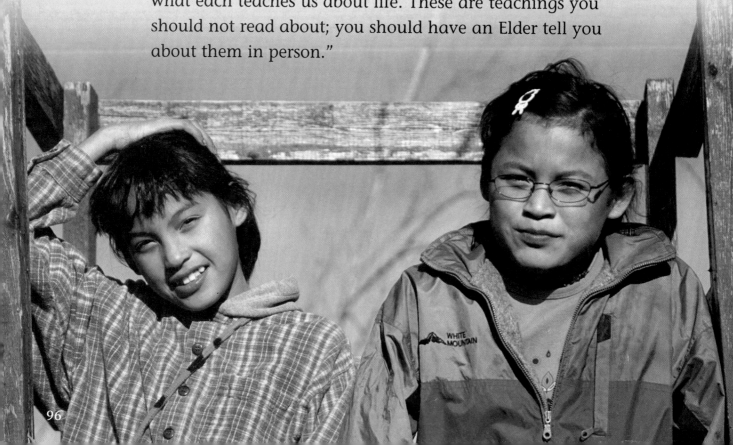

Alberta's Story

The First Nations were the original people to live in Alberta's natural regions. In this chapter, you will find out about how the different land and resources shaped ways of life for each First Nation. These ways of life are still important today. You will learn how each First Nation has its own culture, language, and stories that continue to be part of Alberta's identity. You will also find out about some values and beliefs that are shared among First Nations.

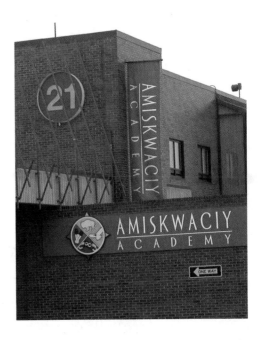

? Inquiring Minds

Here are some questions to guide your inquiry for this chapter:

- Which First Nations first lived in different areas of the province?
- How are the First Nations important to Alberta's identity?

Look for answers in this chapter. If you want to know more, look in other sources as well.

How will I make meaning out of the information I find out about Alberta's First Nations? I will

- make a web
- add information about First Nations
- look for similarities and differences

Who Were Alberta's First Peoples?

Imagine this! Imagine you could go back in time thousands of years. You are travelling across Alberta. There are no towns or cities, as there are today. Yet there are many people who live in the area. There are groups of people living in each of Alberta's natural regions: in the forests, in the parklands, in the foothills, and on the grasslands. There would also be people in the mountains and far to the North, on the Canadian Shield. ◆

Many Nations, Many Cultures

The First Nations were the first people to live in the land that became Alberta. Even though the term "First Nations" is sometimes used to refer to all of the first peoples, each nation was different. This is still the case today. Each nation has a unique culture and its own language. There are 46 First Nations of Alberta. Each nation is also part of a larger cultural group. The main cultural groups of the First Nations of Alberta are shown below.

FIRST NATIONS CULTURAL GROUPS OF ALBERTA

Woodland Cree	Nakoda [na-KO-da]
Plains Cree	Siksika [sik-sik-AH]
Dene Suline [deh-NEH SU-li-nay]	Piikani [pee-KHA-nee]
Dunne-za [duh-NEH DZA]	Kainai [KI-NI]
Dene Tha' [deh-NEH DHA]	Tsuu T'ina [tsoo-tina]

Note: The Siksika, Piikani, and Kainai belong to a group of First Nations known as the Blackfoot.

Some First Nations of Alberta

The map below shows the traditional areas in which each of the nations lived. Some First Nations people still live in these areas today, but some have moved to other parts of the province. Even though they live in many different ways, they still keep their cultures, traditions, languages, and ceremonies.

Nation	Greeting	Meaning
Blackfoot: Kainai, Piikani, Siksika	*Oki*	Hello
Cree	*Tan'si*	Hello
Dene Suline	*Edlanete*	How are you?
Dunne-za	*Neeah*	Welcome
Tsuu T'ina	*Da ni t'a da*	How are you?
Nakoda	*Abawastet*	Good day

First Nations of Alberta, About 1750

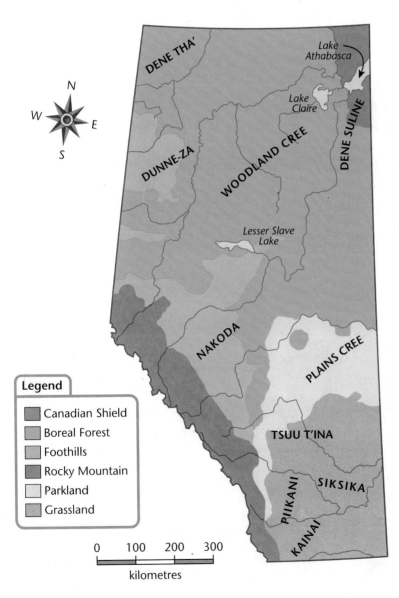

Legend
- Canadian Shield
- Boreal Forest
- Foothills
- Rocky Mountain
- Parkland
- Grassland

0   100   200   300
kilometres

I will print "First Nations" in the middle of my web and add some of the First Nations around it. As I read the chapter, I will try to add more information about each First Nation.

How Did Land Shape Ways of Life?

In each First Nation, people shared a deep connection with the land they lived on. This connection gave them unique ways of life and cultures. Look at the photos of the different regions. What natural resources can you identify in them? How might these resources have been part of different ways of life?

There are many differences in the ways of life of First Nations, just as there are many differences in the landforms, wildlife, and natural resources in the different regions of Alberta. You will read in the following pages about the connection between the people of different First Nations and the land they lived on.

Living in the Rocky Mountains and Foothills

Look back at the map on page 99 to see the traditional land of the Nakoda people. What does the following account tell you about the way people lived with the land in this region?

ALBERTA VOICES

A Land of Plenty

The land was vast, beautiful, and rich in abundant resources. Except during the winters, we spent most of our time migrating along the foothills in search of food, preparing for the cold months ahead. People who migrate require many types of shelter. Our seasonal dwellings, generally used during the summer, were spruce bark teepees. There were also moveable dwellings, used as my people travelled from place to place. These were teepees made from the tanned hides of buffalo, moose, and elk. Other shelters were pole and moss dwellings, cool in summer and warm in winter.

John Snow, Nakoda First Nation

This photograph of teepees was taken in the early 1900s. The hides that covered the teepees were made beautiful with powerful and important symbols that also told a story. Even the colours used had a meaning. For example, yellow often represented the sun, red represented the earth, and blue represented the sky or water.

Skill Smart

- What do you already know about the Nakoda First Nation?
- What do you want to know? (Hint: Use the question words from Chapter 2.)
- Look on the Internet or in books to find answers to your questions. Try to find out about Nakoda communities in Alberta today.
- Share what you have learned.

Living on the Grasslands

The Grassland region is the traditional home of the Piikani, Siksika, Kainai, and Tsuu T'ina people. There were many resources in this region, but the **bison**, or **buffalo**, was most important. At one time, there were as many as 60 million buffalo on the North American grasslands. A herd of buffalo stampeding across the Prairie could sound like an approaching thunderstorm!

ALBERTA VOICES — The Creator's Gift

The Blackfoot people believe that the buffalo was the Creator's gift to us. The buffalo was our primary food, and much more. We didn't hunt randomly. Before a group would go out to hunt, the people would conduct a ceremony.... They would pray for the people going to hunt, and for the beings to be hunted. They would give thanks to the buffalo for giving himself to us for so many things we needed. They would sing a buffalo song. Then they would go to the buffalo jump. So there was a ceremony, and prayer, and song, and then the hunt.

Sandra Crazy Bull
Kainai First Nation, interpreter, Glenbow Museum

Entrance to pound

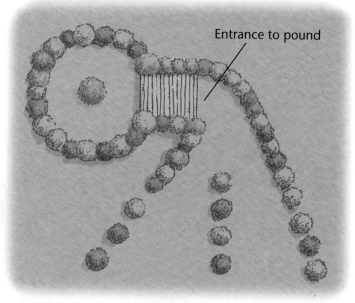

Entrance to pound

Hunters also built buffalo pounds, like the one shown here. They would surround a small group of buffalo and force them into the pound. There, the hunters could kill just as many animals as they needed.

Meat, including heart, liver, kidneys, tongue—food

Skin (hides)—clothing, bags, horseshoes, knife sheaths, drums, saddles, bridles, bedding, teepee covers, saddlebags

Sinew—threads, strings for hunting bows, games

Hair—braided into halters, stuffing for saddle pads

Tail—brush to kill flies and mosquitoes

Hoofs—boiled for glue, rattles

Bones—saddle horns, implements for dressing skins, needles, games

Horn—spoons, drinking cups, ladles

Brains—tanning hides

Ribs—arrow shafts

Shinbones—knives, fleshing tools for scraping hides

Teeth—necklaces

Rough tongue skin—combs

Beard—decorating hunting bows

Stomach—cooking pots, water buckets

Bladder—food bags

Dung—fuel

Shoulder blades—digging tools, hammers

Skull—painted and used in sacred ceremonies

Bone marrow—fat, fuel for fires

Bone-ends—paint brushes

Hide from neck—shields

Read about the many uses of the buffalo. Think about what this tells you about the daily lives of the people. How did they cook? How did they travel? What clothing did they wear? How did they have fun?

Skill Smart

The First Nations followed and hunted buffalo herds on foot. Some horses arrived in the Grassland region around 1730. These horses came from First Nations south of Canada. How do you think horses changed travel, hunting, and other ways of life in the region? Write a paragraph to share your ideas.

ALBERTA VOICES

After the Hunt

The buffalo was our way of life. He provided our people with everything. He gave us food, shelter, and clothing.

Lorraine Good Striker, interpreter Head-Smashed-In Buffalo Jump

Although teepees are not often used for living in today, they are still an important sign of identity. This teepee was built in 2002 for a special exhibition in the Sir Alexander Galt Museum in Lethbridge, to celebrate traditional Kainai culture.

words matter!

A **travois** was a frame used for moving a teepee and for carrying belongings. One end was pulled by a horse or a dog; the other dragged on the ground.

Connections with the Land

What does the following story tell you about the connection of the people with the grasslands?

ALBERTA VOICES Knowing All the Places

We travelled around, but we were not moving around aimlessly. The river was the wintering place, where there was shelter and water. In the spring, people would find out where the rain was, where it was getting warm. The berries start there. The roots and herbs start to grow. The grass is plentiful, so then the buffalo come.

So our people knew where to go to find things, depending on the climate. They knew all the places they moved to. The whole tribe didn't move together; clans and families moved around and spread out over the land. This let them share the land, and protected the territory from other people.

Frank Weasel Head, Kainai First Nation

Setting up camp near Belly River, in 1887. The horse is pulling a frame called a **travois**. The travois was made of skins and poles from a teepee. It was an easy way to move a teepee, but it also carried belongings. What natural resources were used to make a teepee and travois?

Living on the Parklands

The Parkland region is the traditional home of the Plains Cree people. They lived closely with all the life in the region. There were many animals, but the buffalo was most important here, just as it was in the Grassland region.

Plains Cree people used bows and arrows to hunt the buffalo. After about 1730, horses became an important part of their way of life. Later, Plains Cree people hunted on horseback, using guns brought by Europeans. Look at the chart below to find out more.

Winter	• Buffalo herds migrated north, to shelter in the forests.
	• Plains Cree people followed buffalo herds northwards, to be sure of a food supply for the winter.
	• Hunters often chased buffalo into the snow. The animals sank, but the hunters could move on the snow because they wore snowshoes.
Summer	• Buffalo herds migrated southwards, to graze on the grasslands.
	• Plains Cree people followed the buffalo.
	• Hunters sometimes chased animals into marshy areas, where the animals could not easily get away.

This scene was painted by Peter Rindisbacher in 1922. It shows Plains Cree hunting buffalo. What information can you get from the painting?

Inside a Teepee

This illustration of a Plains Cree teepee shows items that might have been used by people living in it. Which natural resources were used?

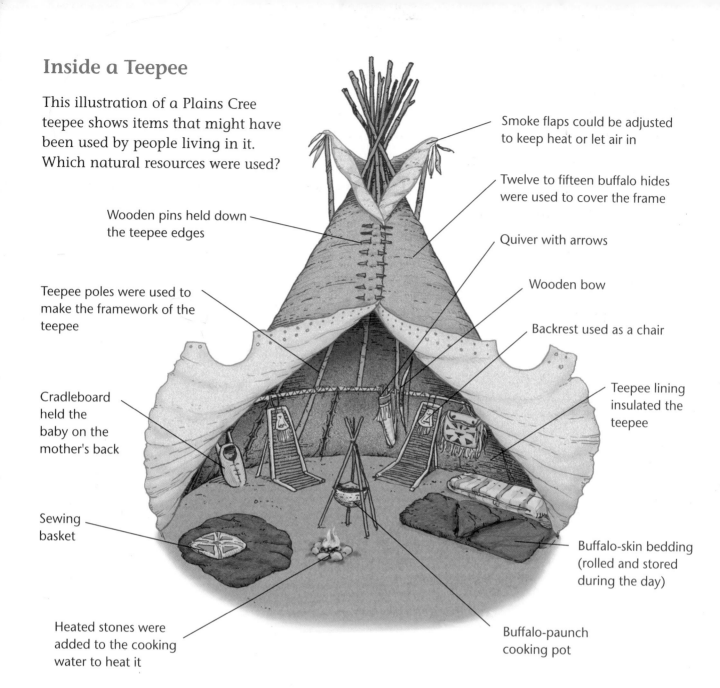

Wooden pins held down the teepee edges

Teepee poles were used to make the framework of the teepee

Cradleboard held the baby on the mother's back

Sewing basket

Heated stones were added to the cooking water to heat it

Smoke flaps could be adjusted to keep heat or let air in

Twelve to fifteen buffalo hides were used to cover the frame

Quiver with arrows

Wooden bow

Backrest used as a chair

Teepee lining insulated the teepee

Buffalo-skin bedding (rolled and stored during the day)

Buffalo-paunch cooking pot

I want to find out about various teepee designs, symbols, and colours. I will add the information about Plains Cree and my research to my web.

ALBERTA VOICES

A Trade Centre

This area, Edmonton, was an established trade centre. People came from all over and from a long way away. They would set up shop and trade there. People from northern Alberta would bring tanned moose hides. They would trade moose hides for buffalo robes, because there were fewer buffalo up north. People traded for clothing, ornaments, beads, later for horses—for all kinds of things.

Billy Joe Laboucan, Cree First Nation

Living in the Boreal Forest

As you can see from the map on page 99, the Woodland Cree and the Dene Tha' lived in the Boreal Forest region. Hunters were taught respect for the land and the life that lived on it. What can you tell about ways of life from the story below?

ALBERTA VOICES

Working Together

We worked the land together, the men and the women. If it was net fishing in the lake, the women would be at the other end from the men, gathering the nets as they were pulled in. On the shore, the men would do the cutting and scaling of the fish. The women would smoke or dry the fish. Nothing was ever wasted. Scales were very important, because they were used as decoration on clothing, shoes, and pictures. Nothing was destroyed. Even the guts from cleaning the fish were buried in the ground, because you must return things to Mother Earth, and we knew this was good fertilizer. When you take out, you must put back!

Myrtle Calahaisn, Saddle Lake

Some Forest Resources

The following animals are all found in the Boreal Forest: moose, deer, elk, ducks, and geese.

THEN **AND** NOW

Then (left): Preparing a moose hide. *Now* (right): Working in Fort McKay. How can you tell that natural resources are still important?

words matter!

Technology refers to any of the tools or ways of doing things that people use to get tasks done or to make their lives easier.

The **environment** includes all aspects of nature that surround us.

Thinking It Through

Look at the examples of traditional Dene Tha' technology. How have they been adapted today? Which of them have you used?

Look at these examples of traditional Dene Tha' **technology**. How do they show you that the Dene Tha' lived in harmony with the boreal forest **environment**?

Traditional Dene Tha' Technology

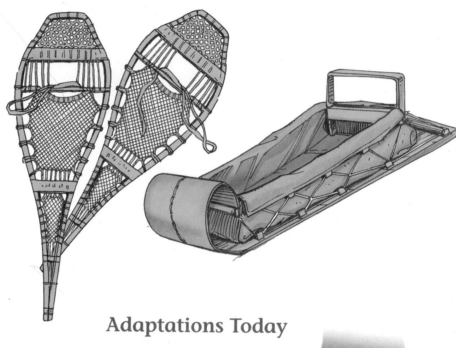

Adaptations Today

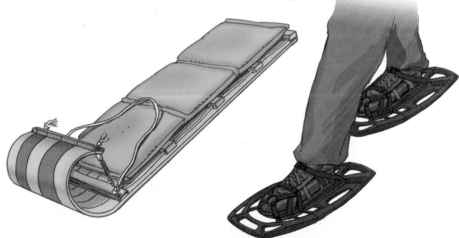

ALBERTA VOICES

It's the Land That Makes Us

One of my Elders told me a situation. He said we can get rid of all the Dene people in Denendeh [our land]. We can all die off for some reason, but if there was another human being that came stumbling along and came to Denendeh, the environment would turn him into a Dene person. It's the environment and the land that makes us Dene people.

Roy Fabian, Hay River

Living in the Canadian Shield

The Canadian Shield region is the traditional homeland of the Dene Suline. In the region's rivers and lakes, there are many fish and water birds that provide food. On the land, there are moose and caribou, and at one time there were many wood buffalo. You will learn more about wood buffalo in Chapter 9.

The spectacular beauty of the Canadian Shield has been an inspiration to many artists. Alex Janvier is from the Le Goffe First Nation, near Cold Lake. Do you see any signs of nature in his painting below?

I will add Alex Janvier's name to my web. What other First Nations artists, musicians, or authors are from Alberta? I will ask my teacher to help me find out more.

Morning Star by Alex Janvier. The artist created this painting for a ceiling in the Canadian Museum of Civilization in Gatineau, near Ottawa. He explained the title with these words: "My people used the morning star as a guide light in the early mornings of the winter hours. According to the stars in the sky… they have an idea of the direction they are going."

Connected with Living Things

Each First Nation has its own culture, but some values and beliefs are shared.

ALBERTA VOICES

A Shared Belief

We are connected to the plants, the animals, everything. We need each other. We depend on each other. We share the essence of everything around us. This goes all the way down the chain of life. We are connected to the mountains, the trees, the grass, the rivers, the animals with two legs, the animals with four legs, the animals with wings, the finned animals, even the creeping animals. We are all interrelated. This connection of all living things—this is part of the connections among all First Nations.

Michael Merrier, Edmonton

The Calendar Months	The Dene Suline Calendar
January	Cold month (edzahi zaghé)
February	Big bird month (det'anichogh zaghé)
March	Goose month (hah zaghé)
April	Frog month (ts'élti zaghé)
May	Egg month (eghézé zaghé)
June	Hatching month (eghéz yéhóli zaghé)
July	Moulting month (echedh zaghé/?idetzc)
August	Birds going back month (na?idéli zaghé/?echeth zaghé)
September	Moose breeding month (dení etkénadíhi zaghé)
October	Winter month (haye zaghé/nhaye zaghé/itts'szi zaghé)
November	Crazy day month (eyune dziné zaghé)
December	Praying month (tettéghe yati zaghé)

Dene Suline calendar. How can you tell that there was always a strong connection between people and nature?

How Do We Know About the First Peoples?

The cultures of the First Nations have been passed down from generation to generation. Let's look at some of the ways in which this has happened.

Traditional Knowledge

First Nations people have used stories to pass on their traditional knowledge of the land and their culture to the next generation. Children learn by listening to stories and being shown the ways of nature, often by the **Elders** of the nation. This way of remembering and telling about the past is called **oral teaching**.

Elders are greatly respected. They have knowledge and understanding that cannot be found in any other source.

ALBERTA VOICES

Listening to Elders

Cree Elder Myrtle Calahaisn

At the Native Friendship Centre in Edmonton, a group of Elders meet once a week to talk to young people about their traditions and culture. They make this statement about traditional knowledge:

If you are young, it is important to sit with Elders, to try to learn where you came from. We try to give our youth their history, love, and compassion [caring]. The old ways can give them that. To learn, you should speak to an Elder in person.

Elders Myrtle Calahaisn, Evelyn Ashley, Amelia Baptiste, Louise Bear, and Theresa Bakker

Stories are part of the tradition of all First Nations. This needs to go on my web.

Skill Smart

Stories are important to all cultures. They also help to tell the story of Alberta. In a small group, try finding more stories about the province. Record the Internet sites, CDs, or books where you find information.

Learning Traditional Knowledge

Myrtle Calahaisn tells how she learned the traditional knowledge that she now passes on to young people in Edmonton. This is a story of her childhood in Saddle Lake, about 70 years ago.

Sometimes our family would travel to other families to hear stories. We would travel from house to house, and all the children from different places would sleep in the same house. The women would get together to speak as the children listened, and then we would go to pick berries together or to collect things that were needed. Then we would come back and take the berries and go from house to house, canning fruits and meats and other things, so that each household had enough to eat over the winter.

The children were taught the importance of being together and working together. They were taught how to survive in the forest. My grandmother taught me and my brother how to survive with her stories and by taking us into the bush. She always had a long apron, and she would have us help her gather up all the twigs in it, all the small wood for starting the fire. Every morning she would have us go with her to get things we needed.

Amelia Baptiste, Louise Bear, Theresa Bakker, Evelyn Ashley, and Myrtle Calahaisn at the Native Friendship Centre in Edmonton. They talk about their culture as they work at sewing beads into clothes or moccasins. The beads are worked into patterns that have been known by families for many generations.

Stories On Stone

Oral teaching is not the only way in which First Nations people pass on knowledge. At Writing-On-Stone, rock paintings and carved images in the rock record the past. These carvings show important events in the lives of the people who lived nearby. Some of the carvings are at least 3000 years old. Writing-On-Stone is still a sacred and spiritual place. Today it is also protected as a provincial park.

There were no horses in this area until about 1730. What does that tell you about this carving of a horse and rider?

ALBERTA VOICES

Story Robes

Some groups store information in pictographs [symbols that tell a story]. For example, a Kainai band might have someone make a robe that has symbols on it. Sometimes these symbols form the shape of a circle on the hide and each new symbol stands for what was very important that year. If the robe has 40 or 50 symbols, that means 40 or 50 years of the most important things that happened.

James Dempsey, University of Alberta
Member of Blackfoot First Nation

A tsinikiisoka'sim [tsee-nik-ee-so-ka-sim], a Kainai story robe, made in the mid-1900s

113

Remains of the Past

words matter!

Archeologists study buildings and objects from the past. These objects are often buried, and archeologists dig carefully to uncover them.

Artifacts include items that were made or used by people long ago. Some Aboriginal artifacts are known as **historical cultural items**.

Thinking
It Through

- What do you think artifacts can tell about ways of life?

- Why is it important to learn about the past? Share your ideas in a small group.

There is another way to learn about Alberta's past. In some parts of the province, scientists have uncovered remains of objects that were used by people who lived here in the past. These scientists are called **archeologists**. The remains that they uncover are called **artifacts**. Artifacts include items that were made or used by people. Archeologists use scientific methods to find out when artifacts were made. They piece together the artifacts' remains, and information about the artifacts, to build a picture of how people may have lived in the past.

Archeologists have found teepee rings in the grasslands, like the one shown in the photograph below. Teepee rings are circles of stones that once held down the bottom edges of teepees. Archeologists can tell that these teepee rings are thousands of years old. Why do you think just the stones have been found, but none of the other parts of the teepee?

There are tens of thousands of teepee rings across Alberta. This photograph shows a teepee ring at the Cranford site. The ring has been boxed off to protect it. The measuring stick (one metre long) is placed to give archeologists a sense of the size of the ring when looking at the photograph.

Learning in Many Ways

Look back to the description of the buffalo jump on page 102. How do you think we know about the way buffalo were hunted in the past? Try to think of at least two ways. At Head-Smashed-In Buffalo Jump, an interpretive centre has been built so that people can learn about this part of Alberta's heritage. The interpretive centre shows how knowledge of the area has come from both oral history and archeology. At the site, Elders and archeologists have combined their knowledge to preserve and celebrate this unique site.

ALBERTA VOICES

Sharing Learning

The archeologist who digs here shares what he learns with me. Our site is very rich in artifacts [such as hunting tools]. It offers remarkable proof of prehistoric life. My Blackfoot Elders pass on to me a lot of information about jumps and our Blackfoot people.

Lorraine Good Striker, head of interpretation, Head-Smashed-In Buffalo Jump

Alberta on Trade Route

A dig near Purple River tells a fascinating story about Alberta's past. Archeologists have unearthed arrowheads, stone tools, and a lot of bison bones. This evidence reveals that this site was once an important area for hunting.

There's more to the story. The tools and arrowheads are made of materials that come from North and South Dakota, in what is now the United States. Archeologists believe that long ago there was probably a trade route between that area and Alberta.

Archeologists working on the site are excited by what they are learning. So are their students, many of whom are from local First Nations. They are happy to find out more about their own ancient past and Alberta's history.

Head-Smashed-In Buffalo Jump

I felt really proud to be an Albertan when I went with my family to visit Head-Smashed-In Buffalo Jump. It's a World Heritage Site. That means it's important to the whole world!

Being here made it easy for me to imagine what it must have been like to have lived near this spot more than 6000 years ago. We camped at Willow Creek Park in a real teepee! At night, we heard stories about how the Kainai and Piikani people herded bison over the cliff.

In the interpretive centre, you can look way up a cliff and imagine the buffalo falling. Some of the skulls, tools, and other artifacts that the archeologists have found are also on display. It was amazing to think they are thousands of years old.

Organizing Information

Think of a time when it would be helpful to record what you have heard or read. Graphic organizers like Venn diagrams, charts, and webs can help. Jot notes are a good way to record key ideas on organizers. Jot notes can be short phrases or even single words. They can include symbols and simple diagrams.

When gathering information and taking notes, ask yourself questions, such as

- Who or where is the information from?
- When was the information gathered? Is it from the past or the present?
- What are the main ideas?
- Why are they important?
- Which ideas can I leave off my organizer?
- How can I find out more information?
- If I could only share one piece of information, what would I tell?

Practise the Skill

- Review pages 111–116. As you read, organize the information in a chart, using jot notes.

- Find a partner. Use your chart and jot notes to tell what you thought was most important about this section of text.

- Did your chart and jot notes help you share the main ideas? What information could you add or remove to share more effectively?

Viewpoints

Where Do Cultural Items Belong?

Different kinds of historical cultural items and artifacts are put in museums. Alberta has important museums such as the Royal Alberta Museum in Edmonton and the Glenbow Museum in Calgary. Yet, there are different viewpoints on what should be done with some items. Look at these opinions.

Historical cultural items, like this Cree saddle from the early 1900s, belong in museums. Museums can look after them, preserve them, and display them so that everyone can learn from them.

Museum visitor

Some of the things that museums have collected are very sacred to First Nations people. We don't call them artifacts. We refer to them as sacred bundles.

We started returning items because we thought it was important to help people keep their culture alive. It can help spread knowledge through a community and make the culture strong. When a sacred bundle comes into a community, it can move from family to family, and everyone benefits from that.

Dr. Gerald Conaty, Senior Curator, Glenbow Museum

People who say these things should be in museums don't understand our ways. They are looking at it from a different point of view. These sacred bundles are not meant to be studied or put out on display. There is a certain way of looking at them and caring for them.

These things are alive; they mean something. They have to be part of our ceremonies and our way of life. They are part of our education. They teach us about our ways of life—spiritual life and everyday life. They are a whole way of life. You can't take a whole way of life from people.

We look after these things better than museums do. Some bundles I have seen in museums are disintegrating. But a sacred bundle that was at home, being looked after in the traditional way—you would never see it disintegrating like that.

Frank Weasel Head, Kainai Elder

Artifacts should belong to people who find them. Many people like to collect arrowheads like these.

Antique dealer

Over to YOU!

1. Work in a group to discuss the different points of view you have read on these pages.

2. Think of some artifacts that are important to your family or community. Would you be prepared to put them in a museum, or would you prefer to keep them at home or in your community? Explain.

Set Your Skills in Motion

In the News

Find a newspaper, magazine, or online article that tells about First Nations in Alberta today. Look for information about celebrations, events, or issues. Make a chart. Use jot notes to help you understand the main points of the article. Explain the article to the class.

Design a Web Page

Design a Web page that uses words and pictures to celebrate one of Alberta's First Nations. Include

- important historical information
- information about traditional lands
- information about communities today
- a dictionary of at least five words from the language of the First Nation
- one additional item of your choice

Create a Brochure

Research a historic site that preserves and celebrates First Nations in Alberta. How does this place show a connection between the land and the First Nation? Create a brochure to share what you learned. Add pictures and a map.

Write a Biography

Find out more about a First Nations artist, author, or musician from Alberta. Write a short biography about the person. Tell how their work is important to Alberta's culture and identity.

Look What You Have Learned!

The regions of Alberta have various landscapes, wildlife, plants, and other natural resources. These have shaped different ways of life for First Nations. All First Nations share a connection with living things. First Nations also share their traditional knowledge through stories. Traditional knowledge has been passed down from one generation to the next, and is still valued today. First Nations culture, language, and stories are a strong part of Alberta's identity.

Review the inquiry questions for this chapter:
- Which First Nations first lived in different areas of the province?
- How are the First Nations important to Alberta's identity?

Share what you have learned by making a report outline about any First Nation you have read about. Think about the region the First Nation is from, ways of life, and how the First Nation is important to Alberta culture today. Include a title and three headings. Use jot notes to record your ideas as you collect information. If possible, use a computer to make your outline.

Take Time to Reflect

Before you go on to the next chapter, think about what you have done in this one. What types of questions might you ask when you gather your research? How can you use charts and jot notes in the future to help organize and make sense of the information you find?

 Choose something from this chapter to save for your Alberta Treasure Chest.

New Roots for Alberta

In 1807, Marie-Anne Gaboury was on the adventure of a lifetime. Together with her husband and a small group of other fur traders, she travelled from Québec halfway across North America. The only way to make the journey was by canoe.

These people were looking for a steady supply of animal furs. They travelled across huge lakes, up raging rivers, and through thick forests, heading towards the West.

Along the way, Marie-Anne gave birth to two children. Eventually, she and her husband arrived in the settlement that became Edmonton, their home for four years. There, her third child, Josette, was born. She was the first baby of Francophone parents to be born in Alberta.

Alberta's Story

In the last chapter, you learned that the First Nations have lived here the longest. Their **roots** are an important part of Alberta's story. In this chapter, you will discover how the land and natural resources made other people want to come here, too. You will see how Francophone, Métis, and British roots became part of Alberta's story.

? Inquiring Minds

Here are some questions to guide your inquiry for this chapter:

* Why did different groups of people come to Alberta?
* How did Alberta develop Francophone, Métis, and British roots?

Look for answers as you read. Then look further if you want to find out more.

How can I organize my research and questions? I will use a KWL chart to record
* what I **K**now
* what I **W**ant to know
* what I **L**earned

What Drew People to Alberta?

Why do some communities have French names? I will record my question on my KWL chart.

This is Canada's first official postage stamp, issued in April, 1851. Why do you think the beaver was used on the stamp?

Grande Prairie, Lac La Biche, Morinville, Lacombe—these are communities in Alberta today. Can you see what they have in common? If you said their names are all French, you're right! Alberta has many other Francophone communities, too. In this section you will see how these Francophone roots began. There are also communities that have British names. Lloydminster, Dunvegan, and Strathmore are just a few. We'll see how Alberta's British roots formed as well.

The story begins with the trading of some of Alberta's precious natural resources. First Nations had been trading with each other for many years. Around the middle of the 1700s, people from eastern Canada and Europe were also coming to trade. The resources they wanted were the furs from animals such as mink, marten, and muskrat. Most of all, they wanted the thick, soft fur of the beaver.

Hats like these had become very fashionable in Europe. Traders made long, dangerous journeys across land and sea to get as many furs as they could.

What Was the Fur Trade?

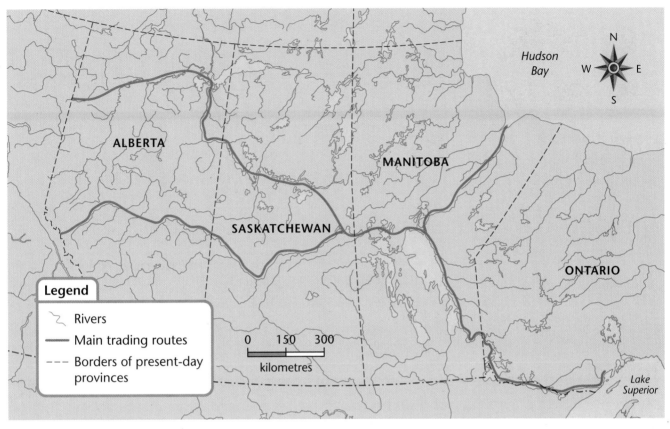

These are the routes that fur traders followed. Look at the map on pages 316–317.
How far did people from Britain and France have to travel to get furs from Alberta?

In eastern Canada, people from Québec and from England and Scotland had been looking for furs for some time. They would meet with First Nations people who knew where to find and trap the animals. In exchange for the furs, they offered First Nations people goods such as kettles, cloth, metal tools, and weapons. This exchange became known as the **fur trade.**

Canadian and European traders began pushing farther west in search of more and better furs. The journey over land to the West was long and hard. Some traders travelled more than 3000 kilometres, paddling most of the way in their canoes.

words matter!

During the **fur trade**, European traders exchanged goods for furs. These furs came from animals trapped by First Nations people. The fur trade lasted from about the 1750s to the 1830s. After that, silk hats became more popular than hats made from beaver.

125

How Did Fur Traders Travel?

How did the fur traders find their way? What did you notice about the trade routes on the map on page 125? They were on the rivers—the highways of the 1700s!

When you are travelling along a modern highway, do you ever have to get out of your car and carry it across some rough land or up a steep hill and down the other side? Of course not, but that's what people had to do then. To get from one river to another, they would carry the canoe and the trade goods on their backs. This was called a **portage**. The canoes were made of light materials, but when loaded, they were very heavy. The men had to be very strong to carry them.

There were advantages to travelling along the rivers. If you were moving in the direction of the river's flow, the current would help to carry you along. If you were going the opposite way, it was hard work. The Cree, Nakoda, and Dene in Alberta had used these trade routes for hundreds of years. The traders from the east wanted to learn from these First Nations and use the same routes.

Voyageurs at Dawn by Frances Anne Hopkins (painted in 1871). How is the canoe being used in this painting?

How Did the Fur Trade Change Alberta?

Imagine this! You are a young man in Montréal looking for adventure. You hear stories about the rugged land of the west. Rushing rivers, steep cliffs, mountains that seem to touch the sky, forests so thick you can barely walk through them. You want to see these wonders and make your fortune. You get a job as a **voyageur** for a fur-trading company, helping to paddle a canoe halfway across the continent.

Whatever the weather, as long as there is daylight, you and your fellow voyageurs paddle the canoes filled with items to trade for furs. You paddle to the beat of the folk songs you learned from your parents and grandparents. Between waterways, you portage with the canoe. You have to carry your pack as well, and it can weigh almost 150 kg! The trip is exhausting, but you see sights that you could never have imagined. If you were this voyageur, how might you feel? What changes might you bring to the land? ◆

I have another question. What did a voyageur's folk songs sound like?

words matter!

Voyageurs travelled by canoe, working for the fur-trading companies. Many of them were Canadiens, from Québec.

Canadiens were Francophones who were born in Canada. Their first language was French.

Yellowhead Pass

Yellowhead Pass is a narrow passage through the Rocky Mountains on the edge of Jasper National Park. It was named after a blond voyageur known as Tête Jaune.

Shooting the Rapids by Frances Anne Hopkins (painted in 1879). What can you tell about a voyageur's life from this painting?

How Did Alberta's New Roots Start to Grow?

The **British Isles** include England, Scotland, Wales, and Ireland. The people from these countries are sometimes referred to as the British, even though each country has its own culture and traditions.

During the time of the fur trade, explorers from the **British Isles** and the United States came to Alberta to try to find routes to push the fur trade farther west. Some explorers were fur traders as well. Others came to make maps of the area. Who were some of these explorers? What contributions did they make to Alberta?

Anthony Henday was born on the Isle of Wight off the southern coast of England. He left on his first expedition to the interior of Canada in June, 1754.

David Thompson travelled widely, making maps. He was known by First Nations people as "the man who looks at stars." Why do you think he was given that name?

Peter Pond was another explorer who made maps and traded in furs. Pond was American, but came to Alberta in 1778 for the huge numbers of furs that could be found here. His journeys took him to the Athabasca area.

Alexander Mackenzie travelled down the river that was later named after him. He made his journey in 1789, hoping the river would take him to the Pacific Ocean. Did it?

In this painting, Anthony Henday is shown entering a Blackfoot camp in 1754. This painting was done by George Franklin Arbuckle in 1951.

Skill Smart

With a partner, find out more about one of these explorers. Look in books or on the Internet. Put your information on a concept map. Add pictures.

Rival Companies

By the time the fur trade reached Alberta, it was controlled by two big companies. One was the Hudson's Bay Company, which was owned by the British. The other was the North West Company. It was based in the city of Montréal in Québec, where most Canadiens lived. Each company tried to get as many furs as it could.

Thinking
It Through

How were natural resources in Alberta used before the fur trade? How did the fur trade change the use of natural resources?

◄ The Hudson's Bay Company became The Bay, with many stores across Canada. The Hudson's Bay Company was famous for its blankets. Why do you think they were so useful?

Many of the people who worked for the fur-trading companies were **Francophones** from eastern Canada. Others were English-speaking people from England, Scotland, or Ireland.

When these people arrived in the area that became Alberta, they brought their culture, their heritage, and their ways of thinking with them. Alberta began to change. Alberta's first Francophone and British roots began to grow.

words matter!

Francophones are people whose first and main language is French. The first Francophones in Canada came from France, but by the time of the fur trade, many were Canadiens—born in Canada.

A Vast Land

Pierre de la Vérendrye and his sons were the first people from Québec to explore the West. They had a Cree guide, who was known as Auchagah (Ow-ka-gah). With his help, they explored Canada almost to the Alberta border in 1732. As a result of their travels, people began to understand just how big North America was.

How Did Trading Posts Develop?

I learned the Canadiens and the British came to Alberta to trap animals and trade furs. I'll add that to my KWL chart.

The North West Company and its Canadien traders set up trading posts along the rivers. The trappers brought the furs to the trading posts and exchanged them for goods offered by the traders.

Look again at the map on page 125. Find Alberta and Hudson Bay. If you were a trapper, it would take you many weeks to take your furs to Hudson Bay to sell them to the Hudson's Bay Company. Why do you think that would be? The North West Company found a way to outsmart its rivals. It built trading posts on rivers. The trappers could get to them much more easily. The Hudson's Bay Company noticed this. It quickly began building trading posts on rivers, too.

Many of these trading posts were called **forts**. Some of the trading posts had thick walls for protection. Soldiers were posted inside.

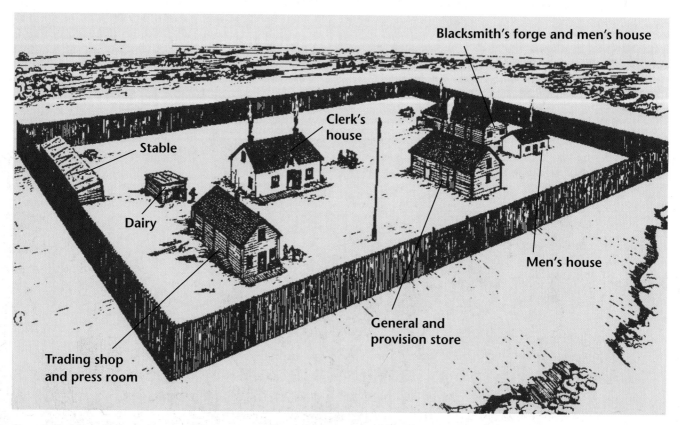

Blacksmith's forge and men's house

Clerk's house

Stable

Dairy

Men's house

General and provision store

Trading shop and press room

An artist's idea of what a fort may have looked like

Rocky Mountain House

Did you know that you can visit a fur trading post? My sister and I went to a trading post that has been reconstructed at Rocky Mountain House. You can visit and watch people in costume relive daily life there.

Rocky Mountain House was the western-most trading post during the days of the fur trade. Both the North West and Hudson's Bay companies were based here. They competed for trade with nine different First Nations, including Blackfoot, Nakoda, and Cree.

When my sister and I went, we took part in the re-enactment of a trading ceremony. There were many steps trading partners had to take to show that they really trusted each other. We got to think about trading through the eyes of different people. I really enjoyed learning about the way trading was done back then.

How Did Today's Communities Grow from the Fur Trade?

The two companies tried hard to outdo one another by building forts farther and farther west along the Saskatchewan River. As soon as one built a fort, the other did, too! They also built forts along the Peace River and Athabasca River.

Look at the map below. It shows where the two trading companies built forts in Alberta. Now look at a map of Alberta today. How many of the trading post locations are still communities today?

Main Fur-trading Posts, Alberta, 1788–1825

Peace River

Fort Vermilion
1788

Fort Chipewyan
1788

Fort Dunvegan
1805

Lesser
Slave Lake
1800

Fort-of-the-Forks
1788

Fort George and
Buckingham House
1792

Fort Assiniboine
1825

Fort Augustus
and
Fort Edmonton
1795

Jasper House
1813

Athabasca River

North Saskatchewan River

Rocky Mountain
House, 1799

N
W   E
S

Present border of Alberta

Hudson's Bay Company Post

North West Company Post

Posts operated by both companies

e.g.
1788   Date when first fort built

0 km   100   200

Skill Smart

Visit a museum, historic site, or library. Find out how your community started. Look at historic photos, diaries, and maps. You could make an electronic chart to share what you learned.

This map shows where trading posts were built. Some were built by the North West Company, and some were built by the Hudson's Bay Company.

Exploring Historical Maps

What are some things you can learn by looking at historical maps? They can help you find out about land and people in the past. You can use them with maps from today. Look to see how some things have changed and how some things have stayed the same.

Practise the Skill

Look at the map on the facing page. Use it to answer the questions below.

1. Which direction did the fur traders first come from? (Hint: Look at the dates.)

2. Name the three main rivers the traders used. Which was used first?

3. What relationship do you see between the rivers and where the forts were built?

4. Name the two forts that are farthest south. What region are these forts in? (Hint: You can check the map of Alberta's natural regions on page 32.)

5. Think about why there were no forts south of this region. (Hint: What animal furs were the traders buying? Discuss your ideas with others in your group.)

How Did Alberta's Métis Roots Begin?

The **Métis** are people descended from British or Canadien traders and First Nations. We use the term **Aboriginal peoples** to talk about First Nations, Inuit, and Métis people together.

Métis Crossing is a community not far from Smoky Lake. Like the Francophone communities we learned about earlier, this community takes its name from the history of the area. Let's see how it came about!

The arrival of the fur trade in the West also led to the birth of a new nation of people. British and Canadien traders married women from different First Nations. The children of these families married one another and had children. Over time, a new nation, the **Métis** Nation, was born.

The Métis Descheneau family are seen here in a formal photograph.

Who Are the Métis?

The Métis were descended from First Nations and Canadien or British traders. Some of their ways of life came from these roots, but the Métis Nation had its own unique identity. Let's look at some of the aspects of its unique culture.

Imagine this! You are living long ago in Alberta. Herds of buffalo roam the prairies. In spring and summer, you see them in the grasslands. As fall comes, the herds move to the parkland and foothills where they can find water and grass to eat during winter. Close your eyes and imagine what it would look like to see thousands of buffalo thundering across the plain. ◆

Buffalo Traffic Jam

My great-great-great aunt talks of having to wait for three days before they could cross the Milk River, as the buffalo were so plentiful. "We would have hundreds of riders [on horseback] galloping at full speed, after a herd of many buffalo, all running at full speed."

Sharon Morin

Métis trading expedition, 1888. The Métis traded buffalo meat and skins, as well as furs.

The Buffalo Hunt

Victoria Callihoo was a Métis from Lac Ste. Anne. She lived from 1861 to 1966. She remembers her first buffalo hunt in this journal entry.

I was thirteen years old when I first joined in a buffalo hunt. We left Lac Ste. Anne after the leaves were out on the poplar trees and our small fields and gardens were seeded or planted.

I used to go with my mother on these trips. She was a medicine woman who set broken bones and knew how to use medicinal herbs. The riders who chased the buffalo were often thrown, sometimes by the bulls charging the riders, or by the horses getting their feet stuck in badger holes.

We always camped close to water. We set our teepees in a larger circle outside the cart circle. A few of the fastest horses were kept in this enclosure and the others were herded all night by a night herder, for horse thieving was a common occurrence. A fast horse was the best possession. A hunter on a fast horse would kill more buffalo than others with less speedy ponies.

Cabin and teepee at Lac Ste. Anne, 1896

Skill Smart

Old diaries, journals, and letters can help explain the past. Reread Victoria Callihoo's journal entry, above. Make a map to show what the camp might have looked like. Use symbols and a legend.

How Did the Métis Help the Fur Trade?

Earlier in the chapter, you learned how the Métis Nation came to be. Many Métis people could speak several languages. Some could speak French, English, or First Nations languages such as Cree or Blackfoot. This meant that Métis people could often translate for European traders when they met with First Nations traders. Some Métis also paddled and piloted the boats carrying furs and trade goods along the rivers of the West.

Food for the Fur Trade

The Métis also provided goods to the traders. From their buffalo hunts they supplied buffalo tongues, which people liked to eat. They also supplied robes made of buffalo pelts. Most important, they used the buffalo to make **pemmican**. Pemmican-making was a skill that the Plains Cree First Nations had. Pemmican was meat that had been dried and pounded. It was then mixed with hot buffalo grease and dried berries. It would become very hard. Traders had to use a sharp knife or even an axe to chop off a piece to eat. Pemmican never went bad and was very nutritious.

THEN AND NOW

The paths used by Métis families to hunt and to work became the highways that cross the Prairies today. They include Queen Elizabeth II Highway and parts of Highway 16.

Thinking
It Through

Why do you think pemmican was so important to the traders?

Drying meat, as shown in this Kainai camp, was one of the steps in making pemmican.

How Did the Métis Solve Their Travel Problems?

Unique Culture, Unique Language

Some Métis developed their own language, Michif. It is a mixture of Cree and French. If you type "Michif" into your search engine, you can find a Canadian government Web site that will let you hear some Michif.

Over time, traders found that their loads were getting bigger and heavier. Canoes were too small and light to carry these loads. Larger boats were needed. Métis traders solved the problem by inventing the York boat.

The York boat could carry heavy loads.

Another Métis invention was the Red River cart (see the picture on page 135). It was made without any metal. Large wooden pegs were used instead of bolts, and small pegs were used instead of nails. There was no grease for the wheels, so the carts made a loud squeaking noise when the wheels turned. It was said that every cart had its own particular squeak!

Skill Smart

- What would you like to know about the York boat or Red River cart?

- In a small group, brainstorm five research questions.

- Look for answers in books or ask a librarian. Keep track of where you find information.

THEN AND NOW

Billy Loutit was a Métis mail carrier. There is a legend that he once delivered a letter from Athabasca to Edmonton faster than a man on a horse! Could someone *really* run that distance faster than a horse? Today there is an annual race in Athabasca called the Billy Loutit Duathlon.

How Did Métis Communities Start?

At first, many Métis people spent most of their time on the trade routes. Then more began to settle in one place. Some lived in or near the fur-trading forts. Others began to farm for part of the year, and hunt buffalo at other times. Soon, there were strong Métis communities.

The song below tells about life in a Métis community. It refers to Gabriel Dumont, a Métis leader. Although he lived in Manitoba, he was well-known among the Métis in Alberta.

ALBERTA VOICES — The "Society of Generous Ones"

In the fall of the year buffalo would run
Gabriel would ride out with his gun
To get some meat for the winter supply
'cause he knew that his people could starve and die.

He'd hunt until he needed no more
Then he'd hunt for the sick and poor
The lame and the old and the ones with no guns
He called it the "Society of Generous Ones."

Don Freed, "Ride Gabriel Ride"

The Métis have a long history in Alberta. You will learn more about that history in Chapter 7. Today, some Métis people choose to live in different areas of the province. Others choose to live in one of eight areas in northern Alberta called Métis settlements. Here, the Métis govern their own communities. There are no official Métis settlements anywhere else in Canada. These Métis communities help to make Alberta unique.

Alberta's Métis Settlements Today

Paddle Prairie
Peavine • Gift Lake
East Prairie
Buffalo Lake • Kikino
Edmonton • Elizabeth
Fishing Lake
Calgary

N
W E
S

Legend
• Métis settlements

0 100 200
kilometres

What Are Some Symbols of Métis Identity?

Many nations have symbols. When you see the symbols, you think of that nation. The Métis Nation, like many others, has a flag as one symbol. Another symbol of the Métis is the colourful sash.

Sashes were worn around the waist. They were woven in beautiful colours, but they had very practical uses. Traders were away from home for a long time. There were no suitcases or backpacks. What did they use? One of the things they used on their travels was a sash.

Traders carried their belongings in a sash, just as you put yours in a backpack. On the trails, sashes were used in many ways—as a scarf, a washcloth or towel, a saddle blanket, or a rope. When clothing tore, the long fringe could be used as thread! Sashes were also used by the East Woodland First Nation and by Canadiens. Each group made its own particular kind of sash. Métis sashes are used today in Métis games and other ceremonies.

Jessie Clemans has a successful business making Métis sashes. She is famous for her "triple arrow" sashes. She uses the old method of finger-weaving to make them.

Preparing to leave on a canoe trip along a fur-trading route from Edmonton to Métis Crossing, to celebrate Alberta's 100th birthday. Why might a trip like this be an appropriate way to celebrate Alberta's Centennial?

ALBERTA VOICES

Métis Symbols

The sash today is usually red, white, and blue. The flag also has the infinity symbol, which means never-ending. So the symbol reminds us of a culture that continues on forever, and the colours of the sash remind us how everything in life is woven together.

Mark McCallum, Métis journalist

How Did Francophone Communities Grow?

While the fur trade was at its busiest, a few people began to see that Alberta had good farmland. In the fall of 1874, two brothers named Frank and Joseph Lamoureux came to Alberta. They were the first Francophone settlers to claim Alberta land for farming.

The brothers settled on the north bank of the North Saskatchewan River in a place that became known as Lamoureux. In 1875, Fort Saskatchewan was built right across the river. Over the years, the brothers brought friends and family members to the new settlement. Other Francophone families followed.

The brothers farmed and raised cattle, and also had several other businesses. Joseph had a pair of pliers, so he was the local dentist! Today, Lamoureux is a small community where about 50 people live.

So many names of our communities come from long ago. I would like to find out about the people who started my community.

Thinking *It Through*

- Why do you think the Lamoureux brothers chose to settle near the water?
- Why would that be an advantage to them?

Fort Saskatchewan, across the river from Lamoureux, continued to grow and is a busy community today.

Where Did Francophone Communities Develop?

Franco-Albertans have always had a strong presence in Edmonton. Remember the story of Marie-Anne Gaboury on page 122? This street in Edmonton is named after her!

Remember the story of Marie-Anne Gaboury on page 122?

These are just a few of the many communities started by Francophones in Alberta.

Skill Smart

Find out more about one community from the map. Make a poster about the community.

- How did it start?
- How did it get its name?
- Include one particularly interesting fact about that community.

In the late 1800s, many Francophones moved from Québec to Alberta. Francophone settlements grew. New ones started in the northern part of the province. Look at the map. Do you live in one of these communities, or have you visited any? If so, you may have seen French signs or heard French spoken there.

How Did Missionaries Build Communities?

A Lovely Place

April 1861—In my travels from Edmonton to Ste. Anne, when I'd stop on a hillside to have my dogs rest, I'd gaze towards a certain hill with a lake in the distance, and just opposite a forest. As I'd gaze, I'd murmur to myself: "What a lovely place for a mission."

Father Albert Lacombe

I wonder what else the missionaries did.

This is how Father Lacombe described the area where he would build the community of St. Albert. Father Lacombe was a Catholic priest who came from Québec in 1852 to work as a **missionary** in the West. He spent many years in Alberta and established Francophone communities here. St. Albert and Lacombe are named after him.

To help the missionaries speak with Cree people, Father Lacombe wrote a Cree dictionary. He started hospitals and played a big part in starting schools in the West.

Father Lacombe also travelled, trying to encourage Canadiens to move to the West.

words matter!

A **missionary** is someone who travels to teach religion to a group of people.

Father Albert Lacombe

What Did the Francophone Missionaries Give to Alberta?

In 1863, the Grey **Nuns** came to St. Albert. These religious women did the work of doctors, dentists, teachers, and nurses. The place where they lived was used as a school and a hospital. They looked after children who had no parents. They learned to speak Cree and wrote a Cree grammar text. Whenever the people had a need, the Grey Nuns tried to meet it.

The Francophone missionaries started small communities called missions. They also built hospitals and schools. They became known for their tradition of caring that many Albertans still value today. The photos on the following page show some of the ways in which the tradition continued.

words matter!

A **nun** is a member of a religious community of women. The nuns spend their lives in prayer and service to others. The Grey Nuns were founded in Montréal in 1738. They are named for their long, grey robes.

Skill Smart

Look at the photographs and captions on the following page. What did the Francophone missionaries give to Alberta? Record your ideas using jot notes.

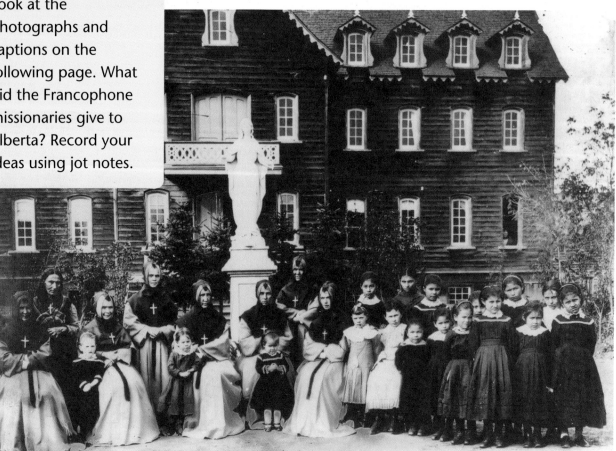

The Grey Nuns and some of the children they taught outside the convent in which they lived, in the late 1880s

144

A TRADITION OF CARING

The Grey Nuns set up a hospital ward in Fort Calgary. That ward became Holy Cross Hospital. The hospital closed in 1996. Do you have any relatives who were treated there?

The Grey Nuns also founded the Edmonton General Hospital, the first hospital in Edmonton. How do you think sick people were cared for before this hospital was founded?

The oldest school in Calgary is St. Mary's. It was started at the Rouleauville mission, which is now part of the Mission district of Calgary. The school taught children of all ages, but today it is a high school. Would you like to go to a school with such a long history?

Later in his life, Father Lacombe founded the Lacombe Home to care for elderly people and orphans. The hospitals founded by many religious orders in many parts of the province are part of the tremendous contribution by Francophones to the development of our province.

Who Were the Protestant Missionaries?

I will ask my teacher to help me search the Internet to find out more about Protestant missionaries.

Francophone missionaries worked to keep their Catholic faith and their language strong. There were also English-speaking missionaries in Alberta. Most were British and belonged to Protestant churches. Some of these missionaries also started schools. The first English-speaking missionary was Robert Rundle. He came from England to Fort Edmonton in 1840. Later, he built a mission on Pigeon Lake. You can still visit the mission buildings today.

Many of the Protestant missionaries travelled around, taking their teaching from one place to another. They learned First Nation languages, so that they could speak with the people they met. These missionaries brought British ideas and values to parts of Alberta.

The Protestant mission at Morley was started by George McDougall and his son, John. This drawing shows the mission in 1875.

Are There Different Opinions About the Missionaries?

There is no question that the missionaries played a very important role in making Alberta what it is today. Yet, there are different **perspectives** on their work. Read the following accounts to see what they are.

ALBERTA VOICES

A Francophone Perspective

Father Lacombe came here to teach the Métis. Those were the French speakers he came here to teach. He wanted to share that with others. He founded and ministered in many churches all over Alberta in the 1800s. People were grateful to have a place to practice their religion in French. They called him our wise elder and they looked up to him. His missions were the gathering places for French-speaking communities.

Émilie Chevigny, Plamondon

An Aboriginal Perspective

The missionaries tried to get rid of Aboriginal spirituality, which is an important part of the culture. They convinced the government not to allow the Sundance. It was very important to people so they still did it, but they hid it. Today, many priests in our city are highly regarded. It's not a problem—we can be Christians and also follow our own spiritual ways.

Laura Vinson, co-executive director, Ben Calf Robe Society, Edmonton

Some missionaries taught in the French language and helped to keep it strong in Alberta. That's one of the reasons why the French language is still spoken in Alberta today.

Thinking *It Through*

Sometimes different people can see the same events in different ways. Why do you think this is so? Use the Alberta voices on this page to support your view.

Lac La Biche Mission, in about 1850

Viewpoints

How Can Place Names Help Us Remember Our Past?

What is the name of the street you live on? What is the name of your community? What do those names mean? Where do they come from, and why does it matter?

Read this newspaper story and letters to the editor to find out what some people think about these questions.

GRADE 4 CLASS SUGGESTS NAME CHANGE

Grade 4 students at the town school have an idea and they're taking it all the way to town council. The students asked the council to change the name of a nearby street to remind people of the history of the fur trade that is part of our town.

"Across from our school is a street called Third Street. We looked at old maps with our teachers. Part of that street was a route that voyageurs in the fur trade travelled to get to the river.

Most people don't even know that," says Violet Beaupré.

"If the town renames the street Voyageur Trail, people will start to ask questions and want to learn more about our history," her friend Trevor Lewis added.

With their teacher's help, the students sent a letter to their town councillor. They hope to send two people to share their viewpoints at the next town meeting.

Some people had opinions about the students' idea, and they wrote letters to the editor of their local newspapers.

To the Editor,

Re: Grade 4 Class Suggests Name Change

I think we should focus on names that relate to the group that settled in an area. This area was settled by the British and many still live here. Let's use an early British family's name!

Sincerely,
R. Kent

To the Editor,

Re: Grade 4 Class Suggests Name Change

I see that the Grade 4 students at our local school want to change the name of the road near their school to Voyageur Trail to remind us of the voyageurs. My family would like to see street names that remind us all of the First Nations who were here long before the fur trade. Things change all the time. We can't change names for every change that happens. We should select names from our history so that we always remember.

Sincerely,
Mrs. R. Sage

Over to YOU!

1. Why do you think the students wrote to the town council? Whom would you need to contact if you wanted to make a suggestion like this one?

2. As a class, discuss the different viewpoints. Take a class vote to decide if the street name should be changed.

3. What areas or streets in your community are named after people or events? Do you think your streets should be named differently to remember the past? Give reasons for your views.

Set Your Skills in Motion

Use a Historical Map

Many Métis came from the Red River area, now in Manitoba.
Use the historical map below and answer these questions:

- From which province did the Métis start to move west in about 1870?
- When did a group go to Edmonton?
- How do you know that groups went to Edmonton and Calgary around the same time?
- Did any Métis go to the United States? How do you know?

The Spread of Métis Communities

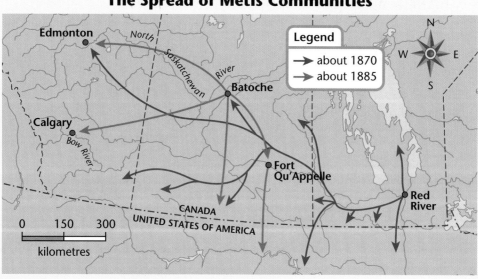

Be a Responsible Citizen

Who is a responsible citizen helping to build a community in Alberta today? With a partner, look on the Internet, in a newspaper, or in a library database. Give a speech to share your findings. Include ways in which you, too, can contribute to your community.

Complete Your KWL Chart

Scan the chapter again. Record what you learned on your KWL chart. Can you think of any new questions to ask? Look in a variety of sources to find answers.

Look What You Have Learned!

Alberta has Francophone, Métis, and British roots. People from Québec, France, and Britain came to Alberta to trade goods for furs with First Nations peoples. Some of the fur traders stayed and married First Nations women. A new nation grew from those unions—the Métis Nation. Different languages and cultures are part of Alberta's past. They are still part of the province's identity today.

> Review the inquiry questions for this chapter:
> - Why did different groups of people come to Alberta?
> - How did Alberta develop Francophone, Métis, and British roots?
>
> Share what you have learned by writing a report. Choose one group you read about. Where can you see their roots today? Consider languages, religion, and traditions. Try to find "Then and Now" photographs or make drawings to illustrate your report.

Take Time to Reflect

Before you go on to the next chapter, think about what you have done in this one. How did you use maps to learn about the past? How might a KWL chart help you in the next chapter?

 Choose something from this chapter to save for your Alberta Treasure Chest.

Preparing for New Settlers

On August 11, 1883, William Sanford Freeze watched the first train to the West arrive in Calgary. He was amazed at the thundering sound of the approaching train, and the squeal of the metallic wheels screeching to a halt. He had never seen such a large machine up close before. Great clouds of steam covered him and the rest of the people who were also there. It was a day never to forget!

William owned a grocery store. He knew the train would bring many changes. Until then, it took four weeks to get a letter from Calgary to Winnipeg by horse. It also took four weeks to order goods for his store, and just as long to get the goods delivered. All that was now about to change.

Calgary 1883
Compliments
Hugh B. Gilean

Alberta's Story

The fur trade brought many changes to the area that became Alberta. Yet even greater changes were still to come. In this chapter, you will find out about people who settled here after the fur trade and how British ways of life became part of Alberta. You will also learn what the changes meant for the people already living here.

? **Inquiring Minds**

Here are some questions to guide your inquiry for this chapter:

- How did important events of this time shape Alberta?
- How did ways of life change for the people?

Look for answers in this chapter. If you want to find out more, explore some other sources as well.

How can I keep track of where I find my information? I will record
- book titles
- Internet sites
- names of people

How Did Alberta's British Roots Grow?

Imagine this! It is the 1860s, and the fur trade is ending. The First Nations live here, along with some Francophone, Métis, and British settlers. The Hudson's Bay Company owns much of the land. Then, in 1869, the Canadian government buys the land because it wants many more settlers to come to the West. Look at the map below to see how far the land stretches. ◆

As you can see from the map, Canada was very different. Until 1867, Canada was a group of British colonies. This meant the British government in England made most decisions. People from Britain had settled in parts of Canada, but they were still British and loyal to the King or Queen of England. Then in 1867, some of the colonies joined together to form the new country of Canada. It had its own government in Ottawa. It was similar to the British kind of government. The same kind of government was set up in the West as settlers began to arrive. Our government today still follows many British traditions.

Thinking
It Through

Do you think all the different groups of people you have learned about were happy with a British style of government? Why or why not?

Canada in 1870. Rupert's Land was owned by the Hudson's Bay Company and was sold to Canada in 1869. Can you find the area that would become Alberta on the map?

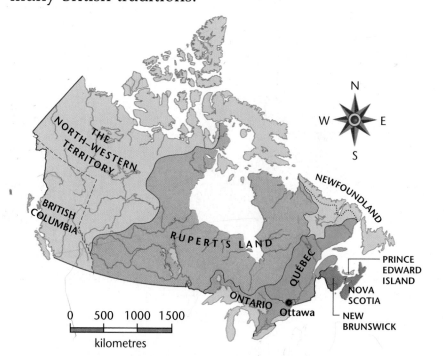

Why Was the Land for Sale?

Why do you think the Hudson's Bay Company was willing to sell its land? The answer can be found in the changes to the fur trade.

Think about how people sometimes like to change the kinds of clothes they wear. Fashions that were once in style become unpopular. People were pretty much the same in the 1800s. Silk hats became the fashion. No one wanted beaver hats any more.

What would this change mean for the fur trade? What would it mean for the First Nations and Métis trappers, and for the people living in the trading posts? What other ways would people find to make a living in Alberta?

Skill Smart

How would the end of the fur trade affect the First Nations and Métis trappers? Write a paragraph to share your thoughts.

ALBERTA VOICES

Green to Black

They say there was an old lady long ago. She was sitting on the prairie in her teepee, and she said, "The next people after us will hardly see the green grass. All this land is going to be turned over, and it will be black." She meant the earth was going to be cultivated, and, you know, all there is around here is farming and ranching.

Katie Bull Shield-Wells
Kainai First Nation

THEN AND NOW

Left: Trading post at Stand Off, around 1880. *Right:* Standing guard at Fort Macleod, a post that has been restored today as a historic site. Why do you think some trading posts have been restored as historic sites?

Why Was Settlement Difficult?

Canada's first prime minister, John A. Macdonald, believed that people had to settle on the land to make Canada a strong country. The first step, he thought, was to build a railway across the land, from the east coast to the west. Why do you suppose he thought the railway was so important? What difference would it have made to

- farmers and ranchers in western Canada?
- settlers in Francophone communities?
- people in eastern Canada who wanted to move west to start a new life?

Before the railways, people often travelled by river or by Red River cart. Some carts were pulled by oxen or donkeys, like the one shown here in Wetaskiwin, 1895.

I'll make a list of these four difficulties. I will look for and record information as I read.

Why Was the Railway Important?

The railway would make it much easier for settlers to come to the West. Yet there were still difficulties. It was a huge challenge to build a railway across Canada. In addition, many people believed that the West was a violent place, without law and order. The huge herds of buffalo presented another problem. How could a railway be built and how could fields be planted with buffalo roaming the prairies? The Canadian government had to find a way to build settlements on lands where the First Nations lived. Let's take a closer look.

Why Was It Difficult to Build the Railway?

Imagine that your family is building a house. What would you need to build it? The government in the 1870s knew that settlers in the West needed all kinds of supplies for building their homes and farms. They knew a railway could transport these goods. It would also help farmers send their crops to market quickly. But no railway had ever been built through such difficult country.

Imagine what a task it was to build a railway. There were deep valleys where bridges needed to be built. There were swampy muskegs that the railway had to go around. There was the hard rock of the Canadian Shield and many kilometres of open prairie to cross.

Thinking
It Through

Look at the photograph below. What can you tell about the way bridges were built in the late 1800s? How would building a bridge look today?

Building a railway bridge over Beaver Dam Creek, near Castor

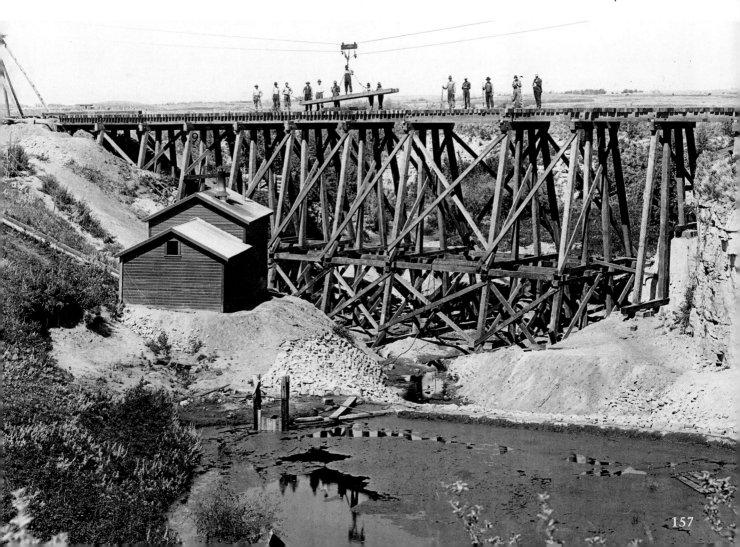

Why Were Law and Order Needed?

Would you move to a place if you heard it was not safe? In the 1870s, southern Alberta was a dangerous place.

Whisky Traders

The problem began in about 1865, with whisky traders. They were men who came from Montana, an American state to the south. They came to trade furs, but they didn't trade with blankets, pots, or guns. Instead, they offered "whisky," a mixture of alcohol, pepper, and red ink. The whisky poisoned many people. Whisky traders often took advantage of the First Nations people who lived in the area.

Wolfers and Disaster at Cypress Hills

Another problem at this time was caused by "wolfers." They were trappers who got furs by putting out poisoned buffalo meat to kill wolves and coyotes.

Then a group of wolfers did something no one could forgive. They were searching for some missing horses in the Cypress Hills. They came across a group of Nakoda who were camping peacefully nearby. Although the Nakoda had not taken the horses, the wolfers attacked them, killing 30 people.

The government in Ottawa knew it was time to bring law and order to the West.

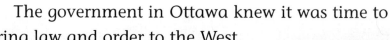

THEN AND NOW

Fort Hamilton, just outside present-day Lethbridge, was an American fort. Since its main business was selling whisky, it became known as Fort Whoop-Up.

Fort Whoop-Up is now an interpretive centre, where people can go to learn about Alberta's early history.

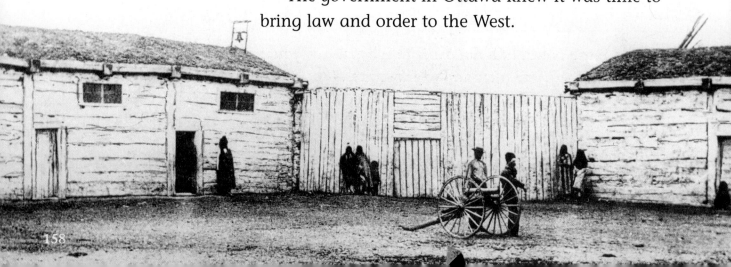

The North West Mounted Police later became the Royal Canadian Mounted Police. You probably know them as the "Mounties." Today, they are seen as a symbol of Canada around the world.

In 1873, the government set up a police force called the North West Mounted Police (NWMP). The first group of police trained in Manitoba. In July 1874, they began a long trek west. The company formed a line about 4 kilometres long. It included 275 armed men, 114 Red River carts with Métis drivers, field kitchens, mowing machines, plows, 339 horses, 142 oxen, and 93 beef cattle. Jerry Potts, a Métis guide, helped them find their way to Fort Whoop-Up.

The NWMP followed a British approach to law and order. Their red coats reminded everyone of their connection to Britain, whose soldiers also wore red uniforms. Their arrival began to change Alberta's identity. The British influence was growing stronger.

Were the NWMP successful at getting rid of the whisky traders? Here's what Chief Crowfoot of the Blackfoot First Nation had to say.

Skill Smart

- Visit the library or a museum to find out how the North West Mounted Police came to Alberta. Try looking at historical photos.

- Create a chart on the computer to show your information. Add illustrations.

ALBERTA VOICES

Police Protection

If the police had not come to the country, where would we all be now? Bad men and whisky were killing us so fast that very few of us would have been left today. The police have protected us as the feathers of the bird protect it from the frosts of winter. I wish them all good, and trust that all our hearts will increase in goodness from this time forward.

Chief Crowfoot, Blackfoot First Nation

Why Were the Buffalo a Problem for the Government?

Do you remember how huge the buffalo herds of Alberta were? How do you think these herds would have made it difficult to build a railway? What do you think the government would do about the buffalo? Here is one explanation. Once you have read this story, look for more accounts from other people at this time.

ALBERTA VOICES

A Way of Life Ends

In the days of my ancestors, there was no shortage of buffalo. The buffalo, which we call "iini," helped my people survive for thousands of years. There were so many buffalo that it took a couple of days for them to move through an area. The European people have a different perspective than my people. When they came, they wanted the buffalo out of the way. After the government took control, they wanted to build a train across the country. The goal was to kill off the buffalo to open the land for farming. I have seen photographs of European men shooting buffalo from horses, trains, and on foot. It became extremely difficult for my people to survive. When the buffalo were gone, so was our way of life.

Sandra Crazy Bull, Kainai First Nation
Glenbow Museum Interpreter, First Nations
Programs

Sandra Crazy Bull, shown here in traditional dress worn for a special presentation

Working with Graphs

People often use graphs to show change over time. You can read a graph to find out how things compare at different times, or how quickly a change happens.

We now have buffalo in North America. The few that were left in the 1880s were protected, and their population has grown. Today, many buffalo live on farms. The following figures tell about the rise in the number of buffalo in North America.

Numbers of Buffalo 1845–1940

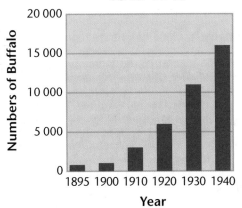

Numbers of Buffalo 1950–1999

1950	22 000
1960	38 000
1970	50 000
1980	150 000
1989	250 000
1999	350 000

Practise the Skill

Try using a computer to make your own bar graph with the figures for 1950–1999. Notice that the numbers grow all the way from 22 000 to 350 000. How will you solve the problem of showing these numbers?

Now answer these questions about the two buffalo graphs.

1. What change does the first graph show? How do you know?
2. List two pieces of information you can tell from the first graph.
3. What change is shown by the graph you made? How do you know?
4. List two pieces of information you can tell from the graph you made.
5. How many more buffalo were there in 1999 than in 1960? Solve with a calculator.

How Did Life Change for the First Nations?

I want to learn more about what happened to the buffalo. I'll ask the librarian to help me find some sources that will give me different points of view.

What does Sandra Crazy Bull mean when she says, "When the buffalo were gone, so was our way of life"?

Between 1871 and 1875, North American hunters killed ten million buffalo. By the mid-1870s, no buffalo could be found north of the Red Deer River. Americans who counted the animals in 1886 found only six buffalo!

In Chapters 4 and 5, you saw how important the buffalo were to the way of life on the prairies. They provided food and many other items. They played a part in spiritual life. How would the people live after the buffalo were killed?

Skill Smart

Skim through Chapters 4 and 5 to find the sections on the buffalo. Make jot notes about why the buffalo were so important. Record the section titles and page numbers for your information.

Buffalo hunters from Canada, the United States, and Europe killed buffalo for sport, and left them to rot. The piles of bones, like the ones shown here in about 1880, were so thick, they looked like snow on the prairie ground.

Why Were Treaties Made?

The government saw that many First Nations people were starving. It thought the problem could be solved if First Nations people changed to a farming way of life. The government also knew that settlers needed land to start farms. It made a plan that would help reach both of these goals.

The government began talking to the First Nations about making treaties. A **treaty** is an agreement between two nations. The government wanted to take the land for settlers, but made promises to the First Nations in return. The First Nations would move onto areas of land called reserves. In return, the government promised to provide food, health care, farm equipment, and schools.

words matter!

A **treaty** is an agreement between two nations. Every treaty is unique, depending on the situation. To the First Nations, treaties are solemn and sacred agreements that still apply today.

Thinking It Through

Why can a treaty be a good way to solve a problem? Discuss your thoughts in a small group.

ALBERTA VOICES Treaty 7

Each treaty was given a number. Here are two different views on Treaty 7. What do they tell you?

Government Minister, 1877
This Treaty… is certainly proof of the [fair] policy of the government of Canada towards the First Nations. [It also shows] the confidence of the First Nations in [our] promises and [fair] dealing….

Sandra Crazy Bull, 2006
My people were presented with a document written in English. It was a foreign language to us at that time. Government officials spoke through interpreters. We were told that we would help newcomers adjust to life here. We would share the land and we would get health benefits, education, and other benefits. My people also believed this was a peace treaty, and we still refer to it as such. It changed our lives forever.

Chief Crowfoot, also known as Issapomahksika [is-a-bo-mah-xi-ka], was one of the Blackfoot leaders who signed Treaty 7.

How Did Perspectives Differ?

Have you ever made an agreement with someone and then found out that there was a misunderstanding? Perhaps you saw the agreement from one point of view, and the second person saw it from another. As you read in Chapter 5, the point of view of a group of people is called a perspective. In what ways do you think the government and the First Nations might have had different perspectives?

To the First Nations, a treaty is a solemn and sacred promise that would last forever. Before, First Nations had made many treaties with each other. In their experience, treaties had helped both parties who signed them. To the British, they were legal documents, but they were not sacred.

The government believed it could own the land, and then divide it into lots that settlers could farm. Read the quote below to learn more about the perspective of the First Nations.

First Nations leaders who signed Treaty 8 received one of these silver medals to mark the occasion. What does it show?

ALBERTA VOICES

We Can't Give Land

Our people accepted Mikastoo (Red Crow) as a leader and looked to him for wise decisions. When asked if he would give up the land, Mikastoo held up a handful of earth. He said he could never give away that which belonged to Creator. He then plucked a tuft of grass and told the officials his people would willingly share that with the newcomers.

Sandra Crazy Bull

Treaty 8 negotiations at Lesser Slave Lake

Who Signed the Treaties?

In the area that is Alberta today, three treaties were signed by different First Nations and the government. The map below shows the area covered by each treaty. It also shows the reserves where each nation settled. There are still First Nations in these locations today.

I wonder if the Internet has more about Alberta treaties. If I find anything, I will record the site in my notebook.

Treaty Areas

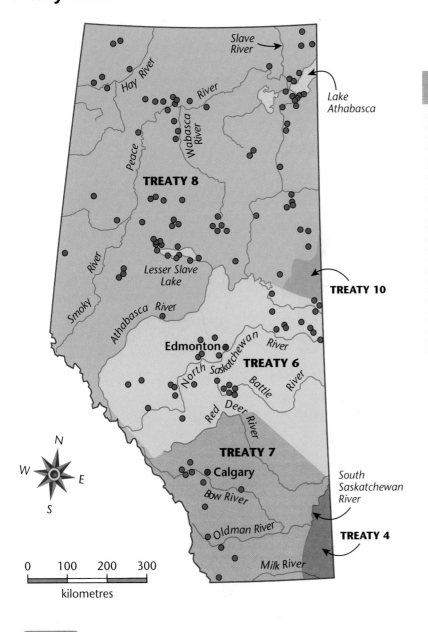

Slave River

Hay River

River

Peace

Wabasca River

TREATY 8

Lake Athabasca

Smoky River

Lesser Slave Lake

TREATY 10

Athabasca River

Edmonton

North Saskatchewan River

TREATY 6

Battle River

Red Deer River

N
W E
S

TREATY 7

Calgary

Bow River

South Saskatchewan River

TREATY 4

Oldman River

Milk River

0   100   200   300
kilometres

Legend
● First Nations reserves created by treaties

Treaty Timeline	
1876	Treaty 6: Signed with the Plains Cree and Woodland Cree
1877	Treaty 7: Signed with the Siksika, Kainai, Piikani, Tsuu T'ina, and Nakoda
1899	Treaty 8: Signed with the Cree, Dunne-za, and Dene Suline

Skill Smart

What are some different perspectives on Treaties 6, 7, and 8?

- In a group, look on the Internet or in books or conduct interviews.

- Make an electronic chart to compare perspectives. How can you explain the similarities or differences?

Right after the Treaty we were put on reserves. An Indian Agent was appointed to each reserve. He dictated what life would be like on the reserve. On some reserves, people were not allowed to leave without a special permit.

The treaties pushed us onto a smaller part of our land. They separated us from our sacred lands. To participate in traditional practices, we had to go to the sacred places. But now we were not allowed to. There was a loss of culture, language, and identity. We know we are part of the land, part of the Creator's creation. This gives a sense of belonging. That was cut off.

So treaties cut the people off from the land they belonged to, and from their families and language. They cut the people off from their whole culture, from a whole way of life. We were disconnected from the ways of our people.

Sandra Crazy Bull

This is a permit or pass that allowed a person to leave the reserve.

This photo shows Cree Chief Piapot [pie-a-pot] ▶ in 1885. He said, "In order to become sole masters of our land, they put us on small reservations as big as my hand and made us long promises, as long as my arm, but the next year the promises were shorter and got shorter every year until now they are the length of my finger, and they keep only half of that."

How Did Life Change for the Métis?

While the First Nations were offered treaties, the Métis were offered **scrip**. Scrip was a coupon that people could exchange for land or money. The Métis could get 240 acres (about 100 hectares) of land or $240. The system was not explained very well, so many Métis did not realize that by taking scrip, they were letting the government take over their lands for settlement.

There were people around at the time who knew how to make money out of buying and selling land. Some of them forged the signatures of Métis people, in order to take their scrip. Others persuaded the Métis to sell their scrip for much less than it was worth. The government had not taken enough care to make sure these kinds of things did not happen. Many Métis were left with no land and no money.

I'll go back to the notes I made at the start of this chapter. I should be able to see what steps the government took to solve some of the difficulties.

words matter!

Scrip is a coupon that can be exchanged for land or money.

The government set up offices, some in tents like the one shown here, to issue scrip. This photograph was taken in Fort Dunvegan in 1899.

Thinking
It Through

Through scrip, the Métis were offered land lots that were very spread out. They could not live close to one another. How might being spread out across the land have affected Métis communities and culture?

How Does Our Past Help Us Know Who We Are Today?

You have read about the coming of the railway, the killing of the buffalo, the treaties, and scrip. These events all cut Aboriginal peoples off from their land, their culture, and their ways of life. Today, many Aboriginal peoples are working to reconnect to their heritage. Look back to Chapter 4 to find at least two examples. Then read on.

This painting is called *Look Back to the Land That Once Was Yours*. The artist is George Littlechild, who was born at Hobbema First Nation. His work is inspired by his Cree traditions.

Mary Jane Sayazie, from Cold Lake, Alberta, says, "Let us maintain our Dene language and culture for the future of our children."

Student Helps Preserve Aboriginal Language

Dorothy Pawlina, a student from the University of Alberta, is working with others on a project to preserve the Nakoda language. Nakoda is one of the many Aboriginal languages at risk of being lost forever. The project team has worked with Aboriginal groups to create books and activities for children learning Nakoda.

Researchers are also trying to create a Nakoda dictionary. "For some people, losing a language is like losing a part of themselves, and it's a really serious situation," said Dorothy Pawlina.

Tom Jackson creates TV shows based on traditional Aboriginal characters. His shows appear on APTN— "the first national Aboriginal television network, with programming by, for, and about Aboriginal peoples, to share with all Canadians."

> My grandpa always says that knowing about our past helps us know who we are now. I think that's true for all of us.

Over to YOU!

1. How does each of these examples help keep a culture alive?

2. In a group, look at Alberta First Nations or Métis Nation Web sites. How do these sites help keep cultures alive?

3. How is your culture kept alive in Alberta? How does it enrich your life? How does it enrich Alberta?

How Was the Railway Built?

In the library, I looked at a book that told me that hundreds of men died building the railway. I'll write down the name of this book and where I found it.

Across the prairies, crews lowered lake levels, flattened hills, and blasted through rock. On July 28, 1883, tracklayers recorded almost 10 km of finished railway in one day.

After the treaties were signed, the way was clear for the railway to be built. Yet there were still many challenges. The next time your family drives across a railway track, take a quick look in both directions. The tracks seem to go on forever into the distance. To the people who built the railway, it probably felt as though the work went on forever, too!

ALBERTA VOICES

Working on the Railway

In the daytime there was the usual labour, such as drilling holes in the rock to blast it with powder. The explosion sometimes threw the heavy stones a hundred yards into the foaming river. We would dodge behind trees and get into sheltered places until the shot was fired, then come out again and take away the broken rock. We would hammer the larger blocks to pieces and shovel the smaller ones into the carts.

Morley Roberts, British writer

What Changes Did the Railway Bring?

So many people were needed to build the railway that workers were brought from China. Some of these workers were treated very badly, although the railway could not have been built without them. They had no information about the country they were coming to. They didn't have the right clothes for the weather, and they were paid only half of what other workers received. This photo was taken in 1886.

Even before the railway was completed, new people came to Alberta. Many of the workers came from China. Others came from different parts of Canada or from Europe. Once the railway was built, it brought many more settlers to the West. Everyone knew that more changes would follow.

ALBERTA VOICES — Lady Agnes' Ride

*In 1886, Lady Agnes Macdonald, the Prime Minister's wife, took a train ride through the Rocky Mountains. She didn't ride **in** the train, however. Instead, she had herself tied on a chair to the cowcatcher on the front of the train. This is what she wrote about her ride:*

There is glory of brightness and beauty everywhere, and I laugh aloud… just because it is all so delightful.

Kicking Horse Pass

When the British were surveying Alberta, James Hector set out to look for mountain passes. One of his horses kicked him and knocked him out. His guides thought he was dead and began to dig his grave. Luckily, he recovered. That's how Kicking Horse Pass got its name!

My Steam Train Ride

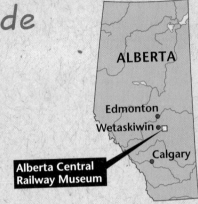

ALBERTA
Edmonton
Wetaskiwin
Calgary
Alberta Central
Railway Museum

What do you think it would have been like to ride on a steam train from long ago? I found out when I visited the Alberta Central Railway Museum, which is near Wetaskiwin. I took a ride on a 1926 passenger train there. The train wheels sound like thunder when they roll across the tracks! It is a fun trip, but bumpy.

I'm glad I didn't have to sleep and eat on the train for days, like the settlers did. On the other hand, I wish I could have seen all the land they travelled across.

The station was my favourite place to visit. The museum is a mini-version of the 1907 Wetaskiwin CPR depot.

There is a waiting room, baggage room, and telegraph office. The telegraph sends messages by making lots of long and short clicking noises. I even got to use it! I learned that trains brought many new people to the province. Trains were also used to ship Alberta's wheat to other parts of Canada.

How Did Ranching Begin?

Settlers were coming out West, but how could they make a living? The land in southern Alberta was too dry for farming, but the grasslands were good for cattle. There were streams where the cattle could drink, and coulees where the animals could find shelter from bad weather. Now that the railway was built, the time was right to begin ranching.

At that time, farms in Britain were not doing well. Many young men from British farming families came to Alberta to try ranching. Others came from France to start ranching at Trochu. Some ranchers also came from the United States to start a new life in Canada.

My great-grandpa told me about living on a ranch when he was a child. I will write down the story. It is part of Alberta's history.

ALBERTA VOICES — **Ranch Country**

I haven't yet found a better country for a ranch: splendid hay, half as nice as nowhere else, an indefinite space for the animals.

Armand Trochu, writing about Three Hills, June 15, 1903. Armand Trochu came from France. He helped to found Ste. Anne's Ranch, which later became the town of Trochu.

Giorgio Pocaterra was an Italian adventurer who wanted an exciting life in a new country. He came to Alberta, and in 1905 started the Buffalo Head Ranch, shown here. The ranch is still operating today.

Why Did More British Settlers Come?

Early ranchers in Alberta started to do well. The Canadian government wanted to encourage more people to settle in Alberta, especially British immigrants and Canadians with British roots.

To attract British ranchers, the government made it very easy for them to get huge areas of land for ranching. In this way, the government hoped to fill the province with English-speaking people who would be loyal to the King or Queen.

Working in Alberta

Many young people came from Britain. Some immigrants were interested in ranching, but some wanted to find other ways to make a living. Many had a good education. They contributed to the province by helping to run schools and hospitals.

Cattle Roundup

In the roundup of 1885, there were 500 horses. Thousands and thousands of cattle were gathered. What a sight they were! When I close my eyes I can still see them plunging into the rivers, swimming with the current, and scrambling out on the opposite bank. I can hear the cries of the riders and the bawling of the calves again. Crossing the river with such a herd was a scene I'll never forget!

Fredrick Ings, cattle breeder

Cattle roundup, Mosquito Creek, 1890

How Did a New British Community Begin?

In the early 1900s, a minister named Isaac Barr started a new British settlement. He worked with another minister named Exton Lloyd. They advertised for settlers in England. More than 2000 people answered, saying that they wanted to come to Alberta. They came to settle in a British colony that later became the city of Lloydminster. Find Lloydminster on a map. What do you notice about its location?

The many British immigrants who came to Alberta at this time brought British ways to our province. These ways are an important part of Alberta's heritage.

A Combined Name

Lloydminster's name combined Exton Lloyd's last name and the word "minster," which means "mother church."

I can see now why we have so many British names in Alberta, like Strathmore, Barrhead, and Coronation.

Lloydminster is divided between Alberta and Saskatchewan. Until 1930, Lloydminster had two of everything—fire department, local government, and other services. In that year, the two halves of the town combined.

175

Set Your Skills in Motion

Create a Bar Graph

Like the bison population, the bear population changed in Alberta. In the 1800s, there were about 6000 grizzly bears. Use the numbers below to show the change over time on a bar graph.

1988	575	1996	765
1990	547	1998	807
1992	669	2000	841
1994	700		

- How many more grizzly bears were there in 2000 than in 1988? Use a calculator to solve.
- Why has the population changed? What is the current population? Are grizzly bears protected? What regions do they live in? Look in books or on the Internet.
- Tell others what responsible citizens can do today to protect the grizzly bear population.

Research an Important Event

Choose one of the following events and find out how that event shaped the place where you live:
- Did the railway go through your community or through an area close by? How did it change life in the community?
- What role did your community have in the buffalo trade?
- What treaty covers the area where you live? What did the territory look like before the treaties?

You might try making a PowerPoint presentation.

Make a Venn Diagram

In what ways were the buffalo important to the First Nations and Métis peoples? How were they important to other hunters? Make a Venn diagram to compare similar and different uses of the buffalo. Try doing your diagram on the computer.

Look What You Have Learned!

Many important events happened in Alberta during this time. The government wanted to bring settlers to the West. The way was cleared for the railway and settlers when the buffalo were killed. Treaties and scrip allowed the government to use land for settlers. The government also started the North West Mounted Police to keep law and order. Many of the settlers came from Britain, so Alberta's British roots grew. Whole ways of life changed for Aboriginal peoples as a result of the treaties and scrip.

Review the inquiry questions for this chapter:
- How did important events of this time shape Alberta?
- How did ways of life change for the people?

Write a report to share what you have learned. Think about how the railway and government affected the Aboriginal peoples. What are some British ways of life that became part of the province's identity? Look in books to search for more information. Keep track of where you find your information.

Take Time to Reflect

Before you go on to the next chapter, think about what you learned in this one.
- How do graphs help show changes over time?
- How can you keep track of the information you find?
- How do you think what you learned will help you in the future?

 Choose something from this chapter to save for your Alberta Treasure Chest.

More Settlers Arrive

Have you ever moved to a new home? What did you think when you first saw it? Petro Dvarich came with his parents from Ukraine, in eastern Europe, in the late 1800s. They stayed with friends who had said that Petro and his family would make a good life on the Prairies.

Petro describes his first sight of his new home: "I could not believe my eyes; the house was a pigsty, the stable but a crude shelter, both covered with sod. Our hearts sank with what we saw. We turned to our [friends] and began to scold them."

Six months later, he wrote in his journal: "My parents were very satisfied with the harvest. My father now felt like a wealthy man and would not return to the old country for anything."

Alberta's Story

Many settlers came from different parts of the world to live in Alberta. In this chapter, you will find out how they cleared and farmed the land. You will learn how they began new communities in many parts of the province. You will find out how this was a time of huge change for Alberta.

? Inquiring Minds

Here are some questions to guide your inquiry for this chapter:

- How did settlers shape Alberta?
- How did the land and resources affect ways of life?

Look for the answers as you read. If you want to learn more, look further.

How can I find out more about Alberta's story during this time? I will
- look at old photos
- interview historians and elders
- read journals and diaries

Who Were the Settlers?

By looking at the photo and reading the caption, I can tell ranchers are part of Alberta's story. They still are today!

Ranching was already important in southern Alberta. Some ranches raised horses to sell. Eaglesplume, shown here in 1893, was one of the most famous horses born at the Quorn Ranch, a British ranch near Sheep Creek.

Thinking
It Through

Think about what you already know about the land and natural resources. What could you tell others to convince them to settle in Alberta in the late 1800s?

Imagine this! It is the late 1800s. The railway you read about in Chapter 6 is ready to bring new people to Alberta. There are settlements here already and lots of land. This land is good for ranching and for farming. Imagine you work for the government of Canada. It is your job to find a way to bring more people to live in the West. What would you do? How would you persuade people to come? ◆

Planning for Settlement

You learned in Chapter 6 how the government cleared the way for more settlers to come to Alberta. Now the government needed a plan to encourage more people to move here. In Europe, there were farmers who could not find land. In the United States, much of the land had already been settled. There were Americans looking for land that was still open. How could the government of Canada attract such people to come to the West?

Why Come to Alberta?

The government decided to offer free land to some of the people who agreed to **immigrate** to the West. They sent posters to be displayed in different parts of the world, telling people about the land in Canada's West. They put up posters in the United States, where people were looking for land. They put up posters all over Europe, in countries such as Ukraine, Poland, and Germany. People there had been farmers for generations. If these people came to Canada, they would bring their farming skills with them.

In some European countries, there were people who could not afford to buy land. Some wanted more land for their children to farm. Some were not allowed to own land in their own country. Imagine how they felt when they saw posters advertising free land in Canada's West!

Ukrainian settler, Redwater, 1912. The government knew that immigrants from eastern Europe would work hard to make a better life for their families.

181

Analyzing Advertisements

Here is a poster that was used to advertise for settlers. We need to ask questions before we do what advertisements suggest.

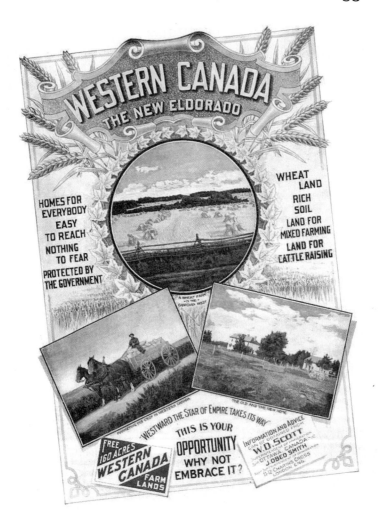

Practise the Skill

1. What facts can you see in this poster? What information is true? How do you know?

2. What does the advertisement suggest about Western Canada? Does it give a complete picture of what it was really like at that time?

3. Is there any information about the land or the weather that the government might not have wanted people to know? Why?

4. How can you use what you've learned here to analyze advertisements you see around you?

A New Life in Alberta

As part of its plan, the government divided the Prairies into townships. Each township was then divided into 36 sections of land. Each settler received a quarter section (160 acres or 65 ha) called a **homestead**. In return for the free land, settlers had to agree to live on it for three years, to build a house there, and to prepare the land for farming. All that the settlers had to pay was a $10 registration fee.

words matter!

A **homestead** was the quarter section of land that the government granted to settlers who were willing to live on the land and farm it.

Homesteaders were the people who lived on the homestead.

Goods Settlers Were Advised to Bring

- canned food
- cooking items
- tools
- a stove
- clothing
- a sewing machine
- medicines
- a cream separator

Homesteaders Mr. and Mrs. E.A. Smith at their first home, a tent, near Beaverlodge, 1909

Settlers who came to farm these lands were called **homesteaders**. A quarter section was only enough land to grow crops to feed a family. Settlers could buy more land for $3 an acre. That gave them a chance to develop large farms and grow enough crops to sell. By the mid-1890s, thousands of settlers were coming to Alberta.

Thinking
It Through

What can you tell about homesteading from the list of items settlers were asked to bring?

What Do Stories Tell About How Settlers Came?

Sarah Ellen Roberts' family came from the United States in 1906 as part of a huge wave of immigrants from that country. They homesteaded about 100 km east of Stettler. This is how she described the journey from Stettler.

ALBERTA VOICES

The End of the Fences

We had not gone far before fences became almost unknown and the trail wound over what seemed to be a vast, endless prairie. Occasionally, the trail wound down into and up out of great ravines, which are called coulees. The trail itself was usually a pair of bare tracks worn by the wheels of wagons, but between these tracks grew buffalo grass. This grass must have been well named, for in many places we saw, stretching across the prairie, the deep paths in the sod that had been worn long ago, by the buffalo.... I am sure we saw many hundreds of buffalo skeletons and skulls, bleached white by years of sun and rain.

Left: Spruce Coulee, Innisfail, before 1905. Coulees were difficult for settlers to cross. *Right:* Homesteader with wagonload at Wainwright, 1910.

Settlers who came from countries such as Ukraine, Poland, Germany, and Russia made a long trip by ship from Europe to Canada. A Polish immigrant describes his family's experience of coming to Alberta from Poland in 1903.

ALBERTA VOICES

The Journey by Ship

There were many children travelling on the two-for-the-price-of-one adult fare. Two people had to share one bunk and one meal. There were four of us and only two plates. It was crowded on the deck; there were always many people waiting to sit down if anyone dared to leave their place. The only time we were able to get an individual meal was when someone was seasick and unable to come to the dining area.

Many families who took the train rode in carriages called "Colonist Cars." The backs of the benches in the cars could be pushed down to make more space to sleep. Settlers had to bring their own bedding and food. The journey to Alberta took about eight days.

Settlers got off the boat in Halifax, Nova Scotia, or Montréal, Québec. Then they had to take a train all the way across Canada to Alberta. Look at a map of Canada to see how many of today's provinces they would pass through.

Where Did Communities Start?

Many American immigrants came to Alberta in the early 1900s. They helped to change Alberta's farming history. A community of Mormons, a religious group from the United States, settled around Cardston. They knew how to irrigate the dry land in that part of Alberta. They helped to turn southern Alberta into a rich farming area. After the Mormons came, southern Alberta was able to grow sugar beets. It became an important crop for Alberta.

Some Francophones also came from the United States. They had moved there from Québec. When they found all the land had already been bought, some came to Alberta. Plamondon was settled by Canadiens who came from Michigan.

Other groups came from the United States as well. A group of black settlers came from Oklahoma, hoping to escape unfair treatment there. They settled in Amber Valley. Look for it on a map. Is it anywhere near where you live?

Skill Smart

- In a small group, scan the photos in this chapter.
- Skim the captions and use jot notes to make a list of communities.
- Pick three places from your list. Use the Internet to find out three facts about each community.
- If possible, organize your information in a computer file for others to read.

Bobbie Crump and family, Edmonton, 1918

As Ukrainians settled into their communities, they began building thatched cottages like those in Ukraine. They were called bydas [boo-dahs].

◀ Churches were often at the centre of a community. They were places for people to pray, but they also helped keep traditions, language, and culture alive.

What about settlers who came from farther away? Imagine what it would be like to move halfway around the world to a place you didn't know, where people spoke different languages. Have you ever had an experience like that?

People often went to areas where others from their homeland had settled. That helped them adjust to their new life. In this way, they built up new communities.

Some people also looked for land that was similar to the land back home. That's what many people from Ukraine did. They settled in the parkland region. It wasn't as good for farming as the grasslands, but it reminded them of home. Many settled in Edna (later named Star), Mundare, and Vegreville.

ALBERTA VOICES

An Immigrant Farmhand

One Polish settler told about his early days in Alberta:

Getting started in Alberta was tough for me. Not knowing a word of English, I had to take any job that the farmers offered me. That usually meant clearing land of bushes, trees, stumps, and rocks for one dollar a day plus room and board. My bedroom was sometimes an unheated shack.

How Was the Land Changed?

I wonder where settlers went to get homesteads? Were the lines always as long as the one in the photo below? I'll ask my great-aunt if she knows any stories about Alberta's settlers.

After they arrived in Alberta, some settlers went and chose the land they wanted. Others went to areas that had already been marked out for them. They trusted to luck that they would get good land. Many did not. Some of the land was very dry, and some very rocky. In northern Alberta, some land was swampy. In the south, there were coulees.

ALBERTA VOICES

You're On Your Own

What would you do if you found yourself in this situation, as described by one settler?

So there you are and the land guide says, "You are on your land now." No roads or anything else. "Now there you are, boy. Get busy and build your house, put in your garden and look after your horses and you will do all right," and he went away.

Settlers found that oxen were better than horses for pulling plows over rocky ground, because they were less likely to fall on the rocks. ▶

Francophone settlers lined up to register their land, Edmonton, 1909.

What Were Some Perspectives on the Land?

Do you remember reading about perspectives in Chapter 6? You learned how the Aboriginal peoples and the government had different perspectives about owning land. The settlers, too, brought new perspectives.

For thousands of years, the First Nations people had shaped their way of life to suit the land. They had lived with nature. Now the European settlers were clearing the land. They cut down trees and plowed the soil. They changed the land to suit their way of life.

Some Aboriginal people, too, adapted their way of life. Read the two accounts below.

Skill Smart

- Create a picture to show how the European settlers changed the land.
- Write a caption to explain how the settlers changed the land.
- Try using a paint or draw program on the computer.

ALBERTA VOICES

New Ways of Life

After 1890, the Blackfoot unwillingly settled into the routine of farming and gardening. After being pressured by the government to sell large portions of their reserve, the band became the wealthiest in Canada and flourished as ranch and farmland was developed, along with coal mining.

Russell Wright, Siksika First Nation

I drove the horses, and my dad plowed. How many days did we have to do that? Our granaries were full of grain. Every year, we hauled three big loads of wheat down to St. Paul. My dad sold two loads, and with the third he made flour—enough to last all year.

Charlie Blackman, Dene First Nation, Cold Lake

My Day at the Ukrainian Cultural Heritage Village

ALBERTA

Peace River

Lesser Slave Lake

Ukrainian Cultural Heritage Village

Edmonton
Wetaskiwin • • Lloydminster
Red Deer
• Calgary

Did you know the Ukrainians were the second-biggest group of settlers to come to Alberta, other than the British?

I had a great time when I visited the Ukrainian Cultural Heritage Village near Edmonton. The guides were dressed in clothes that Ukrainian immigrants would have worn, so I felt as though I had travelled back in a time machine. I saw how these settlers lived when they first arrived in Alberta.

I visited a byda [boo-dah]—a home like the ones the first Ukrainian settlers lived in. It was neat, but I don't think I'd want to be there in a rainstorm!

The Ukrainians knew a lot about farming and coal mining, so they really made a big contribution to Alberta. My visit made me think about how hard the early settlers had to work to build their lives in Alberta.

What Kinds of Homes Did Settlers Build?

Have you ever seen new houses being built in your community? How long does it take? What kinds of machines are used? Building a house was the first thing settlers had to do, but they had no machinery and little help.

Some settlers built tiny shacks. If they could afford it, they bought lumber to build a frame house. If they had no money, they cut trees and built log houses. If there were no trees nearby, they cut brick-shaped blocks from the earth and built soddies. They lived in these houses until they could afford to build a proper home.

After they had built some kind of shelter, the settlers turned to clearing the land for planting. The land often made life especially hard for the new homesteaders.

To keep log cabins warm, people used old rags, sawdust, or flour to stuff the cracks. Some even used dried manure from the oxen.

Soddies

Soddies were warm in winter and cool in summer, but when it rained, they were very wet. Sometimes garter snakes poked their heads through the ceiling! The settlers learned to make doors that opened inwards. Otherwise, the door would not open against thick snow. How do you think they got out?

Soddie near Coronation (Haneyville), 1907

191

Hear the Settlers' Voices!

Life was often very hard for the thousands of new settlers. Listen to the voices and look at the pictures on these two pages. Do you think it is useful to hear people's stories in their own words? Why or why not?

ALBERTA VOICES

A New Life in Alberta

Delayed by Flooding

When the first group [of Icelanders] arrived in Calgary, they hired Métis guides to lead them to Innisfail, and on west to the banks of the Red Deer River, swollen in the June floods. Here they camped for three weeks before being able to cross the raging waters on a raft they had built from the tall spruce trees, which grew on the banks of the river.

Margaret Rasmussen tells about her parents' move to Markerville.

Red Deer River flooded near Beynon, around 1900

Ukrainian schoolchildren in the mining community of Frank, in southwestern Alberta, around 1920

The Hungry Winters

Life was tough in those first years on the homestead. Sometimes food was scarce. Winter clothing was hard to come by. They had no overshoes or winter boots, so strips of gunny sack were rolled around their feet and tied with binder twine. One winter, the horses were so hungry that they came and stood on their hind legs and ate the straw thatch from the roof of the farmhouse.

Alexander Szpak was a Ukrainian whose family settled on a homestead in northwestern Alberta.

"When you got stuck in Alberta gumbo you were there until it dried out. Or until you could get someone with a team of horses to pull you out."
G.A. Cooper, Peace River District

Sixteen Long Years

On June 1, 1909, Adolf Rachui and his family arrived in Leduc by train. Adolf filed on a homestead near Warburg, but abandoned it after eight months because "the land was of no value [for farming], being nearly all swamp and bush."

Finally, Adolf learned of an abandoned homestead near Buck Lake. After working for several summers clearing some of the heavy timber for grain growing and building a house and barn, he moved his family and his belongings by horse and wagon through bush and swamp to finally settle in their own place. It was 1925, sixteen long years after the Rachui family stepped onto the train station platform in Leduc in eager anticipation of receiving free land.

Richard Stein, about his great-grandfather who came from Russia

Millet is one of the places where Adolf Rachui tried to homestead. This photo shows how it looked in 1911. It is now known as "the prettiest town in Canada." Do you think Adolf Rachui would have seen it that way?

Pests Everywhere!

Then there were the flies and mosquitoes, both of which were, at times, simply frightful. I have no words to tell what a terrible pest they were, for they swarmed into the tent by the thousands, and we had no protection against them.

Sarah Ellen Roberts, whose mother homesteaded about 105 km east of Stettler

Giving Up

Many of the homesteaders gave up. It was just too hard for them. At one point, there were more going out than coming in, especially the ones who didn't have wives. They'd get so lonely that they would simply give up.

Peggy Holmes homesteaded about 100 km north of St. Paul.

I know that wheat is still an important crop in Alberta today. So this is how it all began.

How Did Wheat Become "King"?

Before long, wheat farming became much more important than ranching in Alberta. What do the photos below tell you about the way in which wheat became "king"? Why did wheat farming change the land more than ranching had done?

▲ In 1906, a terrible winter put many ranchers out of business. The snow was so deep that some cattle were lost in it. Others couldn't find food. Many ranchers never got over these losses.

▲ Some settlers started market gardens and sold some of the fruits and vegetables they grew. Families worked side by side for years and years, clearing and preparing more land. They saved the money they made to buy more land so that they could grow more crops.

New inventions helped the settlers. This photo shows an early combine harvester near Nobleford in 1928. On the right is C.S. Noble, an American settler who sold farm machinery. He invented the Noble Blade, which helped to kill weeds. Nobleford was named after him.

▼

At first settlers tried growing flax, beans, barley, and oats (shown here). They found it very difficult in Alberta's climate. Many switched to wheat.

Farmers could save money by hiring travelling threshing crews. The crews brought their own machinery with them and just worked for the harvest. Some people came from the East to work on threshing crews during the early fall.

Viewpoints

How Can We Help Farmers?

Settlers had huge challenges trying to make a living off the land. They did not have modern machinery or tools to plow the land and harvest crops. Hailstorms, floods, frost, droughts, and tornadoes could destroy entire crops the settlers had worked so hard to plant and grow.

Farmers today have similar challenges. They have better machines and tools, but these are very expensive and can break down. Alberta's weather still makes farming very challenging. How can we help farmers when bad weather strikes?

> Farmers grow the food we all need. If they are in trouble, we'll all be in trouble.
>
> *Lori Brown*

> I lost my farm after the terrible drought in 2001 and 2002. With no crops or money, I had to give up the farm. It had been in my family for generations. It broke my heart.
>
> *Sandy Hammel*

> I helped my uncle when his farm and house flooded. We couldn't do much about the lost crops. We did help clean up the barns and house. We had to fix buildings and machines, too.
>
> *Lucas Hunter*

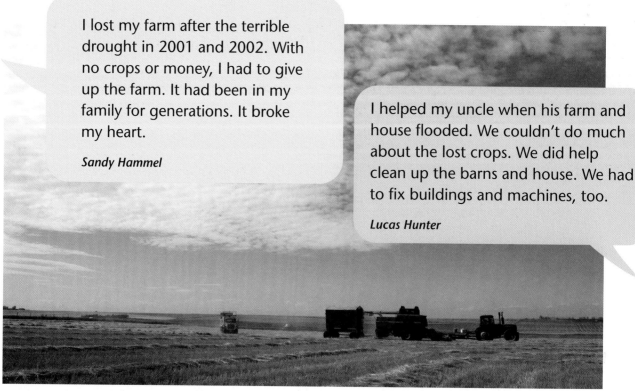

Wheat harvests affected by drought at Crossfield, 2001

My dad is not a farmer, but he helps the community by helping to maintain the dam and irrigation channels so the farmers can water their crops.

Maxine Chong

▲ Hail can completely destroy a crop in just a few minutes.

A funnel cloud touches the ground near Drumheller, June 2001

A tornado flattened my crop. I was devastated because I could not sell the crop and get money to buy things my family needed. The government gave me some money. Right now my new job is selling farm machinery. Next year I will plant another crop and hope the weather cooperates!

Pat Bernier

Over to YOU!

1. What are some things communities can do to help farmers when times are hard?

2. As a class, think of how your community might be affected by bad weather. Then plan a citizenship project that might help your community in this situation. Make a plan of action.

How Did Communities Grow?

Different kinds of communities grew in Alberta. Many had one thing in common: a spirit of cooperation. For most, helping one another was a way of life. People worked together to help their communities grow.

Living Together

People often settled near others with the same homeland or religion. For example, the Mormons settled in Cardston. Scandinavians settled near Camrose, New Norway, Wetaskiwin, and other areas. Many Icelandic immigrants settled in the Red Deer region. Germans first settled in Pincher Creek and Medicine Hat. Then they moved farther north to Bruderheim and Stony Plain. The first Mennonite colony was established in High River. In all these places, people worked together to build places of worship and schools. Grain elevators were built along the railroad tracks so farmers could sell their wheat. Gradually, stores, restaurants and hotels were built.

Over the years, grain elevators became part of the prairie landscape. Some still remain today.

I wonder how my school started? I will interview my principal to find out more.

ALBERTA VOICES

Building a School

People volunteered help and brought lumber. One young homesteader brought a wagon and team and hauled sandstone to lay a stone foundation. Secretary Bates and I cut the logs. We had to plane the siding with an old-time wooden jack-plane and a great amount of "elbow grease." I did my share of the siding and I volunteered until the school was completed.

John Niddrie, settler, Eagle River District, 1905

Francophone Communities

Settlers from Québec built some of the earliest communities. They started coming to Alberta long before the huge numbers of settlers from Britain and other parts of Europe. By the 1890s, many English-speaking settlers had arrived. To keep their own communities strong, Francophone priests decided to bring more French-speaking people to Alberta. They went to Québec, the United States, France, and Belgium, looking for people who would come.

Louis and Josephine Chevigny came from Québec in 1880. They built this house in St. Albert to look like their home in Québec. It still stands on the old homestead and is owned by the Chevigny family.

Putting Down Roots

When they arrived, many Francophone settlers put down roots in St. Albert. Later, they also went to other parts of Alberta, including St. Paul, Vegreville, Bonnyville, and the Peace River area. Edmonton, too, had a strong Francophone community that had existed since the days of the fur trade in Fort Edmonton. Francophones opened many stores, hotels, and other businesses there.

In communities like St. Paul, almost everyone spoke French. School would be called *l'école*. On main street buildings you would see signs such as *La Banque d'Hochelaga* and *boulangerie*. You would read newspapers in French to learn what was going on in Alberta and the world. These communities developed their own culture and identity, unique to Alberta. They became Franco-Albertan.

The Révillon Frères store, Edmonton, 1903. Révillon Frères was a major rival of the Hudson's Bay Company.

Jeannine de Moissac grew up just north of St. Paul. What can you learn from this interview with her about how the community grew in the early days?

Jeannine de Moissac

What was it like to live in St. Paul in the early days?

At threshing time, one thresher would go around to all the farms. So everybody helped everybody else. When my father was very sick, all the farmers around came to milk the cows and so on. Some people were better farmers than others, so they would give their expertise.

We bought our groceries in St. Paul and went to church there. When my brothers grew up, they played hockey there. There were a lot of wedding dances. There was a lot of music in our family. My uncles played accordion, violin, and guitar. That was how we all got together. There are still a lot of connections between the families.

How did Francophones help Alberta grow?

With their energy! My father was a farmer. He had a mission to grow lots of food and feed the world. The Francophones worked hard. And family values are strong. Our ties are getting stronger and stronger.

There is a lot of French in the music in Alberta, and in the art and the literature.

We are proud of who we are. I am proud to be a Franco-Albertan.

Skill Smart

Find out about people who work together to help your community. Look in the newspaper, or listen to a television or radio broadcast. With a partner, prepare a speech to share your information.

Métis Communities

Like the Francophones, the Métis of Alberta built their own identity. In 1932, they formed a group called the Métis Nation of Alberta. Read these stories to see how they built strong communities.

A Place of Our Own

Shelley Jackson lives at the Kikino Métis Settlement near Lac La Biche. She explains how Alberta's Métis settlements came to be.

The Métis had come from all over Alberta and Saskatchewan. A lot of Métis moved into Alberta in the late 1880s, and they had no place... of their own. There were a few gentlemen in the early 1930s who started to talk amongst themselves about how the Métis needed to get together as a group and talk to the government about putting land aside for them. The government agreed to give the Métis a land base. There's a bunch of lakes around here. They'd be able to fish and they'd learn to farm and make their own way.... Settlements came into being in the late 1930s and families started to move into Kikino in 1939.

The Métis community is very large. It's very close knit. I feel fortunate to be a part of it. Anybody would help you, like you were the child of the whole community. That's what it really was like growing up there; it was where you were looked after by everyone.

Marge Friedel, Métis Elder

Thinking *It Through*

How does belonging to a community add to quality of life? Share your thoughts with a partner.

In 2005, the Métis Nation of Alberta helped to organize this wagon trek from Saskatchewan to Métis Crossing, Alberta. It celebrated the great contributions made by Métis communities to Alberta and Canada.

Set Your Skills in Motion

Analyze Advertising

In a small group, look for an ad for your community, another community you have visited, or any local event. Try travel brochures, the Internet, or even the radio or television. Pay careful attention to the ad.

- What message is being sent?
- What questions do you have about this ad or brochure? Is there anything about the ad or brochure that is possibly misleading?

Answer the questions using jot notes.

Picture What Makes It Alberta!

Victoria McDonald lives in Fort MacKay. She tells about the houses in her community. "All the houses were painted red. The First Nations name for Fort MacKay was Red Clay. That's what everybody put on their houses." People coming around the bend of the Athabasca River recognized Fort MacKay because of the colour of its homes. What helps you recognize your community? Draw a picture, take a photograph, make a video, or create a collage to show what makes your community distinct, but still part of Alberta. Tell your class about your work.

Write a Story

Write a story from the point of view of a settler. Use what you have learned and your imagination.

- Where did you live before coming to Alberta?
- How did you travel to the province?
- What did you do when you arrived?
- What challenges did you face? What went well?

Add illustrations or copies of historic photos.

Look What You Have Learned!

Settlers came to Alberta from different parts of the world and Canada. They helped to establish and build communities. Many were based on farming. They brought their knowledge, languages, and culture. Homesteaders worked on the land, building houses, planting crops, and caring for livestock. Alberta became known for its wheat. Ways of life changed for Aboriginal communities in various ways, as well. The stories of different groups of people are all part of Alberta's identity.

> Review the inquiry questions for this chapter:
> • How did settlers shape Alberta?
> • How did the land and resources affect ways of life?
> Show what you have learned by making a web. At the bottom of your page, make a prediction. What do you think will happen to the land and communities next? Check your predictions as you keep reading.

Take Time to Reflect

Before you go on to the next chapter, think about what you learned in this one. What did you learn from the stories of the people? What might you do in the next chapter to improve on gathering information?

 Choose something from this chapter to save for your Alberta Treasure Chest.

Looking Back: Chapters 4, 5, 6, and 7

Anita uses a fishbone organizer to outline what she thinks are the key points in Chapters 4, 5, 6, and 7.

Chapter 4: Living with the Land

- First Nations were the first people here
- many ways of life, based on the land and available resources
- traditional ways still valued
- all First Nations have their own culture and language

Chapter 5: New Roots For Alberta

- Canadien, Métis, and British roots developed
- fur trade with First Nations
- Métis Nation began
- diverse languages and cultures

Diverse people helped shape Alberta.

Chapter 6: Preparing for New Settlers

- British ways of life became part of Alberta (e.g., NWMP)
- railway built across the country; brought new settlers
- ways of life changed for people already here
  - nearly all buffalo killed
  - First Nations sign treaties

Chapter 7: More Settlers Arrive

- settlers from all over; lots of opportunities
- brought their knowledge, languages, and culture
- communities grew; some new ones established
- farming wheat becomes important

Share What You Know

? Inquiring Minds

Study Anita's fishbone organizer closely. Then skim through Chapters 4, 5, 6, and 7 to help you recall what you learned. Turn to page 3 in Getting Started. Which one of the overall inquiry questions for the book is the main focus of these chapters? Why do you think that?

 Work with a small group to prepare an Alberta Treasure game show.

Plan to prepare two parts for each question:

- a fact part of the question that asks "who," "what," "where," or "when"
- a thinking part that asks "how" or "why," such as
  - Why was this important?
  - Why did this happen?
  - How does this make Alberta unique?
  - How did this make a difference?

Retrieve, or recall, what you've learned in Chapters 4, 5, 6, and 7. Check your projects and activities as well.

Process, or think about, your information. Each group member should think of five fact questions.

Create game-show cards by organizing your questions. Choose a thinking question to go with each fact question. Write each two-part question on the front of a card. Put the answers on the back.

Share your questions by presenting them as a game show. Invite your classmates to play.

Evaluate how well you and your group worked together. Were you pleased with your game show? Did others seem to like it? What would you do differently next time?

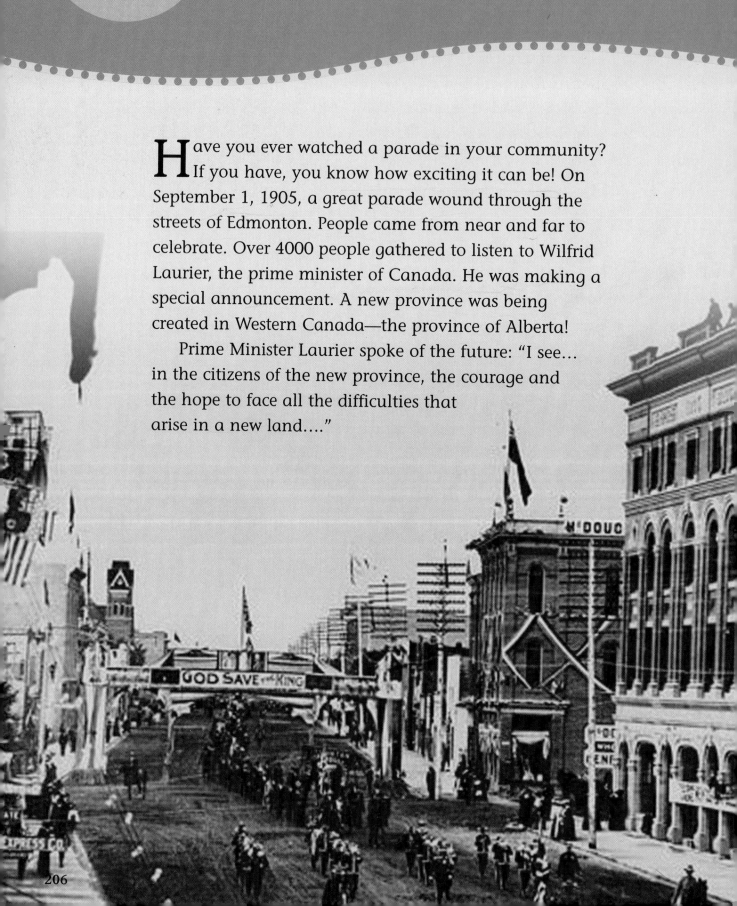

Becoming a Province

Have you ever watched a parade in your community? If you have, you know how exciting it can be! On September 1, 1905, a great parade wound through the streets of Edmonton. People came from near and far to celebrate. Over 4000 people gathered to listen to Wilfrid Laurier, the prime minister of Canada. He was making a special announcement. A new province was being created in Western Canada—the province of Alberta!

Prime Minister Laurier spoke of the future: "I see… in the citizens of the new province, the courage and the hope to face all the difficulties that arise in a new land…."

Alberta's Story

In 1905, Alberta became a province. New industries, towns, and cities began to grow. In this chapter, you will discover how and why this happened. You will find out how Alberta got its borders and its name. You will also learn how Alberta became a place where people from many different places felt they belonged.

Stephen Avenue—a historic street in Calgary

? Inquiring Minds

Here are some questions to guide your inquiry for this chapter:

- How did Alberta become a province?
- What do major events and stories tell us about Alberta's past?

If you want to know more, try some other sources.

How can I use technology to help me with the research process?
I will
- gather information in computer files
- use electronic webs, charts, or spreadsheets
- record interviews
- take photographs

How Did Alberta Become a Province?

words matter!

A **legislative assembly** is made up of leaders who represent the people. They make decisions about running a territory or province.

Thinking
It Through

Look at the map on pages 316–317. Is Regina close to or far away from Edmonton and Calgary? Do you think people in Regina would be in a position to know what was best for people in Alberta? Why or why not?

Imagine you are travelling in Canada. If someone asks you where you live, you would probably say, "Alberta." You would use the name of your province. At one time, Alberta was not a province. It did not have the borders that it has now.

Think back to what you learned about Canada in Chapter 6. The government had bought a vast area in the West, but this land was not yet part of Canada. Alberta was part of an area known as the North-West Territories.

As more settlers arrived, the government in Ottawa needed a way to take care of what was happening in the North-West Territories. It set up a **legislative assembly** in the city of Regina. Which province is Regina in today? Back then it, too, was part of the North-West Territories. The legislative assembly was based on the British form of government. It is a system of government we still have today.

Regina was the capital of the area that included Alberta and Saskatchewan.

Why Become a Province?

As more settlers arrived, towns and settlements grew. Many services, like roads and schools, were needed. The government in Alberta had been collecting taxes from the people. Still, there was not enough tax money to pay for all the services that were needed. The government did not want to ask for more taxes. If the settlers had to pay more, they might move away.

Every year, Alberta asked the Canadian government for more money, just as you might ask your parents for an allowance. Parts of Canada that had already become provinces didn't have to ask for money. They were given money each year. If Alberta became a province, it would also receive money without having to ask.

ALBERTA VOICES

A Growing Town

There were now three parallel streets and four avenues.... The Trader's Bank had set up offices and amusement halls. A cinema showed films three days a week...There were three grain elevators and a stockyard for loading cattle in railroad cars, and an enormous drugstore where everything could be found.

Marcel Durieux, Stettler, 1908

THEN AND NOW

Stettler in 1908 *(top)* and today *(bottom)*. What changes can you see? Who do you think arranged for many of these changes to be made?

Who Had Control?

I did some research. I found out that in Alberta in 1881, there were only 1000 settlers. By 1901, there were 73 000 settlers! I will type this into a new computer file called "Alberta's Population."

There was another way Alberta could get more money. It could take more control of its resources. Alberta had coal, wheat, and timber, but the land was controlled by the government in Ottawa. That meant money from these resources went to Ottawa. Then Ottawa decided how much of it Alberta should get back. How do you think people in Alberta felt about this?

Albertans also saw that the provinces could make many of their own decisions and their own laws. Soon some people were saying that Alberta should become a province, too. They wanted Alberta to control its own resources and make its own decisions.

Frederick William Haultain was premier of the North-West Territories. He thought the West should have more control over its resources and development. He worked hard to make Alberta a province.

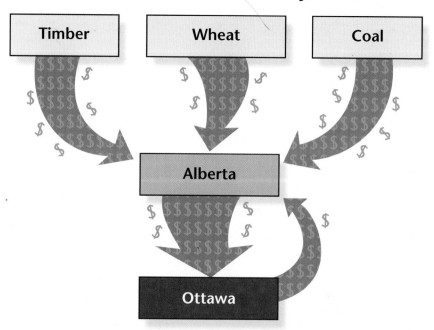

How Ottawa Controlled Alberta's Resources and Money

Skill Smart

- Look at a map of Canada. Use the scale to find the distance between Ottawa and Edmonton.

- Why might it have been difficult for Ottawa to make the right decisions for Alberta? Remember that trains were the fastest way to travel, but even they were slow.

Where Will the Borders Be?

There was much discussion about the new plan for Alberta to become a province. People had different opinions about how the land should be divided.

- Frederick Haultain wanted one large province covering the whole area. Why do you think he favoured this plan?
- Wilfrid Laurier, prime minister of Canada, wanted to split the area in two. Why do you think he had this point of view?
- Some citizens liked the idea of one big province. They thought the government in Ottawa would pay more attention to a large province.
- Other citizens wanted two provinces, so that each provincial government could be closer to the people of the province.

Eventually, the plan for two provinces was chosen.

Thinking It Through

- Look at Map A. If Province Three had become Alberta, which cities would not have been in this province?
- How might your life be different if Province Three had become Alberta?

Map A

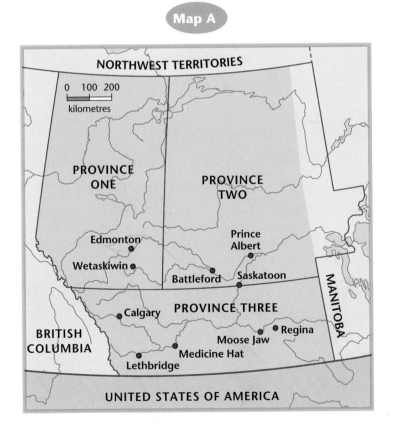

Map B

Map A shows one idea for splitting the area into provinces. Map B shows how Alberta and its borders look today.

What About Schools?

The Clearwater School in the Beaumont area taught in French. What else can you tell about school life from this photograph? How does this classroom compare with yours?

Thinking It Through

In the 1880s, many English-speaking people moved to Alberta from Ontario. Some of them wanted the West to be English-speaking only. By 1892, French was not allowed in the legislative assembly, the courts, or the schools. How do you think Francophones felt about this?

If Alberta became a province, it would have to follow Canada's laws. The laws on schools almost made Alberta change its mind about becoming a province.

Most Francophone children went to Catholic schools that taught in French. Some politicians in Ottawa argued that the government should not give money to Catholic schools. In 1905, it was decided that Protestant and Catholic schools could receive money from the government. It was also decided that English was the language of education. The Catholic schools would have to teach in English.

Some Catholic schools, started by Francophone priests and nuns, continued teaching in French. Many French-speaking Albertans sent their children to these private schools. They had to pay tuition and school taxes. They were determined to keep their language, culture, and identity strong.

Alberta or Buffalo?

Do you like your name? What does it tell about you? Why are names important?

The plan to make a new province went ahead, but the province needed a name. Once again, there was much debate. Frederick Haultain wanted the new province to be called Buffalo. Why do you think he considered this a suitable name? Some people wanted the name Alberta, to honour Princess Louise Caroline Alberta. She was the daughter of Queen Victoria, who had been the queen of England and Canada. The princess was also the wife of John Campbell who had been Canada's **governor general**. As you know, Alberta was the name that was finally chosen.

Princess Louise Caroline Alberta. Lake Louise, the town of Caroline, and Mount Alberta were also named for the princess.

Choosing a Capital City

The new province needed a capital city. Several communities put their names forward. In 1906, Edmonton was declared the winner. Why? Edmonton had been settled since it was a fur-trading post more than 100 years earlier. It was also the largest community at the time and was located in the centre of the province.

Capital Cities?

These cities put their names forward. How would you have liked your community to be Alberta's capital?

Calgary	Vegreville
Red Deer	Wetaskiwin
Banff	Edmonton

Skill Smart

- With a partner, suggest three names for your classroom.
- Have others rank your ideas from favourite to least favourite.
- Record your results on a spreadsheet.

Mount Alberta

Alberta Becomes a Province!

It took years of discussion and debate to answer all the questions. How many provinces would there be? What would the borders be? What should be done about schools? During this time, people wrote letters and reports to Ottawa. They held meetings. They debated with each other.

At last, in 1905, Alberta became a province, with its own provincial government. Now the new province could make decisions for its people.

ALBERTA VOICES

A Parade!

On September 2, 1905, the Calgary Herald *described the parade in Edmonton. This parade celebrated Alberta's becoming a province.*

Perhaps the best part of this parade was the presence of about 1800 school children. They rode in decorated floats, with such mottoes as "We'll Grow" and "Prairie Flowers."

Governor General Earl Grey watched the parade from the balcony of the Edmonton Club. He was especially pleased to see all the children.

First Nations Perspectives

Do you think many Aboriginal peoples celebrated the birth of a new province? Why or why not? Alberta could make many of its own decisions now, but what about the First Nations?

I will make a chart on the computer. I can compare how First Nations lived before and after the settlers arrived.

Gathering grain on a Kainai farm in southern Alberta

ALBERTA VOICES

A New Way of Life

First Nations people on reserves were cut off from traditional ways of life. Some became successful farmers, but they faced many difficulties. Here is one view written by the members of the Blackfoot Gallery Committee at the Glenbow Museum.

In 1889, the Canadian government...decided that each adult could farm only one acre and care for one or two cows. Our people were allowed to use only simple tools such as hoes, rakes, cradles, sickles, and flails. They were not allowed to work together cooperatively [as a community].

The Indian Agent had absolute control over all aspects of our lives. Our people could not buy seeds, sell crops, or sell or butcher livestock without his permission.

From **Nitsitapiisinni: The Story of the Blackfoot People**

Thinking *It Through*

- How would it have helped the First Nations people to be able to farm and ranch without all these rules?
- How would it have helped the rest of Alberta if the First Nations had been able to farm freely?

How Did Alberta Begin to Change?

Naming Places

Communities were springing up all along the CPR line. It fell to the railroad to name all these new places, so they did it in alphabetical order. North of Calgary, for example, these communities all begin with A's and down south with C's, and so on.

Marjorie Winspear McEnany, settler, 1917

Find Calgary on a map. Why do you think it became a centre for ranchers? When the railway reached Calgary in 1883, it was a small town. Soon many new ranchers arrived. Calgary grew so quickly, it became a city just a year later.

By 1905, wheat farming was important. Calgary grew more as farmers brought their wheat to be traded. All over Alberta, towns and cities were springing up. Alberta was changing. It had been a farming province. Now most people lived in towns and cities.

Skill Smart

- Where could you find proof to support what Marjorie Winspear McEnany says?

- With a partner, make a list of sources you might look at. Check out two sources from your list. Were you able to find proof? If so, what?

THEN AND NOW

Top: Calgary in 1906. *Bottom:* Calgary today. What similarities and differences can you see?

From Trading Post to Capital

Why do you think Edmonton was a good place to build a trading post? In 1891, the railway was built from Calgary to Edmonton. It gave fur traders another way to move their goods. Edmonton was booming because many people were passing through on their way to the Yukon, where gold was found. Some people stayed in Edmonton. Others came to build hotels and stores for the gold miners. In 1904, Edmonton became a city.

Edmonton grew quickly again, once it became Alberta's capital city.

I used my digital camera to take photos at Fort Edmonton Park. I can't wait to share this information with my class!

Edmonton's high-level bridge was completed in 1913. It was one of the largest bridges in Canada at the time.

Fort Edmonton Park was rebuilt in a new location along the North Saskatchewan River. Today, many people come to visit this historic site.

Louis Trudel, a Francophone, was president of Trudel Furs in Edmonton. He was known as the Buffalo King because he made buffalo fur coats for the North West Mounted Police.

Fact and Opinion

Different kinds of information help us learn about the past. We often rely on facts to tell us about events. **Facts** tell us about something that is true. **Opinion** is what someone thinks or believes. Opinions give us only one point of view. We can't always rely on opinions to tell us what happened. The facts might be different. Opinions can still help us understand the past, though. They show us what people believed.

Practise the Skill

The headlines below have been translated from the Alberta newspaper *Le courier de l'ouest (Western Mail)*. They appeared in 1906 and 1907.

TELEPHONE LINE COMPLETED BETWEEN LACOMBE AND STETTLER

Calgary Will Host the Dominion Exhibition in 1908

Everyone who attended presentations by theatre troupe Fanning à l'opéra enjoyed them very much!

Scientist in New York believes Canadian West is rich in diamonds

BOYS' SHOES ARE SELLING FOR $1.75 TO $2.50

Edmonton streets will need to be paved. Carts and other vehicles are turning them into mud pits on rainy days.

- Which of these headlines give facts? Which give opinions? How do you know?
- What do these headlines tell about life in the early 1900s?

How Did Logging Towns Begin?

As you learned in Chapter 7, many settlers used logs to build their homes. At first, they cut their own wood, but soon logging camps and sawmills opened to provide the lumber that settlers needed. The railway brought more people who needed to build homes. The railway also needed wood to support the steel train tracks.

This sawmill was at Pigeon Lake. What can you tell about the equipment that was used?

Before long, people came to the logging camps and sawmills to find work. Logging towns sprang up on the edges of forested areas all around the province. Which regions of Alberta do you think were the best for logging? Why?

Building a church in Rivière Qui Barre. How can you tell that communities worked together?

Thinking
It Through

The name of the settlement at Rivière Qui Barre is French for a Plains Cree word meaning "river that blocks the way." How could lumber help solve this problem?

219

How Did Mining Towns Begin?

words matter!

Towns and cities are called **urban areas**.

Look at the picture of the train. How can you tell it is a steam train? All trains that ran on the new railway were powered by steam. The steam was produced by burning coal. Alberta was lucky because it had lots of coal. Before long, many mines opened to dig out the coal that was needed for the new railway. Coal was also used to heat homes and other buildings. Soon towns grew up around the coal mines as people came to find work. Alberta was becoming more **urban**.

This is a steam train. Coal heated the water in the train's boiler. The water turned to steam. The steam pushed the rods that made the train wheels move.

Lethbridge was the centre of the coal industry. The Blackfoot named it *Sik-okotoks*—"place of black rocks."

Thinking It Through

How do you think lumber and coal added to quality of life in the new province of Alberta?

ALBERTA VOICES

Keeping Warm

The log house was heated by a large potbelly stove. There was a large hole in the living room ceiling to allow the heat to rise to warm the bedrooms during those long, cold winters. It was a long trip in the fall by horse and wagon to go to Starkey Coal Mine...where they got...coal to feed the potbelly stove and the kitchen stove during the winter.

Eileen Skinner, a settler's granddaughter

Some Logging and Mining Communities

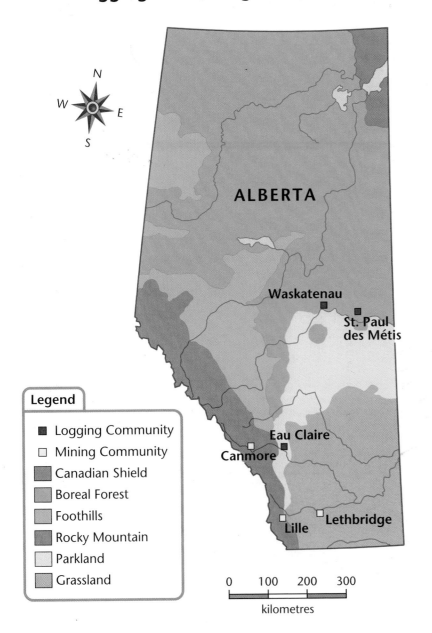

ALBERTA

Waskatenau

St. Paul des Métis

Eau Claire

Canmore

Lille   Lethbridge

Legend

- ■ Logging Community
- □ Mining Community
- Canadian Shield
- Boreal Forest
- Foothills
- Rocky Mountain
- Parkland
- Grassland

0   100   200   300

kilometres

I will make an electronic web to show what I've learned about logging and mining communities. I can use the text, this map, and photographs for information.

▲ Lille was a mining town from 1901 to 1912. This photo shows the coal mine *(bottom)* and the homes of the miners *(centre)*. Many miners came from Europe to work and settle in Lille.

◄ This is a lumber mill in Eau Claire, a logging camp near Calgary on the Bow River (1901). Eau Claire was the main source of lumber in the Calgary area. It closed down in 1945.

My Day in a Coal Mine

ALBERTA

Edmonton

Red Deer

Drumheller

Medicine Hat

Atlas Coal Mine

Did you know that until 1913, some children worked in Alberta's coal mines to help earn money for their families? I got to imagine what it was like when I went to the Atlas Coal Mine near Drumheller. Kids like me used to go down into the mine, where the air was full of coal dust. They worked for 10 hours at a time!

Seeing people in costume who were re-enacting the past helped take me back in time. We tried pushing one of the coal carts on a reconstructed railway. Wow— was it heavy! Then I took a ride in the coal car, which used to take the miners to work. When I finished the tour, I went to the wash house. I imagined what I would be like after a day of working underground.

My visit gave me lots to think about. I'm glad people decided that work for kids should be in school, not in mines!

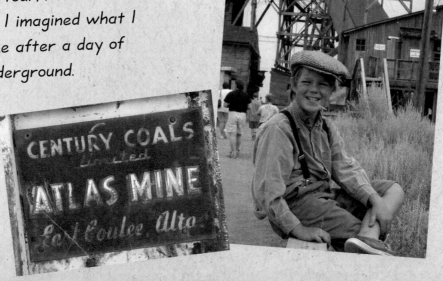

CENTURY COALS
Limited
ATLAS MINE
East Coulee, Alta.

What Happened to Wheat?

Alberta's cities were growing quickly in the early 1900s. Even so, about half of all people who lived here still worked in agriculture. Most farmers grew wheat. Wheat was still "king." People said the Prairies were the "breadbasket of Canada." When they thought of Alberta, they thought of wheat. It was part of the province's identity.

Wheat fields near Cereal, in 1920. What can you tell about the crop from this photograph?

The Dust Bowl Years

Without warning, everything changed. In the late 1920s, a terrible **drought** hit the Prairies. It lasted 10 long years. The land dried out. Fierce winds made matters worse. They blew the soil away. Huge dust storms turned the skies black. The Prairies were renamed the "dust bowl."

words matter!

A **drought** is a long period with far less rain or snow than usual.

ALBERTA VOICES

The Land Blew Away

The wind blew all the time.... [My wife] said the wind used to make the house vibrate...a hot sucking wind. It sucked up all the moisture. So this wind just blew and blew, and we had dust storms...The land just blew away.

Prairie farmer, 1930s

Grasshoppers Everywhere!

The hot, dry weather brought massive clouds of grasshoppers that ate any wheat the farmers did manage to grow.

How Did Alberta Recover?

The whole province suffered during the drought of the 1930s. Starving families had to sell their land or simply abandon it. Many people moved to the cities, even though it was hard to find work there. Yet, by the 1940s, the quality of life had improved for many people. How did that happen?

Think back to the story of Leduc in Chapter 3. The discovery of oil in 1947 brought changes to Alberta. Many people had already begun working in logging and mining. Now more began working in the oil and gas industries. Alberta had a new identity. It became known as an "oil province."

Prairie dust storm near Lomond in the early 1930s. Compare the dust bowl field below with the field shown on page 223.

How Did Alberta Become More Diverse?

Who lived in the new cities that were springing up? After Alberta became a province, its **population** became more **diverse**. People came from different cultures and from many different countries. Some immigrants came from the United States, Scotland, Ireland, and Belgium. Others came from Russia, Germany, Italy, and China. They brought their families and their traditions to Alberta.

Some settlers who came to farm didn't do as well as others, so they moved to the cities. Sometimes workers who had built the railway stayed once it was finished. Some people planned, from the start, to live in towns and cities. They came to open shops and other businesses, or to work in schools or hospitals.

ALBERTA VOICES | A New Beginning

Pauline Stein's grandson, Richard Stein, describes his grandmother's experience:

Pauline was excited and relieved, but apprehensive [scared] as she stepped onto Canadian soil at Halifax on a warm September day in 1912. Excited because she and her children...were finally in their chosen country. Soon they would be reunited with her husband, Daniel Stein, who had gone ahead six months earlier to find a place to live. Relieved because it had been a difficult three-week journey from her home village in Russia. She was tired and weak from seasickness and caring for her children. Apprehensive because she spoke only German and was worried about the long train trip in an English-speaking country.

Pauline and her family in Canada in 1922. Before the Steins came to Canada, they were German immigrants living in Russia.

Why Was Alberta a Land of Promise?

Where did the children on these pages come from? Why did their families want to come to Alberta? What kinds of work were they looking for? Imagine you are one of these children. In your journal, write how you feel about moving to Alberta.

My name is Natalie Masson. It is 1906. My father is a farmer, and we live in Québec. We have farmed here for many years, but now we cannot grow enough for our family.

Last Sunday, a priest visited our parish. He told us about French-speaking communities in Alberta with Catholic churches, schools, and rich farmland. He said that Francophone families are needed in the West. Now my parents are talking about moving there.

My name is Peter Helt. It is 1903. I live in Budapest, a city in Hungary. My father works on a boat on the Danube River. He loads and unloads freight from the busy docks. It's hard work, but he's strong and doesn't mind it.

My mother's cousin wrote a letter from Canada. He is in a place called Crowsnest Pass. He is working as a coal miner. He says lots of miners are needed, and the pay is much better than it is here.

My name is Kristina Nilson. It is 1904. I live in Minnesota, in the United States, but my family comes from Norway. Our farm here is not doing well. It's too small, and we can't afford to buy more land.

Last week, my uncle was in the general store. He saw a poster about Alberta. There are lots of jobs there and plenty of land. My dad and my uncle thought they could go logging in the woods. My parents told me there are many Norwegian communities in Canada's West. Perhaps we'll also move there.

My name is Hiroki Tanaka. It is 1910. I live in Japan. My family owns a small farm. There isn't much land in Japan that's good for farming. Most farmers, like us, build terraces up the steep hills to make room for more crops. But there's no room to grow!

We are going to move to Alberta. My aunt and uncle and my cousins are all living there. They grow sugar beets for the sugar factory in Raymond. My uncle has written to tell us that there is flat farmland as far as the eye can see!

My name is Kaari Lehtinen. It is 1907. I live in Finland. My parents are worried about the changes happening here. There has been a lot of trouble lately.

My uncle went to Alberta to see what life would be like there. He works in a coal mine at a place called Canmore. He says it's beautiful. He told us there is lots of wide-open space in Alberta. It makes you feel like you have room to grow!

Helping Alberta to Grow

For many immigrants, Alberta was a place where they could make a good life for themselves and their families. Look at the information below. How did immigrants help Alberta to grow?

People left China because there wasn't enough land to grow food. At first, many worked on the railway. Then they went into business for themselves. They opened restaurants and grocery stores. They worked hard and brought their families to Alberta and to other parts of Canada.

A Russian Jewish couple, Judah and Chasia Shumiatcher, started a hat-making business in Calgary. It still exists today. One of their hats became the official hat for the winter Olympics in Calgary in 1988.

Little Italy

Some of the Italians who came to Alberta found work in the railway, in the mines, and in the forestry camps. Many who worked in the mines settled in the Drumheller Valley. Some moved to cities like Edmonton and Calgary. A part of Edmonton where many Italians settled and still live today is called "Little Italy."

Keeping Francophone Culture Strong

Most of the immigrants who came to Alberta began to learn English. What do you think this would mean for Alberta's Francophones? Most of them were more determined than ever to keep their culture, language, and identity strong. They opened private French schools, and they started French-language newspapers. Today, more than half of Alberta's Francophones live in the Calgary and Edmonton areas.

Today the town of Falher offers services in English and French. Many residents are Francophones.

Francophone children outside their school in 1909. Their teacher, Dellamen Plamondon, is standing at the doorway. She is only 12 years old!

Le Progrès was founded in Morinville in 1909. It was one of four French newspapers published at the time. Another newspaper, *Le Franco*, is still published today.

In 1940, French radio programs ran for only six minutes a day! Alberta's French language radio station, CHFA, opened in 1949.

I'm going to record some interviews with my neighbours to see if they moved here from somewhere else.

Keeping Aboriginal Cultures Strong

As Alberta's cities grew, they drew in many more people. Aboriginal peoples, too, began moving to the cities. They also helped the cities grow and become more diverse. Yet, they also remembered their traditional ways of life.

Emma Minde was a Plains Cree woman who was born in Saddle Lake in 1907. Later, she went to live with her husband in Hobbema. She shares her memories of how her people used to live.

ALBERTA VOICES

Remembering a Way of Life

Emma Minde

From the time I was a child, I saw my parents and other people, other parents, work so hard at making a living. These are things they used to do. They used to hunt so they had meat, and they also used to trap…. And they also used to fish.

And today these skills are greatly missed…. You just go to the store now; you just go and try to buy something. This is why I am asked to tell about it, so that the young people would know how the old people back then used to run their lives…. Everything used to be hard to obtain, but for them it was not hard because they were used to it. They were happy to do these things….

The life of long ago was certainly good, but you probably could not live like that today, for there is too much damage to the earth. There is so much cultivation all over.

Emma Minde

Honouring the Past

Aboriginal peoples worked to build communities and organizations that would keep their cultures strong. You learned about some of these efforts in Chapter 4 and Chapter 6. Over time, Aboriginal organizations also began talking to governments. They wanted to make sure that promises made to their peoples at the time of the treaties were not forgotten. They want to be sure that their contributions to Alberta are recognized.

ALBERTA VOICES — Celebrating Our Heritage

I am proud of my Métis heritage: I am Scottish and Cree... I want Alberta to be a place where all people can feel proud of who they are and where they came from—a place where we are all encouraged to celebrate the things that make us unique. Many Albertans share that vision. People from across the province are finding ways for Aboriginal people to honour, celebrate and preserve their wonderful and unique heritage....

Colleen Klein, volunteer and wife of Ralph Klein, premier of Alberta, 1992–2006

Colleen Klein

First Nations Conference, Ottawa, March 9, 1984. Representatives of First Nations and Métis peoples met with the Canadian government. Since then, there have been many other meetings.

Viewpoints

How Can a Growing City Respect the Past?

Alberta's cities have continued to grow and change. Some people want to make sure we don't lose the heritage of our cities as they grow. Let's look at one example.

Rossdale Flats is an area in Edmonton on the banks of the North Saskatchewan River. For 8000 years, it was a meeting place for First Nations. During the fur trade, two forts were busy in the flats. Many people were buried here—First Nations people, Métis, Francophone fur traders, voyageurs, and European settlers.

City of Edmonton

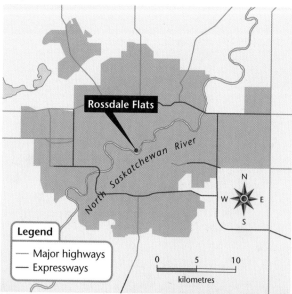

Rossdale Power Plant

In 1903, a power plant and a water treatment plant were built to supply Edmonton with electricity and clean water. Later, bridges, exhibition grounds, and a ballpark were built. A paved road covered part of the burial grounds. When Alberta needed more power, plans were made to expand the Rossdale Power Plant.

Over time, there have been many meetings about what to do with this area. In one discussion, people expressed the following points of view.

> I've heard people say that the site is almost the birthplace of Alberta...It would be lovely to see the Power Plant shut down.
>
> – *Catherine Garvey, Historical Board of Edmonton*

> It may cost $600 million to build the plant somewhere else. The community needs the new plant.
>
> *— Power Plant official*

> We have to honour that site…. But some people are saying, "Oh, it was just a cemetery, just leave it, and don't put anything on it." If we do that, in 50 years it will be forgotten.
>
> *— Philip Coutu, Métis representative*

> I wish they would turn that building into an education centre…. My ancestors are buried on this site…. I would like to have a monument there.
>
> *— Fran Gosché, descendant*

> We should make more parkland and green space in the area, or put in some small shops or restaurants. A community centre, tennis courts, or a public swimming pool would be a good addition to the neighbourhood.
>
> *— Some responses in a survey of Rossdale residents*

These decisions were made for Rossdale Flats:

- Operate the water treatment plant, but shut down the power generator.
- Make the burial grounds a historic cemetery.
- Protect some buildings as historic sites.
- Put up a monument to honour the people buried there.

Over to YOU!

1. Discuss the different views. Talk about reasons for the differences.
2. What does "compromise" mean? Do you think the results were a compromise? Why or why not?
3. Are there any monuments or areas in your community that preserve and respect the past? Why are they important?

Set Your Skills in Motion

Display Some Headlines

Look through a local newspaper. Cut out stories, headlines, or letters to the editor about current events in your community or in the province. Sort your findings and post them on a bulletin board under the headings "Fact" or "Opinion." Look at the clippings other students posted.

- Is everything under the correct heading?
- How do you know?
- Why is it important to be able to tell the difference between fact and opinion?

Say How You Help

You have seen that, at one time, children worked hard. They helped build the province. How do you contribute to Alberta today? Do you contribute by going to school? If so, how? How do you contribute by other actions, either at home or in the community? How could you do more? Write a journal entry to give your views.

Protect a Special Site

Research a historic area in your community. As a responsible citizen, inform others about what they could do to protect and preserve this site. Try using technology to create a brochure or poster.

Make a Flow Chart

Make a flow chart. Show how groups of people have used the land over time. Think about First Nations, fur traders, and settlers before and after 1905. What events caused these changes? Try using a computer to make your chart.

Look What You Have Learned!

Many settlers came from around the world to live and work in the province. They made their living as farmers, coal miners, and loggers, and in the new jobs that were opening up in towns and cities. Communities grew quickly. Some people moved from rural to urban centres. In 1905, Alberta got its name and joined the other provinces in Canada. Alberta had a provincial identity.

Review the inquiry questions for this chapter:
- How did Alberta become a province?
- What do major events and stories tell us about Alberta's past?

Show what you have learned in this chapter by using a computer to make a graphic organizer. Save your organizer in a database for others to view.

Take Time to Reflect

Before you go on to the next chapter, think about what you have learned in this one. What have you learned about fact and opinion that will help you in the future? How can you use technology to help you in your inquiries?

 Choose something from this chapter to save for your Alberta Treasure Chest.

Preserving the Land

In a dark cave in the Rocky Mountains, warm water from deep inside the earth bubbled up in hot springs. For centuries, people of the Kootenay First Nation had known the cave as a sacred place of peace. In 1883, three men helping to build the new railway discovered the cave. They made a plan for it. They wanted to start a spa—a place where people could come to enjoy a dip in the warm water. The spa would make them rich.

Instead, two years later, the Canadian government made the area into Banff National Park. Most of the land would be preserved exactly as it was. Banff was the first national park in Canada and only the third in the world. The area was set aside so all the people of Canada could enjoy it forever.

Alberta's Story

You have read that people in Alberta use the land for agriculture, mining, and forestry. People also use the land and water for activities such as skiing, fishing, hiking, and camping. In this chapter, you will discover how Alberta tries to protect some of its land. You will find out how parks and protected areas help to preserve Alberta's heritage, land, plants, and animals.

? Inquiring Minds

Here are some questions to guide your inquiry for this chapter:

- Why are provincial parks, protected areas, and national parks important?
- How do we protect Alberta's land and heritage?

Look for answers in this chapter. If you have other questions, explore more!

How can I share some of the things I find out? I will

- think about my audience. Who am I sharing this with?
- try using graphic organizers like Venn diagrams or webs
- try writing a report, giving a speech, or creating a slide show

Why Do We Need to Protect the Land?

words matter!

Habitat is the place where an animal makes its home in nature. If the habitat is changed or cleared, animals might leave to find a home somewhere else, or they might die out.

Some of Alberta's endangered plants and animals:
1. western spiderwort
2. western blue flag
3. northern long-eared bat
4. whooping crane

Do you remember reading about the prairie grasslands in Chapter 1? Two hundred years ago, many different types of animals and native plants were found on the grasslands. Now the land is filled with farms and cities. Most of the original animals and plants are gone. The native grasses have been dug up, and the animal **habitats** have been cleared.

Now think about how natural resources are used in Alberta. Huge areas of the boreal forest are cleared to mine the oil sands. Forests are cut for lumber. How could using the land in this way affect the natural environment?

Look at the plants and animals below. They were once common in Alberta. Now there are so few of them left, they might die out. How can we protect them, and other plants and animals that are in danger?

How Can We Preserve Land for the Future?

To protect plants and animals, governments have set aside some parts of the province they call **protected areas**. Some protected areas also preserve landforms, such as hoodoos in the badlands.

Different Types of Protected Areas

Some protected areas allow visitors. National and provincial parks are protected areas where people can go to enjoy the landscape, plants, and wildlife. Other protected areas are closed to people. In all protected areas, there are strict limits on how the land is used. Hunting, fishing, logging, drilling, and mining are banned in some areas. Even though people can use some of the resources, large areas will be protected for the future. Protected areas help to sustain the natural environment of Alberta.

Thinking
It Through

Think about the last time you visited a park.
- What did you do there?
- How would your quality of life be different if there were no parks? Explain.

ALBERTA VOICES

A Gift to My Grandchildren

I think about a time when I sat on a wildflower-covered ridge and watched 31 mountain goats, large and small, in Willmore Wilderness Park. I hoped that my grandchildren would one day sit in the same meadow to watch the goats' grandchildren.

Ray Rasmussen

Enjoying nature in Willmore Wilderness Park

239

Who Created Parks and Protected Areas?

Look back to the story of Banff on page 236. Who was responsible for creating Banff National Park?

The government of Canada protects some parts of the country for all citizens to enjoy. Since Banff was created, many more **national parks** have been established. There are now more than 40 of them across every province and territory in Canada. They preserve natural features that are important to all of Canada.

Alberta has five national parks. Do you think this is enough to protect all of the province's unique features and places? In 1932, the government of Alberta decided that the province should also take steps to protect the land. Today, the government of Alberta takes care of more than 500 **provincial parks** and different types of protected areas. In all, the government of Alberta works to protect over two million hectares!

Alberta's Parks and Protected Areas

Provincial Parks
Ecological Reserves
Wilderness Areas
Natural Areas
Provincial Recreation Areas
Heritage Rangelands
Willmore Wilderness Park
Wildland Provincial Parks

Sign welcoming visitors to Jasper National Park. Canada's two official languages are used in national parks.

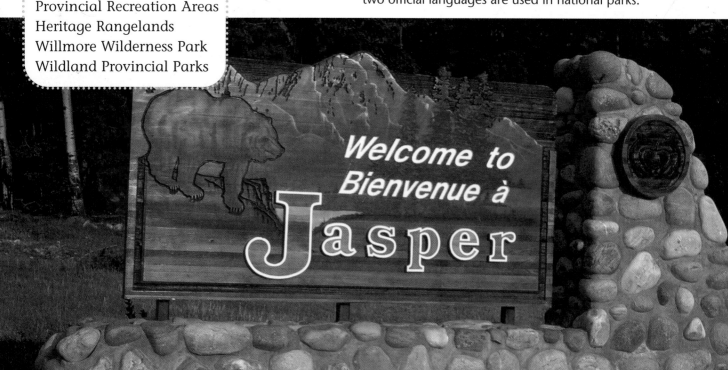

What Do Parks and Protected Areas Do?

The diagram below shows some of the purposes of parks and protected areas. Many parks and protected areas have interpretive centres with displays that tell about special features of the area. Sometimes they tell about the land or about people who have used the area in different ways. In many places, visitors can participate in hikes and other programs with park wardens to learn more about the area. Most parks have campgrounds where people can enjoy being outdoors.

Jasper was named after Jasper Hawes, a North West Company clerk. Mount Edith Cavell was named after a British nurse. I'll make a web to share what I know about Jasper.

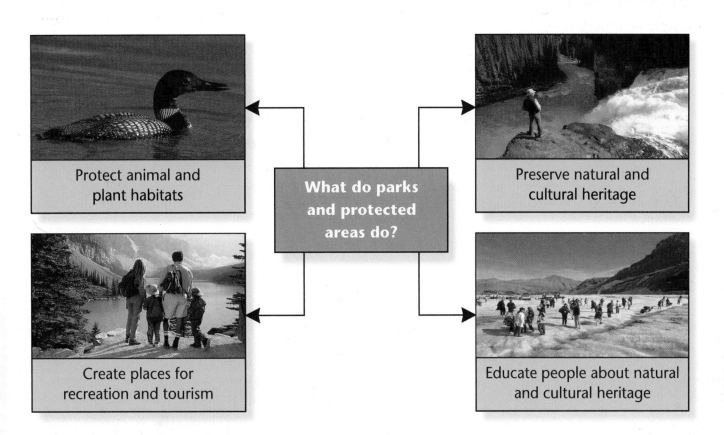

Protect animal and plant habitats

What do parks and protected areas do?

Preserve natural and cultural heritage

Create places for recreation and tourism

Educate people about natural and cultural heritage

Respect for the Natural World

If we hope to preserve our way of life, the first thing we must do is rediscover our respect for the land, the water, and the entire natural world.

Lois Hole, former lieutenant governor of Alberta

Should Logging Be Allowed in Protected Areas?

All protected areas have rules about land, water, plants, and animals. However, different types of protected areas have different rules. For example, logging is allowed in **heritage rangelands**. These areas were created to protect prairie grasslands. Logging is also allowed in **wildland provincial parks**. They were created to allow people to enjoy camping and hiking. Logging is not allowed in **wilderness areas**.

People have different views about logging in protected areas. Let's see what they have to say.

▼ Athabasca Dunes Ecological Reserve

Logging Without Limits!

I think logging should be allowed in all protected areas. More than half of Alberta is forest. We won't be running out of trees anytime soon.

Cutting down trees in protected areas won't affect the environment in the long run. Trees grow back, don't they?

Rock Lake–Solomon Creek ▶ Wildland Park

Is logging allowed in these protected areas?

No Logging!

Logging should be banned in all protected areas. Protected areas were created to protect the environment. We should leave them in their natural state.

Logging could conflict with other activities. I'm a birdwatcher, and logging destroys the birds' habitat.

Logging with Care!

Some protected areas, like wilderness areas, were created especially to protect the forest. We shouldn't log in those areas. But some protected areas were created to preserve other things. So I agree with logging in those places.

We have to be careful about logging in protected areas. There should be a limit to the number of trees cut. We should log only the younger trees and preserve the old ones.

Logging is an important industry for Alberta. What are the advantages and disadvantages of allowing logging in protected areas?

Over to YOU!

1. Work in a group to discuss these viewpoints. What is your opinion? Would your opinion be different if you worked for a logging company?

2. Do you think other activities, like mountain biking or riding snowmobiles, should be allowed in protected areas? Explain your thoughts.

3. With your group, make a list of rules you think people should follow in a natural area near your community. Think about ways you can preserve the land for future generations.

What Do Our National Parks Preserve?

I could create a slide show about Alberta's national parks. I will share my presentation with a younger student.

Let's learn more about Alberta's five national parks. As you read, think about what each park preserves. Look at the photographs to find out more about each park.

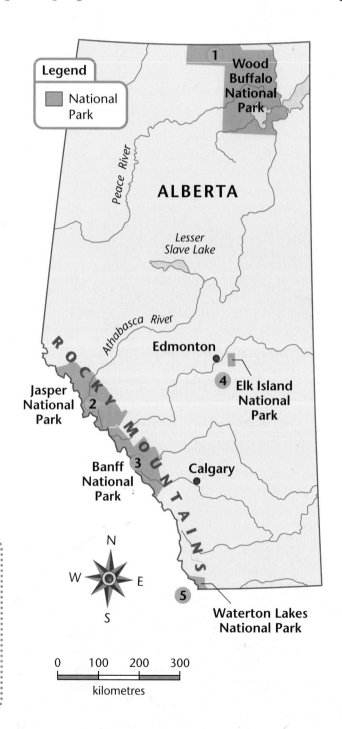

Skill Smart

What do the pictures on the opposite page show about Alberta's natural landscapes? Write a descriptive paragraph about Alberta's national parks. Include information about some of the things the parks protect.

World Heritage Sites

Three of Alberta's national parks are also World Heritage Sites. They are Wood Buffalo, Jasper, and Banff. World Heritage Sites are places of great natural or historic value to the world as a whole.

244

Wood Buffalo National Park is the world's second-largest park. It also has the largest herd of free-roaming buffalo.

Jasper National Park is the largest park in the Rocky Mountains. The Athabasca Glacier is in Jasper National Park.

Banff National Park has mountains, sparkling lakes, hot springs, and forests. It is one of Canada's most popular parks.

Elk Island National Park features the Living Waters Boardwalk, a 150-metre floating sidewalk on Astotin Lake.

Waterton Lakes National Park is in Canada. Glacier National Park is in the United States. Together they form Waterton-Glacier International Peace Park. Canadians, Americans, and Blackfoot First Nations work together to protect the land and wildlife here.

Wood Buffalo National Park

Wood Buffalo National Park was created to protect the buffalo in northern Canada. If you visit, though, you might see more birds than buffalo. The big animals are often in hiding.

Why are there so many birds? The park has huge **wetland** areas that have formed where the Peace and Athabasca rivers come together. Birds use the wetlands as a nesting place. One of the wetland areas is a nesting place for the endangered whooping crane. It is the only nesting habitat in the world for this bird.

Ducks flying over Lynx Strand Creek. The wetlands in the park provide habitats for birds on their long journey to warmer weather.

Salt flats in Wood Buffalo National Park. These huge areas of salt plains are unique in Canada.

Thinking
It Through

Why do you think it is important to protect the buffalo in Alberta? (Hint: Remember the role of the buffalo in Alberta's history.)

ALBERTA VOICES

Who Was More Afraid?

My husband, David, and I were hiking in Wood Buffalo National Park one summer. As I came around the bend, I was surprised by a moose heading right towards me. I jumped, turned, and walked in the other direction. The moose did the same thing. It turned around and ran away! I guess he was as afraid of me as I was of him.

Kim Webber

Jasper National Park

Jasper is the most northern of Alberta's mountain parks. More than two million people visit the park each year.

▲ Pyramid Lake and Mountain, Jasper National Park

▲ Rafting on the Maligne River, Jasper National Park

Protecting the Woodland Caribou in Jasper

Woodland caribou are in danger of dying out in Canada. There are more caribou in Jasper National Park than anywhere else in Canada, but their numbers are getting smaller. To protect the animals, Parks Canada is changing hiking rules in the park. Dogs are not allowed where the caribou roam. During the season when the calves are born, hikers must stay on main trails to avoid the animals.

Skill Smart

With a partner, find out more about the protected plants and animals in Jasper. Look in three different sources. Try books, the Internet, or interview an adult. Use computer files to organize the information you find.

Banff National Park

Banff National Park has a wide variety of natural features. No wonder it has three million visitors every year!

Moraine Lake and the Valley of the Ten Peaks. Banff National Park preserves many natural features for future generations.

Grizzly bears in Banff National Park. Elk and white-tailed deer are among the animals protected in the park.

There is a lot to do in Banff National Park. Would you enjoy this activity?

Lake Louise. This is one of the most photographed lakes in the world.

Thinking *It Through*

How does Banff National Park help protect and preserve Alberta's natural environment?

ALBERTA VOICES   Gold Medal Dreams

I am training to be a downhill skier. My dream is to represent Canada in the Olympics. My favourite place is Banff. The scenery is fabulous, and they say the skiing is the best in the world. I am lucky to live close to the mountains.

Emilie Tremblay

My Visit to Banff

My dad says everyone has a favourite activity at Banff National Park. I had two! The first was a trip in a gondola up Sulfur Mountain. What a great way to travel all the way up the mountain in just eight minutes. And what a great view from the top!

My other favourite activity was our visit to the Cave and Basin Hot Springs, filled with warm water that comes from deep under the ground. The water smells like rotten eggs. Dad said it was because of the sulfur—a mineral that's found in the earth. We weren't allowed to go into these pools because we would disturb the Banff Springs snails. These snails are not found anywhere else in the world, and they are in danger of dying out. I'm glad that the snails are protected. They help to make Alberta unique.

Elk Island National Park

Elk Island National Park is less than an hour away from Edmonton. The park protects an area of wilderness parkland. This is one of the most endangered habitats in Alberta.

Although it is the smallest of Alberta's national parks, Elk Island is home to a host of animals. As well as plains and wood buffalo, it has moose, deer, coyotes, beaver, and at least 250 types of birds. It also has lots of elk, of course, as you can see below.

Visitors to Elk Island National Park can go boating on Astotin Lake. In winter, they can go snowshoeing or skiing.

Bringing Back the Trumpeter Swan

The trumpeter swan is the wildlife symbol of Grande Prairie, about five hours northwest of Elk Island. There used to be many trumpeter swans in Alberta, but they haven't lived in Elk Island National Park for over 100 years. They disappeared because of overhunting. Elk Island is trying to bring the swans back. Future visitors will be able to enjoy seeing this beautiful bird.

Waterton Lakes National Park

Waterton Lakes National Park has beautiful waterfalls, lakes, and prairie grasslands. Because of its climate, it also has a large number of plants and wildflowers. Pygmy poppies have been found only in the Waterton Lakes area.

Red Rock Canyon in Waterton Lakes National Park is known for its red and green layers of rock.

Many types of flowers grow in the park, including pygmy poppies, shown here. These poppies are unique to the area.

Cougars can be found in the park. Bighorn sheep, deer, bears, moose, and many types of birds are also found here.

Skill Smart

Make a table similar to the one below to compare any two national parks in Alberta. Use books, magazines, or the Internet to help you find more information about the parks.

	National Park	_National Park_
Natural features		
Wildlife		
Plants		
Activities		

What Do Our Provincial Parks Preserve?

The parks and protected areas give us so many ways to enjoy the outdoors. They encourage us to visit parts of the province we may not have thought about otherwise.

Provincial parks were created to preserve the variety of Alberta's natural and historical features. What can you tell about the number and range of provincial parks from this map?

Provincial Parks

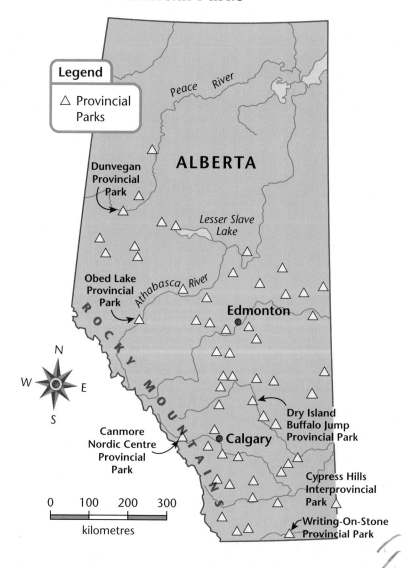

Read on to learn more about six of Alberta's provincial parks. They are located in five different natural regions. As you read, think about how each park preserves a different aspect of Alberta's heritage.

Visit Some Provincial Parks

PRESERVING WILDLIFE AND PLANTS: CYPRESS HILLS

My family and I went on a camping trip to Cypress Hills Interprovincial Park. It's the only provincial park that crosses over two provinces—Alberta and Saskatchewan. As we got closer to the park, the hills just seemed to rise up out of the flat land around it. My dad says the park is sometimes called a forest island in a sea of grass. So the park preserves forests, streams, and hills in the middle of the prairie grasslands. The next day, we rode along the bike trail. We kept an eye out for the wild turkeys and some of the 14 types of orchids that grow in the park.

Gordon Woo

PRESERVING HABITATS: OBED LAKE

Last year, my mom took me kayaking at Obed Lake near Hinton. The park protects a wetland area where many animals and birds live. I used our binoculars to look for birds. I saw lots of them, and I could also see fish under the clear water. I saw some elk, but didn't spot any moose. It was so quiet and peaceful—and fun too!

Daniel Cliche

PRESERVING NATURAL AND CULTURAL HERITAGE: DRY ISLAND BUFFALO JUMP

I live near Huxley. I have been going to Dry Island Buffalo Jump, in the badlands, since I was a little boy. I never tire of seeing the cliffs and thinking of how animals once stampeded over the edge. And I enjoy looking at the hoodoos. When I was a boy, this area was not protected. People in the community worked hard to convince the government to make it a park. I'm glad they did—aren't you?

Louis Whitford

PROVIDING RECREATION: CANMORE NORDIC CENTRE

I volunteer at the Canmore Nordic Centre Provincial Park. People ski here in the winter and ride their bikes in the summer. I like it best when there's a race. My job is to make sure the spectators stay back from the start and finish lines. In summer, my favourite event is the mountain bike race. Some racers go for 24 hours straight! In winter, I really enjoy the cross-country skiing events. I like being out in the crisp air, and the scenery is breathtaking.

Jane Schmidt

A racer at the Canmore Nordic Centre mountain-bike race, held every summer

PRESERVING CULTURAL HERITAGE: DUNVEGAN

My brother and I spent the day at Dunvegan Provincial Park and Historic Site. Dunvegan was one of Alberta's first trading posts and missionary centres. Some of the old buildings have been restored so we can see what life was like back then. There are also gardens where fruits and vegetables are grown as they were in the past.

Sammy Malic

PRESERVING CULTURAL HERITAGE: WRITING-ON-STONE

My parents took me to Writing-On-Stone Provincial Park. It is near the town of Milk River in the badlands. I saw images that First Nations people in this area carved in the rock. Some of the carvings were over 3000 years old! The South Piikani people lived in this area. They believed it was a sacred place. Their drawings show that this place was very important to them.

Olivia Hubahib

The Milk River at Writing-On-Stone Provincial Park

How Can We Preserve Our Parks?

I am going to make a chart on the computer to share what I know about protecting natural areas.

You have learned that governments are responsible for Alberta's parks and protected areas. Who else do you think is responsible?

Millions of people from Alberta and around the world visit the parks every year. Many communities depend on **tourism**. Tourists spend money in the hotels, restaurants, and stores near the parks. Many Albertans work in hotels and museums or as tour guides and instructors. Tourism benefits Alberta, but it can also cause problems.

Think of what might happen in a natural area when many people come to see it. People might leave litter. Their vehicles might cause pollution or injure animals. Careless campers might cause fires. Can you think of other effects tourists could have on parks?

What Can Visitors Do?

Most parks have rules similar to the ones below. How does obeying the rules help preserve the park?

Thinking
It Through

- What are some things you might do to care for the environment when you visit parks?

- Should you show the same care in other natural areas? Why? Explain.

These activities are not allowed:

- Collecting or removing of any natural objects (for example, wildflowers, driftwood, or berries) or cultural objects (for example, arrowheads)
- Hunting
- Fishing without a licence. Certain fish may not be caught.
- Motorized off-road travelling
- Snowmobiling
- Paragliding, parachuting, or hang gliding
- Using personal watercraft

Be a Thoughtful Visitor

Justin wanted to know how tourists and animals can share Alberta's parks. He interviewed Derek Tilson, a Park Warden at Waterton Lakes National Park. Read on to see what he found out.

Does tourism affect animals in the park?

Tourists enjoy the wildlife very much, so they sometimes want to get too close to the animals. Some even feed the mule-deer and big-horned sheep. These animals become used to people, so they aren't afraid to go into the town site. This can be dangerous. Their horns or antlers can get caught in fencing. Some animals are run over by cars, too.

Does tourism affect other animals?

If campers leave food around, bears come looking for it. Then we have to move the bears somewhere else. In the worst case, the bear has to be destroyed. But we try not to do this.

Does the park teach tourists about living with wildlife?

We ask people to put everything in their vehicles when they are not on their campsite. Pots, pans, and even bars of soap attract wildlife. We tell campers when they check in, and there are signs everywhere in the park.

Can tourists and animals share the park?

I think so, but tourists should keep a safe distance away from wildlife. Use binoculars to view them. Respect the wildlife in the park.

Skill Smart

Write down some other questions you would like to ask a park warden. See if you can find answers from other sources.

What Can Residents Do?

People do live in some park areas, but there are rules for these people, too. For example, the town of Banff is located in Banff National Park. There is a rule that Banff cannot have more than 10 000 people living permanently in the town. The residents must have a job there or be related to someone who is working there. Why do you think this rule was made?

People who live in park townsites are careful not to leave food and garbage out, so they don't attract the animals. They also encourage wildlife to stay away. In the town of Banff, the elk are chased away by people waving hockey sticks!

What do you think this sign means?

The town of Banff. Why do you think people might want to live here?

What Can You Do?

Anyone who visits a park or protected area can make a difference. You can obey park rules and learn about the park environment. You can try to leave as little mark as possible on the parks. Even if you have never been to a park or protected area, you can learn about the natural environment, and appreciate the role that parks play. With your support, the parks and protected areas will still be beautiful for future generations.

Take only photographs. Leave only footprints.

Thinking *It Through*

Why do you think it is important to protect parks for future generations? Discuss your thoughts as a class.

SKILL POWER

Communicating Information

Information can be communicated in many ways. You can present what you have to say in any of the ways shown here, and more.

How do you choose which one to use? A lot depends on your purpose for communicating and your audience. Are you planning to inform, persuade, or entertain? Who is your audience? What kind of presentation might best help them understand what you have to say?

Telling
Speech
Oral report
Poem
Song

Writing
Essay
Written report
Web site
PowerPoint presentation

Showing
Posters
Photographs
Drawings
Graphs and tables

Practise the Skill

Look back at the sign of park rules on page 256. Try to communicate the information in different ways. Remember to think about who your audience is first. You could

- give a speech
- create a PowerPoint presentation
- draw a poster

Which format do you think works best? Why?

Set Your Skills in Motion

Communicate Information

Think about the parks and protected areas you learned about in this chapter. Which place would you like to visit the most? Why? Look back to page 259 to see the different ways you might communicate. Pick a format. Use it to try to persuade your teacher to take you to your chosen park or natural area.

Create a PowerPoint Presentation

Work in small groups. Choose one endangered plant or animal in Alberta. Find out how Alberta's parks are helping to protect this type of animal or plant. Plan a short PowerPoint presentation for the class. Include details about whose responsibility it is to help protect these plants and animals. Include details about what responsible citizens can do to protect these plants and animals.

Create a Tourism Brochure

Make a brochure encouraging people to visit a national park in Alberta. What can you see and do? How does the park protect nature? Have fences been built? Are there hiking trails? Add some tips on how tourists can respect nature.

Report on a Newspaper Article

Find a newspaper, magazine, or Internet article on how any Alberta park is preserving its wildlife, plants, or landscape. Read the article once to identify the main idea. Read it again. What different viewpoints are included in the article? Share the main idea of the article and the different viewpoints with your class.

Look What You Have Learned!

Parks and protected areas are important because they preserve the natural landscape, plants, and animals that are special to an area. Tourists can visit parks to learn about Alberta's natural and cultural heritage. Tourism also brings money and jobs to the province. However, it's important that visitors and residents respect the park environment and wildlife and obey the rules. Parks and protected areas are all part of Alberta's identity.

Review the inquiry questions for this chapter:
- Why are provincial parks, protected areas, and national parks important?
- How do we protect Alberta's land and heritage?

Show what you have learned by making a chart. Collect information from the text that answers each inquiry question. If you can, add information from other sources. Be sure you include where you found different pieces of information.

Take Time to Reflect

Before you go on to the next chapter, think about what you have learned in this one. How did you communicate information in different ways? What did you learn that will help you share information more effectively in the next chapter?

Choose something from this chapter to save for your Alberta Treasure Chest.

Celebrate Our Past, Build Our Future

Imagine walking down the school hall and hearing over 30 different languages being spoken! That could happen to you at Connaught Community School in Calgary. What languages might you hear? Here are just a few: Russian, Korean, Amharic from Africa, Urdu from Pakistan, and Mandarin or Cantonese from China.

Connaught School is unusual. Not many schools have students from so many different countries. Some students at the school moved to Alberta with their families. Others come from families who have always called Alberta their home. They all learn in English, but they like to share their home languages, too. They celebrate their cultures at school. Every day is a day to share experiences and culture.

Connaught School shows us that people from countries all over the world are making Alberta their home.

Alberta's Story

In earlier chapters, you read how Alberta's population has grown and changed over time. In this chapter, you'll learn more about people from many different countries who came to join Alberta's communities. You will discover how this history and heritage is being preserved for the future. Together, Albertans celebrate the heritage that has made their province what it is today. Together, Albertans work to build the future.

Connaught Community School

? Inquiring Minds

Here are some inquiry questions to guide your inquiry:

- How have people of many cultures helped make Alberta what it is today?
- What difference can I make to Alberta?

Look for answers as you read. To find out more, explore other sources.

I've learned a lot about the inquiry process that will help me as I do more exploring. I now know
- how to make a plan and ask questions
- where to find information
- how to organize and share my findings

What Makes Alberta's People So Diverse?

Alberta's population is diverse. The First Nations have always lived in the area that became Alberta. Other people have come from almost every country of the world! Some families have been here for hundreds of years, and others are new to Alberta. Everyone has experiences, knowledge, ways of life, and traditions to share. They are all part of Alberta's story. That's something to celebrate!

Where Are Some Albertans From?

Let's look at some of the scrapbook pages Kevin's class made. On these pages are notes from their e-pals, whose families came to Alberta from other countries. Read what their e-pals wrote.

My family came from Vietnam to live in Calgary when I was a baby. My parents were happy to see the Rockies. There are mountains in Vietnam, too! My family speaks English and French, and I go to a French immersion school. We celebrate Vietnamese holidays such as *Tet*, which celebrates the New Year.

HIEN

My great-grandparents came to Alberta in 1949, from Italy. My great-grandfather was a carpenter. When he came to Bellevue, he learned English very quickly. He started his own construction company. My grandmother speaks Italian to me so I will always know the language. I love speaking Italian!

Lina

When I first looked for Canada on a globe, it seemed so far away from my home in the Philippines. We came to Fort McMurray because my mother was offered a job as a nurse. My brother and I learned English in school. There are other people from the Philippines living here. Some of my Philippine friends were born in Alberta. They help me with my English, and I talk to them in Pilipino.

Malaya

Thinking
It Through

- What is the story of your family's background?

- Think about your family's language and the place they first called home. What makes their language and home interesting?

My grandfather was a tailor in Hungary. My grandparents came to Canada in 1958. They settled in Lethbridge, and my grandfather set up a tailoring business. I am very close to my grandparents. When I visit, my grandfather teaches me many Hungarian folk songs.

Alexa

A few years ago, my parents came to Alberta from Algeria, in Africa. We found a home in Calgary. I can see the mountains. My friend from school said his dad would take me skiing there. I go to a Francophone school because our family is used to speaking French. I learned English in school in Algeria. That's why I can write to you in English.

Edouard

I want to find out more about communities that speak other languages. Time to make a new inquiry plan!

Why Are Francophone Communities Important?

There are many languages spoken in Alberta. The French language has deep roots in the province. Most people who speak French have made their homes in Francophone communities. About half of Francophone Albertans were born in Alberta. Some families have been here for hundreds of years, as you saw earlier. About half of the French speakers who live in the province come from other countries in **la Francophonie**. La Francophonie is an organization of French-speaking countries around the world. Alberta's Francophones are a diverse group.

Franco-Albertans celebrating Canada Day

ALBERTA'S FRANCOPHONES COME FROM—
Alberta: They have been here for many generations
Other provinces: e.g., Québec and New Brunswick
Europe: e.g., France and Belgium
Africa: e.g., Tunisia and Rwanda
Caribbean: e.g., Haiti and Martinique

The Franco-Albertan Flag

The Franco-Albertan flag was created in 1982. The wild rose and the colour blue stand for Alberta. The white lily, or fleur de lys, stands for France, the home country of the first

Francophone settlers in Canada. The blue and white stripes show the waters and roads travelled by Francophone explorers. The colour white stands for la Francophonie.

Skill Smart

- How does the flag show what is important to Franco-Albertans?
- Create a flag to show what is important to your family or school.

How Does Diversity Make Alberta Strong?

The people of Alberta have roots in many different traditions, customs, religions, celebrations, and languages. This gives Alberta a rich **cultural heritage** that adds to our quality of life. It means that Albertans can draw from various experiences, stories, and ways of looking at the world. This diversity will help Alberta grow in the future. Imagine Alberta as a tree. The roots are different cultures and traditions. Remembering those roots will keep them healthy. Then the tree and its branches will grow big and strong for the future.

Thinking
It Through

- How do the photos on this page show Alberta's diverse population?
- How does Alberta's cultural heritage add to quality of life?

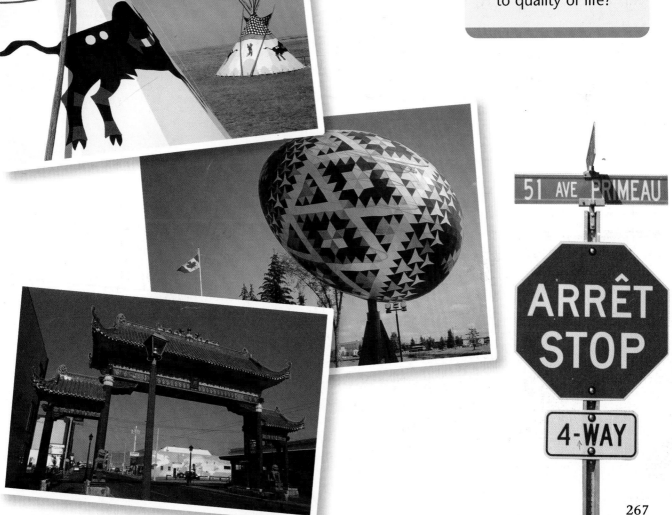

How Have People Made a Difference?

Many people have helped make Alberta a good place to live. Each year, Albertans can nominate people from the past or in the present to be given an award. These people can become part of the Alberta Hall of Fame. Here's a display Marc made showing a few people in the Hall of Fame. How have they made a difference to Alberta?

Victoria Callihoo: Métis Historian

Victoria Callihoo was one of Alberta's most important historians. You can read some of her memories in Chapter 5. She wrote down her memories so that Métis people could learn their history. Without her work, a part of Alberta's history may have been lost forever.

Karl Clark: Inventor

In 1929, Karl Clark invented a way to get the oil out of the Alberta oil sands. He put some oil sands into a large rotating drum. Then he mixed the sands with hot water and lye to separate the oil from the sand. A similar process has been used from 1967 to today.

Dr. Mary Percy Jackson: Wilderness Doctor

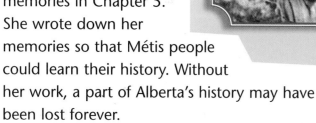

Dr. Mary Percy Jackson used to visit patients by canoe, horseback, or dogsled! She came to northern Alberta in 1929. She took care of people in the Peace River area for over 45 years. She was one of the few doctors in the area.

Joseph Crowshoe: Piikani Elder

Joseph Crowshoe was a respected spiritual leader of the Piikani First Nation. He helped to develop the Head-Smashed-In Buffalo Jump site in southern Alberta, which is now a World Heritage Site. He also preserved his language by working on a Blackfoot dictionary.

Léo Piquette: Francophone Politician

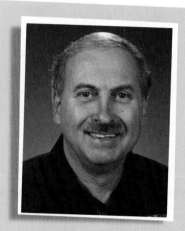

Léo Piquette was elected to Alberta's Legislative Assembly in 1986. He fought for the right to speak French there. He also supported the Francophone community's efforts to exercise its right to run its own schools. In 1993, the Alberta government created three Francophone School Boards.

The Edmonton Grads: Basketball Legends

This women's basketball team was famous from 1915 to 1940. They played in Canadian and North American championships and in the Olympics. They hold an all-time record for any sports team: 502 wins and only 20 losses!

Edward Shimbashi: Farmer

In the 1930s, Edward Shimbashi and his father grew potatoes near the town of Raymond. He brought the first potato harvester into the province. He also found ways to irrigate the land. These changes were a great help to potato and beet farmers.

I wonder which communities have murals. I could check the Internet to find out, or ask an adult, like my teacher.

How Do We Celebrate the Past?

Alberta has many treasures of the past. You have already explored some of them. They help us learn stories of the people and the land. When we know about the past and celebrate it, we have a better understanding of people. We gain respect for them and for the land that is now Alberta.

WHERE CAN WE LEARN ABOUT THE PAST?

Local Museums	Many towns and cities in Alberta have a museum or site that shows the history of that community. Across Alberta, museums collect artifacts and set up exhibits. These exhibits help us remember and learn about the past.
Our Provincial Museum	The Royal Alberta Museum in Edmonton displays the history of the whole province in one place. Many visitors come to learn about Alberta.
Heritage Sites	Heritage sites are fun because they bring history to life. Workers there dress in costumes to show visitors how people once lived. Sometimes you can learn by watching and listening. Sometimes you can learn by taking part!
Historic Murals	Many communities paint murals to tell their stories. Research is done to make sure that the paintings are accurate. Murals are often painted by local artists.

In the Royal Alberta Museum, you can learn about the land, people, birds, and animals of Alberta. In the Natural History Gallery, you can explore Alberta's rocks and minerals. The Wild Alberta gallery shows pictures of Alberta's landscapes.

The Cowboy Trail

How can you see a whole lot of Alberta's past, all on one trip? You can take the Cowboy Trail. It's the best trip I ever took. We drove along the trail and stopped to visit different historic sites.

My favourite stop was the Bar U Ranch near Longview, in the foothills of the Rockies. Visiting the Bar U helped me imagine what ranching was like many years ago. We went to a campfire at night and heard stories about the land. We ate bannock and listened to music. The next day, we went horseback riding. That was so much fun! My horse was named Rocky, after the Rocky Mountains.

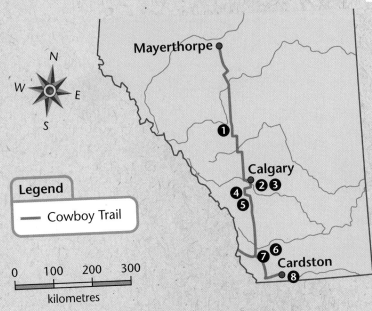

Legend
— Cowboy Trail

Mayerthorpe

Calgary

Cardston

0   100   200   300
kilometres

Main Stops on the Cowboy Trail
1. Rocky Mountain House
2. Glenbow Museum
3. Heritage Park Historical Village
4. Turner Valley Gas Plant
5. Bar U Ranch
6. Head-Smashed-In Buffalo Jump
7. Kootenai Brown Pioneer Village
8. Remington Carriage Museum

What Do Historic Sites Tell Us?

Here is Natasha's slide show of historic sites she discovered on the Internet and in books. See what you can learn from her slides and the information she included in her presentation. Why do you think sites like these are important to Albertans?

This is the Stand Off Rodeo. Rodeos celebrate the work of ranchers and cowboys. In Stand Off, the Kainai First Nation celebrates with a rodeo and fair every summer.

This is a huge mural at Elk Point's Mural Park. It shows people, places, and events of the past. People in the community helped the artist by sharing old photos, stories, and memories.

Here is the Grande Prairie Museum. It shows visitors what life was like when settlers came here in the early 1900s.

272

This is Father Lacombe Chapel. It is Alberta's oldest building. Father Lacombe built it in 1861. The area around it became a Métis settlement. Later the settlement became the city of St. Albert.

Here is the Stephansson House. Stephan Stephansson was a poet from Iceland. He moved to Markerville in 1889. You can now learn about Icelandic culture at his house.

This is the Andrew Grain Elevator Interpretive Centre in the village of Andrew. It is one of the best preserved grain elevators in Alberta. Inside, displays tell the story of agriculture in Western Canada.

Should Grain Elevators Be Preserved?

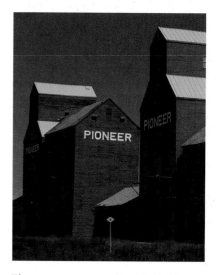

There were once almost 2000 wooden grain elevators in Alberta.

One of Natasha's slides showed a grain elevator that was preserved. It now displays an important part of Alberta's story. Years ago, if you drove through Alberta's Prairies, you would have seen a grain elevator in almost every town. Many of the tall wooden buildings were built in the early 1900s to store grain and to load the grain onto rail cars. They were usually painted in bright colours and displayed the name of the town.

Today, many old grain elevators have been taken down. New grain elevators made of concrete and steel have been built instead.

Should the old grain elevators be preserved? What do you think? Look at some of the arguments:

The old grain elevators are made of wood, so they are fire hazards. They should be torn down.

The new grain elevators are much larger and can process more grain. Why should we keep the old ones if the new ones are better?

The old grain elevators are part of Alberta's heritage. They are a symbol of the farmers' hard work. They are part of our identity. I think we should keep them.

This is a new grain elevator in Carseland, near Calgary.

One School Takes Part

Students at Prince of Wales Elementary School took a stand on this issue. They wanted to keep the story of the grain elevators alive for the future. They met with Walter Danylak, from High River, who has a dream of building a grain elevator museum.

The class wanted to help Walter Danylak. They went on field trips to research the history of grain elevators. They wrote letters to the government about the importance of remembering this part of Alberta's history. They even had a meeting with the premier!

Their work was shown on the Internet as part of the Galileo Educational Network. The students were invited to present their project to the Alberta Grain Elevator Society in Stettler. They even appeared on a TV program in Edmonton. The students were proud that their voices were being heard. They were glad to help preserve part of the past.

Over to YOU!

1. As a group, discuss each of the viewpoints on page 274. Which opinion do you agree with most? Why?

2. Why do you think it was important to the students to help preserve the history of the grain elevators?

3. Identify a symbol of Alberta's past in your community. Do you think steps should be taken to preserve this symbol? Give reasons for your view.

How Can Art Tell Alberta's Story?

Art is another way in which people can tell their stories. See what you can learn from the copies of paintings that Giselle chose for a bulletin-board display to tell about Alberta's places and people.

Edmonton Skyline by Jim Cupido. This painting shows the North Saskatchewan River, which flows through Edmonton.

Plains Cree Way of Life by Nona Foster. In this painting, the artist tells about the life of her Plains Cree ancestors.

Still Playing for the Street Championship by Peter Shostak. His paintings tell about life in Ukrainian communities in the 1940s and 1950s.

Coal Mine at East Coulee, Alberta by Peter Etril Snyder. This is Canada's last wooden coal-mine structure.

How Can We Build for the Future?

I want to organize and share my family's history. My mom has lots of photos in a box. I'll see if she'll help me sort them and put them into an album.

Think of people you have learned about who have made a difference in Alberta. Their actions have helped to build the future. Some people write or paint their stories. Others work to preserve Alberta's fossils. Some protect the resources of the land and Alberta's parks. Some work to save buildings, forests, or creeks. There are people who work to keep their language and traditions strong. Many of us want special events and celebrations to carry on into the future.

All these things, and more, are an important part of our heritage and history. We build our future on them.

This is a mural in Legal. It shows the history of the town in a way that everyone can see—just by walking down the street! This is one of the ways that people in Legal preserve their history and heritage for the future.

Thinking *It Through*

- Is there something in your community that's an important part of its history?
- Why do you think it's important?

What Part Do Celebrations Play in Our Future?

Everyone has something to celebrate. You might be celebrating something today! Not everyone shares the same celebrations. Families, communities, and people of diverse cultures have their own days of celebration. Still, there are some days that most Albertans celebrate. Think of days like Earth Day, Heritage Day, Canada Day, Treaty Days, and Family Day.

Each summer, my community celebrates National Aboriginal Day. I want to find out more about the celebrations for next year. I'll interview my neighbour, who works at the town hall.

Communities often celebrate with special events. This boy is taking part in the Taber Cornfest. What special events, such as festivals or rodeos, happen in your community? What do they celebrate?

Skill Smart

- With a partner, make a chart with all the celebration days your community celebrates. Look on the Internet for clues.
- Take a survey to find out which celebrations students in your class attend.
- Make a graph to share your results.

Celebration days are important. They help us explore and show our respect for other cultures. Celebrations are also a time to remember important events and people that are part of Alberta. Think again of the image of Alberta as a tree. Different cultures and traditions are the roots of the tree. Celebration days can be a way of remembering those roots, keeping them healthy for the future.

Celebrations are also a time to get together to have fun! That's important for our future, too.

How Can I Help?

There are things you can do today that will make a difference to the future. That's what the students in Prince of Wales Elementary School discovered. Read about some other students who made the same discovery.

Reduce Your Waste-Line

One year, almost 100 classes in Alberta took part in the "Reduce Your Waste-Line Challenge." For one week, classes in each school carefully recorded what type of waste was produced. They labelled containers for plastics, paper, glass, juice boxes, organic waste, and garbage. Then they decided how much waste could be recycled, reused, or composted. Most classes discovered that more than half of the waste in their classrooms should not go to landfills! After that, they paid more attention to the three R's.

Schools in Red Deer, Fort McMurray, and other communities won prizes for taking part.

The Three R's

Reduce your use of resources.

Reuse products when you can, instead of throwing them away.

Recycle paper, plastics, metals, and bottles.

Taking Action in Your Community

What can you do all year to reduce waste at school and at home? Here are some ideas. What can you add to the list?

- Reuse school supplies.
- Waste less paper.
- Buy items with less packaging.
- Make sure recyclables don't go in the garbage.
- Start a composting program.

Reduce Reuse and Recycle!

Restore Native Plants

Each year in June, an Emerald Award is given to a school for an outstanding project on taking care of the environment. Dr. E.W. Coffin Elementary School in Calgary recently won that award for their work on saving native plants. These are plants that are part of Alberta's natural heritage.

Rescuing Plants

This project helped me understand why we need to rescue plants in various areas of our city before they are destroyed. They are an important part of our history.

Dimitrinka, student
Dr. E.W. Coffin Elementary School

Students at Dr. E.W. Coffin Elementary School still work in the natural areas planted nearby.

The project started in Whispering Woods, a wooded area next to the school. The students at the school set out to restore an area called the Prairie Amphitheatre. The City of Calgary helped with the project. Students collected seeds of native plants from nearby Nose Hill Park. They grew plants from these seeds, and then planted them around the Prairie Amphitheatre.

The students watered the plants all summer. It wasn't long before the plants were growing well. The students made plans to open the Prairie Amphitheatre for everyone to enjoy. They made signs to name the plants so visitors would know what they were. The area looked beautiful, and more native plants were growing. The students had really made a difference!

Thinking *It Through*

- What ideas do you have now about ways you could make a difference in your community?
- How would your project help build for the future?
- What could you do to get started?

Setting Goals for the Future

The students in each of these schools saw a problem that could affect quality of life now and in the future. They saw what needed to be changed, and they decided how to make it happen. They set a goal that gave them something to work towards.

People often work together towards a common goal. Together, everyone can work to make Alberta a great place to live.

These students set a goal to improve their schoolyard. How are they working towards this goal?

Protecting the Forests of the Future

Alberta's Aboriginal Junior Forest Ranger Program is a summer program for First Nations students. Its goal is to train the students to work as forest rangers. They watch for wildfires, learn about the forest, and gain forestry skills. The Junior Forest Rangers also learn about harvesting plants for medicine. They take part in ceremonies and learn from Elders.

Different communities, such as Fort Vermilion, Sucker Creek, and Fort Chipewyan, host the rangers when they are not in the forest camps.

- Why do you think these communities would be involved in this program?
- Why do you think it is important for young people to learn about the forests in Alberta?

Thinking
It Through

Think about your school or community. What problem needs to be solved? Doing something about this problem could be a goal you share with others.

Solving a Problem

You have learned how some students discovered a problem and found a way to make things better. You can do that, too.

Step 1: Identify the problem. Write it down. That will help keep the problem clear in your mind.

Step 2: Find out more. Ask questions. Research the problem at the library, on the Internet, or in the newspaper. The more you know about the problem, the easier it will be to solve.

Step 3: Brainstorm solutions. To begin, think of as many solutions as you can. For each one, consider the pros and cons.

Step 4: Choose the solution you think is best. Keep it simple. You want a solution you can do. State the solution as your goal.

Step 5: Work together. Tell other people about the problem and your solution. Listen to their ideas. Make a plan to carry out the solution together. Then do it.

Step 6: Evaluate your planning and the action you took. Did things work out the way you intended? Did you meet your goal? What worked well? What would you do differently next time?

Practise the Skill

Talk with your classmates about problems in your school or community. Choose one of these or another problem you know of. Follow the steps above to solve the problem.

Set Your Skills in Motion

Do a Survey

What concerns do people have about Alberta's future? Create a survey to find out. You may want to ask people about the environment or the future of your community.

- Create a list of questions, and make copies of your survey.
- Give the survey to students, teachers, parents, and people in your community.
- When you have the surveys back, gather your results and report them. What are people most concerned about? What are they less concerned about?
- Choose one problem and use the first four steps on page 283 to suggest a solution.

Make a Current Events Scrapbook

Make a small scrapbook or booklet of interesting events that are happening in Alberta.

- Check the newspaper, television programs, or the Internet to find out about current events in Alberta.
- Organize your booklet. Paste in newspaper or Internet clippings, and write summaries of television news. You can also make comments about how you think an event might affect the future.

Create a Hall of Fame

Nominate three or four people you think deserve to be in Alberta's Hall of Fame. Include a person from the past, someone from your school or community, and someone from another part of Alberta.

- Ask people you know for their suggestions. Check newspapers, television programs, and the radio to learn about Albertans in the news.
- Write a short profile of each nominee and include a photo, if possible. Explain why this person belongs in the Alberta Hall of Fame. Post your profiles for others to read.

Look What You Have Learned!

In this chapter, you explored how Alberta's diverse population makes Alberta strong. You read about citizens who made a difference, and considered ways you can do the same. You examined Alberta's story through people's reflections, historic sites, art, and celebrations. All of this is part of Alberta's identity and helps build the future.

Review the inquiry questions for this chapter:
- How have people of many cultures helped make Alberta what it is today?
- What difference can I make to Alberta?

Show what you know on a large building block.
- Make a cardboard cube or use a cube-shaped box. Cover with squares of paper.
- On the sides, tell how people of diverse cultures and ages have helped make Alberta what it is today. On one end, tell why the past is important. On the other end, tell what you can do now to help make a difference. Use written descriptions and illustrations.
- Put your building block next to a partner's to see what story the blocks build together.

Take Time to Reflect

Think about what you have learned in this chapter. When did you use all or part of the inquiry process? How was it helpful? How will the steps in Solving a Problem help you find ways to make your school or community a better place?

Choose something from this chapter to save for your Alberta Treasure Chest.

Looking Back: Chapters 8, 9, and 10

Justin uses a spider map to outline what he thinks are the key points in Chapters 8, 9, and 10.

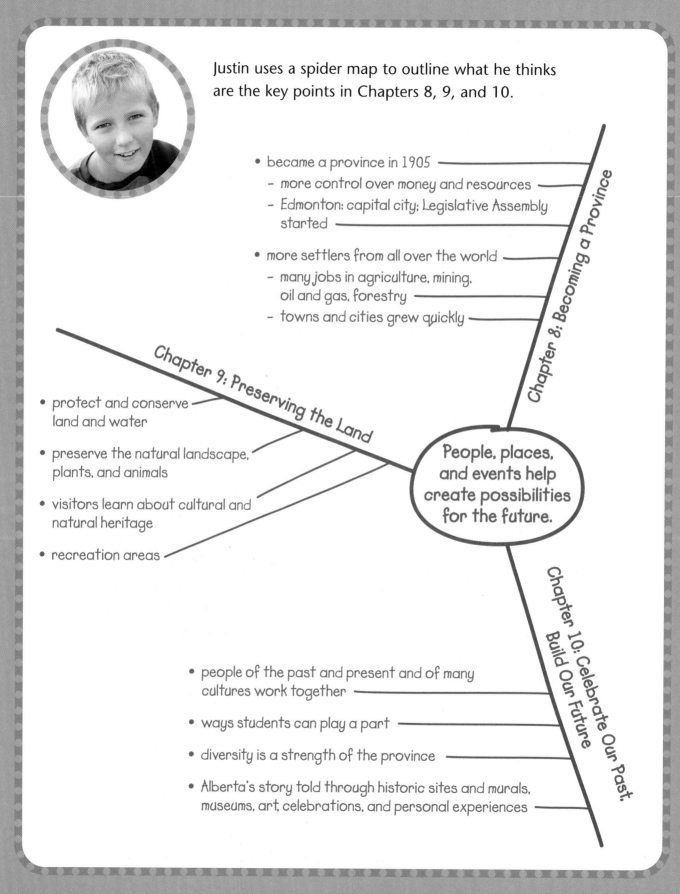

Chapter 8: Becoming a Province

- became a province in 1905
  - more control over money and resources
  - Edmonton: capital city; Legislative Assembly started
- more settlers from all over the world
  - many jobs in agriculture, mining, oil and gas, forestry
  - towns and cities grew quickly

Chapter 9: Preserving the Land

- protect and conserve land and water
- preserve the natural landscape, plants, and animals
- visitors learn about cultural and natural heritage
- recreation areas

People, places, and events help create possibilities for the future.

Chapter 10: Celebrate Our Past. Build Our Future.

- people of the past and present and of many cultures work together
- ways students can play a part
- diversity is a strength of the province
- Alberta's story told through historic sites and murals, museums, art, celebrations, and personal experiences

Share What You Know

? Inquiring Minds

Study Justin's spider map closely. Then skim through Chapters 8, 9, and 10 to help you recall what you learned. Now turn to page 3 in Getting Started. Which one of the overall inquiry questions for the book is the main focus of these chapters? Why do you think that?

Prepare an Alberta Treasure information pack. In it, give some examples of how people, places, and events help shape Alberta's future. Include examples from the past and today.

Plan to include different types of articles like

- a profile of a person who has made a difference
- a newspaper story from a time in history, which describes an important event
- an article you have written
- a map, photos with captions, or drawings
- an interview with students whose project made a difference

Retrieve, or recall, what you've learned about how Alberta is building a future.

Process, or think about, which people or events have made a difference. Select five or more for your information pack.

Create your information pack by organizing your information according to the time in Alberta's story.

Share your information as a booklet, a fold-out accordion book, a folder, or a big book.

Evaluate how well you worked in each of these steps. Are you pleased with your booklet? Did others seem to like it? What would you do differently next time?

Wrapping Up

What better way to wrap up our exploration than with an official Alberta song!

Alberta

Composed by Mary Kieftenbeld

Flatlands, rollin' plains
Clear blue skies, prairie rains;
A tapestry of colours in the fall.
Snow-covered mountain tops,
Wheat fields, canola crops;
Alberta has it all.

Chorus
Alberta is calling me.
Home sweet home, it's where I'm proud to be.
Alberta is calling me.
Livin' right I'm feelin' free.

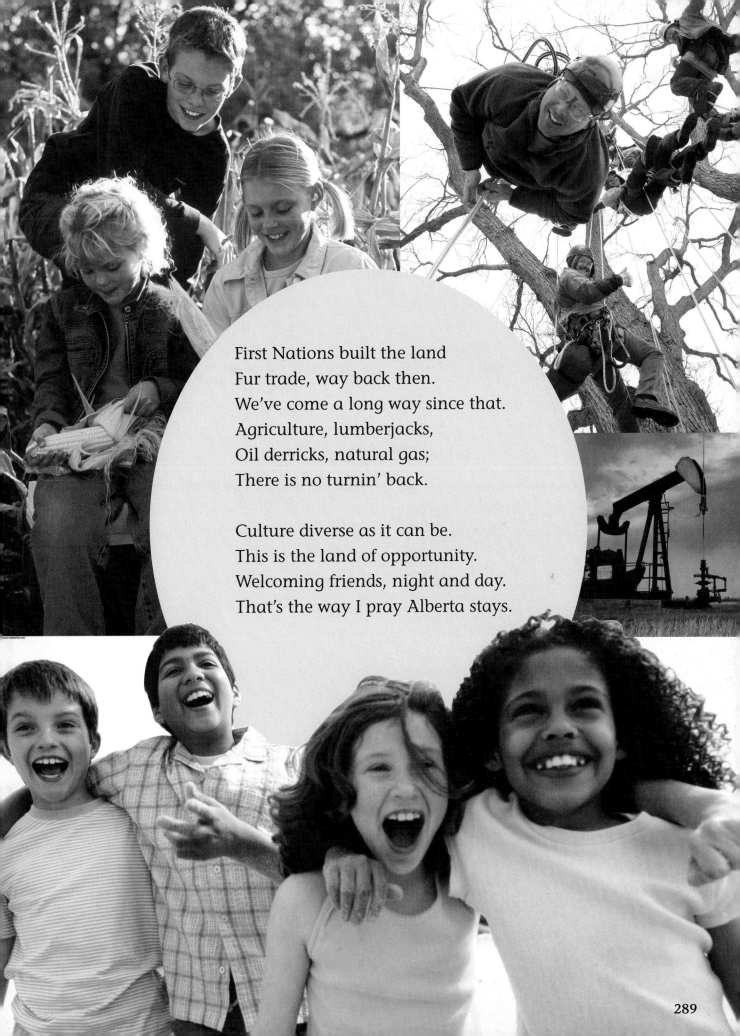

First Nations built the land
Fur trade, way back then.
We've come a long way since that.
Agriculture, lumberjacks,
Oil derricks, natural gas;
There is no turnin' back.

Culture diverse as it can be.
This is the land of opportunity.
Welcoming friends, night and day.
That's the way I pray Alberta stays.

Alberta: People, Places, and Possibilities

I wonder what the words to some of Mary's other songs are. I could check in a music store, or I could write to her on her Web site.

In her song, composer Mary Kieftenbeld tells a story of Alberta.

Mary has a story, too. It is part of Alberta's story. She was born and raised in Calahoo, northwest of Edmonton. When she was only six years old, she sang in her church choir. When she was ten, she picked up the guitar and has been singing and playing ever since. Mary now lives on a farm in Alberta near Rivière Qui Barre with her husband, Ed, and their four children.

In many of her songs, Mary sings about her life and the things that are important to her. Her songs tell young people that life is full of possibilities and that we can all make a difference in the world. She says it doesn't have to be something big, and you don't have to be perfect to do it! Even small actions can count for a lot.

Is This Like Being a Good Citizen?

Mary Kieftenbeld is making a difference by bringing a positive message to people through her music. She's doing something to help make people's lives better. That's part of being a good citizen.

Mary Kieftenbeld

How Can You Make a Difference?

Citizenship also includes showing respect for
- people's cultural heritage
- the rights, opinions, and points of view of others
- the diverse cultures and languages in Alberta
- Alberta's history and historic sites
- our environment

It's all part of making a difference. It's all part of citizenship.

How Does Good Citizenship Add to Quality of Life?

Treating people fairly makes them feel happy and like they belong. It makes them feel comfortable with who they are.

If we take care of our environment, we will have the things we need that affect our health and shelter—like fresh water, clean air, and healthy forests. Caring for the land will also help Alberta continue to be a land of opportunity. All this contributes to quality of life now and in the future.

How can I make a difference? Maybe I can get some ideas by thinking about what people in our school have done to make it a nice place to be.

Skill Smart

In Chapter 10, you read about students making a difference by caring for and respecting the environment. Design a poster or a display to encourage respect for one of the other points in the list above.

Why do you think planting trees is an example of good citizenship?

Alberta's Story

In Getting Started, we said that the story of Alberta is really not just one story—but many. Mary Kieftenbeld's story is one of them. Your story is one of them, too. In this book, you have explored many stories about how Alberta came to be what it is now.

Here are some of the stories you've explored.

How the land was formed

Alberta's fossil heritage and natural resources

How the people who were here first, and others who came later, make Alberta a place of diverse cultures

How Alberta became a province and what that meant to people who lived here

Preserving our land and resources for the future

Alberta's celebrations and challenges

Stories like these make Alberta unique. They show how we can build on the past and the present to help create the future. We can be proud to be part of Alberta!

Skill Smart

Create a citizenship poster. Use words and illustrations to encourage people to make a difference to the health, safety, happiness, or future of others.

? Inquiring Minds

Throughout your exploration of Alberta, you have asked questions and searched for information. You have used the inquiry process introduced in Getting Started.

> Before, I used to do a project and then that was it! Now I spend time on the Evaluating step and think about what I've learned. I even think about how I did things and what I might change for my next project.

> I've always liked to do reports and add photos, drawings, and charts. But now in the Sharing step, I do other things, too. I like to create slide shows, dioramas, posters, and songs. It's more fun now!

Evaluating

What can I learn from this inquiry that will help with my next inquiry?

Do I need to take action based on my information?

Sharing

Am I going to share what I've found?

If so, how will I share it?

Thinking *It Through*

Reflect on how you have used the inquiry process over the year.

- What did you find difficult at first?
- In which of the six steps have you improved the most? Explain.
- What changes will you make in your next inquiry?

I used to just think about what my topic was and then go and search for information. I didn't really have a Planning step. Now I write down some questions. Then I think about how to follow the inquiry steps to get the answers.

Planning >

What questions do I need to ask?

Retrieving

How will I find the information?

Reflecting

Thinking About Your Inquiry

How will I record my information?

Is my information accurate and reliable?

How will I organize my information?

Do I need to ask other questions?

Processing

Creating <

I didn't know it was important to find information in more than one place. In the Retrieving step, I learned to use all kinds of sources—the Internet, books, and ideas from other people. Now I can get better information and check to see if it's correct.

At first, in the Processing step, I wrote out too much information. Then I started to use jot notes, but I didn't write them in any special order. Now I use headings, a web, or a fishbone organizer.

Set Your Skills in Motion

Create a Personal Story

Your story is part of Alberta's story because you are part of Alberta. Think about the places, people, and events that are important to your story. Think about what your story might be like in the future. What might you want to do? How will you make a difference in the world? Choose a way to tell your story. You might want to use words or pictures with captions. Perhaps you could use a timeline or a flow chart.

Write an Alberta Song or Poem

Think about what Alberta means to you. Jot down your ideas. Review them, and then add other ideas. Choose descriptive words and arrange them in an order that seems natural. Put these ideas together to create a song or poem. Your poem doesn't have to rhyme, but you can write in rhyme if you want to. When you're ready, make a final copy to share with others.

Make an Alberta Zine

A zine is a small do-it-yourself magazine produced by one or two people. People create zines to share ideas on a topic.
- Choose a topic from one of your Alberta inquiries. Gather ideas from activities you have done, or write about a new topic.
- For your zine, you'll need a cover with the name of the zine and a contents page. Include articles such as stories, reports, viewpoints, interviews, and poems.
- You'll also need illustrations such as drawings, charts or diagrams, photos, clip art, or pictures cut from magazines.

Look What You Have Learned!

This year, three main inquiry questions have been guiding your exploration of Alberta.

- How do the land and its natural resources affect quality of life for people in Alberta?
- How do stories, history, and culture give people in Alberta a sense of identity and belonging?
- How do people and events help to change Alberta over time?

It's time to find out how much you have learned.

With a small group, brainstorm points to give general answers to each of these questions. You don't need to give specific examples.

- Record each point on a large sticky note and place the notes on a table, on the floor, or on the chalkboard.
- Reorganize your sticky notes into groupings that make sense.
- Then make a web or chart to display your points. Save it for the activity on page 298.

Take Time to Reflect

Now that your exploration of Alberta is coming to a close, think about what you learned.
- Which inquiry question could you answer most easily?
- Which question did you find the most difficult to understand? Why?
- What really helped you in discovering answers to these questions?
- What do you think will help you in other inquiries?

Choose something from this chapter to save for your Alberta Treasure Chest.

Putting It All Together!

Look back at the web or chart you saved from the activity on page 297. Choose one inquiry question. As a group, recall stories that can be used as examples to explain the points listed on your web or chart.

Create a mural with captions, a slide show presentation, or a report with drawings or photos to answer the inquiry question.

 Prepare for an Alberta Treasure Day. This is a celebration day! You can show other classes or invited guests what you have learned in your exploration of Alberta.

Plan your celebration. Check with your teacher to see what might be possible.

Retrieve, or collect, samples showing what you have done this year.

Process, or think about, what to display. Make it something that helps tell the story of Alberta— something you are proud of.

Create a display by organizing your items. Get together with others in your class to see if you want to combine displays.

Share your Alberta Treasures on a bulletin board, table, shelf, or desk. You may want to plan an oral presentation to explain some items.

Evaluate how well you organized and set up your display. Does it represent important things you learned about Alberta's story? Did people learn more about Alberta? What would you do differently next time?

Atlas

What Is a Map?

A map is a drawing of the Earth on a flat surface. Maps do not show what the land actually looks like. For that, you need a picture. Instead, maps use symbols and colours to show some of the features of the land. Look at the picture and the map of the same area below. In what other ways is a map different from a picture?

Picture of Mary's Bay

Map of Mary's Bay

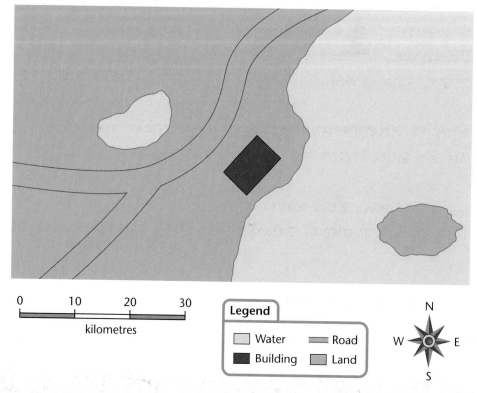

0   10   20   30

kilometres

Legend	
Water	Road
Building	Land

N
W   E
S

Reading a Map

Map makers add special features to maps to help us understand the maps. Following these steps will help you with your map reading.

Step 1 Read the title. It tells you what the map is about. Then look at the whole map to get a general idea of the information it gives.

Step 2 Find the legend for the map. Sometimes a legend is called a key. The legend explains the colours and symbols used on the map.

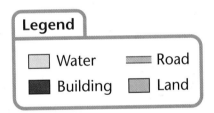

Step 3 Look for different colours on the map. Colours show different features. Check what the features are by matching the colours to the legend. Remember that blue is used to show water features such as lakes, rivers, and oceans.

Step 4 Find the compass rose. It will show directions on the map. North is always near the top.

Step 5 Look at the scale.
It will tell you about distance on the map.

Using Scale to Measure Distance

The scale of the map tells you about the actual distance between the places. Follow these steps to use a scale to measure distance between two points on the map. The example below shows the distance between Calgary and Edmonton. Practise the steps by finding the distance between other communities on the map on the opposite page.

Step 1 Mark the locations of the two places on the edge of a sheet of paper.

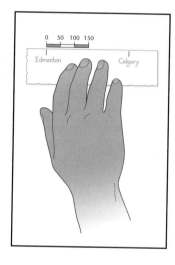

Step 2 Place the edge of the paper against the map scale, with the first mark at 0.

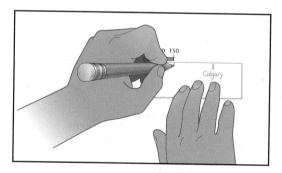

Step 3 Make a mark on your paper at the right end of the scale.

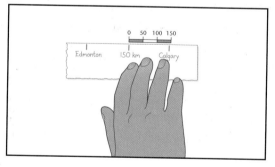

Step 4 Move your paper so that your mark lines up with 0 on the line scale. Measure the next distance. Now add the distances together to find the total distance.

Alberta: Major Communities

N
W · E
S

Hay River

Slave River

Peace River

Wabasca River

Lake Athabasca

ALBERTA

Fort McMurray

Lesser Slave Lake

Grande Prairie

River

Smoky River

Athabasca River

Cold Lake

Fort Saskatchewan

St. Albert
Spruce Grove
Stony Plain
Edmonton

North Saskatchewan River

Lloydminster

Leduc
Wetaskiwin
Camrose

Lacombe

Red Deer

Red Deer River

ROCKY MOUNTAINS

Drumheller

Cochrane
Airdrie
Banff
Canmore
Calgary

South Saskatchewan River

Okotoks
Bow River
Brooks

Oldman River

Medicine Hat

Lethbridge

Legend

- ● More than 100 000 people
- ● 10 000–100 000 people
- • Less than 10 000 people
- ∿ Rivers
- — Provincial boundary

0   100   200   300
kilometres

Reading a Physical Map

A physical map shows the features of the land. Most physical maps use colour to show the height of the land. Mountains, hills, and areas of flat land can be identified.

You can get an idea of what the land looks like by using a "slice" through the land. The diagram below shows a cross-section along the dotted line (from "A" to "B") on the map on the opposite page. How would the slice be different if "A" to "B" was from Jasper to Lake Athabasca?

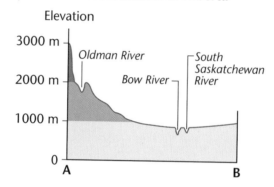

Cross-section of Alberta

Follow these steps to read a physical map.

Step 1 Identify any areas that are patterned to show the height or shape of the land.

Step 2 The legend of a physical map will often tell you the height of the land, in metres. Use the legend to identify which areas are higher and which are lower. Notice that lower land is generally green. Map makers often use green for lower land and brown for higher areas.

Step 3 A physical map helps you to tell which ways the rivers flow. Rivers flow "down" from higher areas of land to lower areas.

Alberta: Physical Map

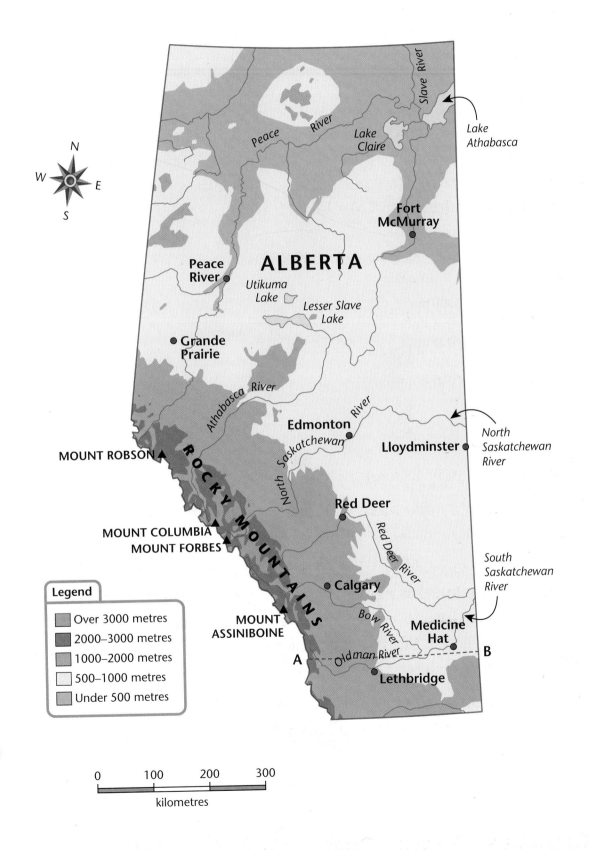

N
W · E
S

Slave River

Peace River

Lake Claire

Lake Athabasca

Fort McMurray

Peace River

ALBERTA

Utikuma Lake

Lesser Slave Lake

Grande Prairie

Athabasca River

MOUNT ROBSON ▲

ROCKY MOUNTAINS

Edmonton

North Saskatchewan River

Lloydminster

North Saskatchewan River

MOUNT COLUMBIA ▲
MOUNT FORBES ▲

Red Deer

Red Deer River

South Saskatchewan River

MOUNT ASSINIBOINE ▲

Calgary

Bow River

Medicine Hat

A   Oldman River   B

Lethbridge

Legend

▨	Over 3000 metres
▨	2000–3000 metres
▨	1000–2000 metres
☐	500–1000 metres
▨	Under 500 metres

0   100   200   300

kilometres

Alberta: Some Major Tourist Attractions

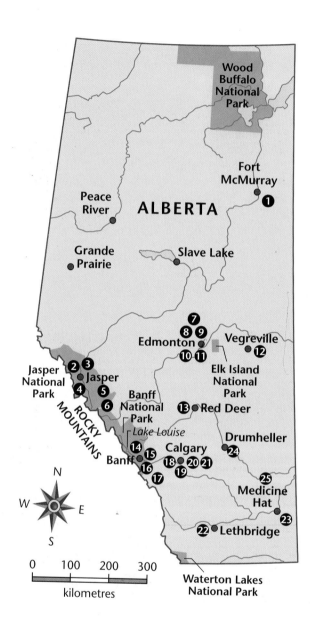

Legend

1. Heritage Park
2. Jasper Gondola
3. Jasper Park Lodge
4. Athabasca Falls
5. Maligne Lake
6. Columbia Icefield
7. Devonian Botanic Garden
8. Edmonton Art Gallery
9. Muttart Conservatory
10. West Edmonton Mall
11. Telus World of Science
12. Ukrainian Easter Egg
13. Alberta Sports Hall of Fame and Museum
14. Banff Upper Hot Springs
15. Banff Springs Hotel
16. Banff Gondola
17. Kananaskis Country
18. Calgary Science Centre
19. Calgary Zoo, Botanical Garden, and Prehistoric Park
20. Nakoda Institute
21. Stampede Park
22. Nikka Yuko Japanese Gardens
23. World's Tallest Teepee
24. Royal Tyrrell Museum
25. Dinosaur Provincial Park

National Park

Alberta: National and Provincial Parks

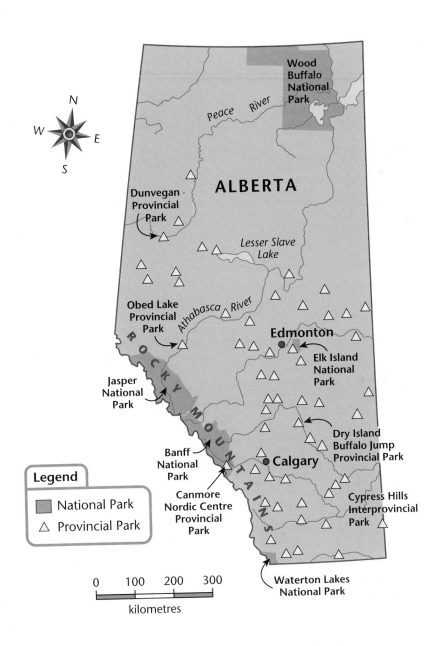

Wood Buffalo National Park

Peace River

ALBERTA

Dunvegan Provincial Park

Lesser Slave Lake

Obed Lake Provincial Park

Athabasca River

Edmonton

Elk Island National Park

Jasper National Park

ROCKY MOUNTAINS

Dry Island Buffalo Jump Provincial Park

Banff National Park

Calgary

Canmore Nordic Centre Provincial Park

Cypress Hills Interprovincial Park

Waterton Lakes National Park

Legend

▨ National Park

△ Provincial Park

0   100   200   300

kilometres

Tangle Falls, Jasper National Park

Alberta: Historic Sites and Museums

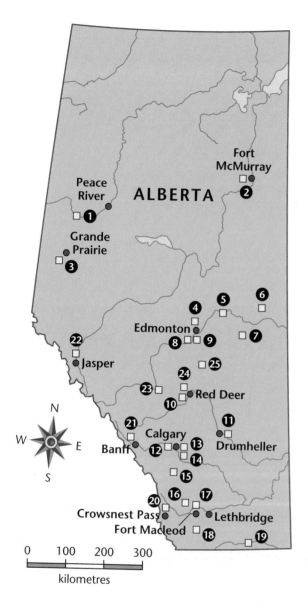

ALBERTA

Fort McMurray

Peace River

Grande Prairie

Edmonton

Jasper

Red Deer

Banff

Calgary

Drumheller

Crowsnest Pass

Fort Macleod

Lethbridge

N W E S

0 100 200 300
kilometres

Legend

1. Historic Dunvegan
2. Oil Sands Discovery Centre
3. Grande Prairie Museum
4. Father Lacombe Chapel
5. Victoria Settlement
6. Fort George and Buckingham House
7. Ukrainian Cultural Heritage Village
8. Fort Edmonton
9. Royal Alberta Museum
10. Stephansson House
11. Royal Tyrrell Museum
12. Canadian Olympic Park
13. Glenbow Museum
14. Heritage Park Historical Village
15. Turner Valley Gas Plant
16. Head-Smashed-In Buffalo Jump
17. The Fort—Museum of the North-West Mounted Police
18. Stand Off
19. Writing-On-Stone Provincial Park
20. Frank Slide Interpretive Centre
21. Cave and Basin National Historic Site
22. Jasper Park Lodge
23. Rocky Mountain House
24. Fort Normandeau
25. Reynolds Alberta Museum

☐ Historic Site or Museum

Royal Alberta Museum

Alberta: Facts and Figures

Area   661 190 square kilometres

Highest point   Mount Columbia: 3747 metres

Lowest point   Slave River: 152 metres

Largest lakes   Lake Claire, Lake Athabasca

Longest rivers   Peace River and Athabasca River

Annual precipitation   Lowest   Medicine Hat (335 mm)
                            Highest   Jasper (620 mm)

Average temperature   Lowest   Fort Smith (–24°C in January)
                            Highest   Medicine Hat (19°C in July)

Population   3 223 400 in 2005

Oil and gas   Ninth-largest oil producer and third-largest natural gas producer in the world

Agriculture   Over 20 million hectares

Forestry   Forests cover over half of the province

National parks   Banff, Elk Island, Jasper, Waterton Lakes, and Wood Buffalo

World Heritage Sites   Wood Buffalo National Park, Canadian Rocky Mountain Parks (includes Banff and Jasper), Waterton Lakes National Park, Dinosaur Provincial Park, and Head-Smashed-In Buffalo Jump

Pelican Rapids, Slave River

Alberta: Symbols

Flag

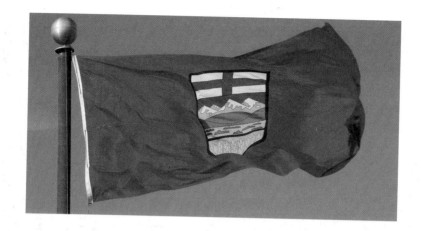

Coat of Arms

Motto: Strong and Free

Provincial flower:
Wild rose

Provincial tree:
Lodgepole pine

Provincial grass:
Rough fescue

Provincial mammal:
Rocky Mountain bighorn sheep

Provincial fish:
Bull trout

Provincial stone: Petrified wood

Provincial tartan (cloth)

Green for forests

Gold for wheat fields

Blue for lakes and skies

Pink for the wild rose

Black for coal and oil

Canada: Historical Maps

Canada at Confederation, 1867

- Nova Scotia
- New Brunswick
- Québec
- Ontario

Canada, 1876

- Nova Scotia
- New Brunswick
- Prince Edward Island
- Québec
- Ontario
- Manitoba
- British Columbia

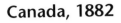

Canada, 1882

- Nova Scotia
- New Brunswick
- Prince Edward Island
- Québec
- Ontario
- Manitoba
- British Columbia

Canada, 1905

- Nova Scotia
- New Brunswick
- Prince Edward Island
- Québec
- Ontario
- Manitoba
- Saskatchewan
- Alberta
- British Columbia
- Yukon Territory

Canada

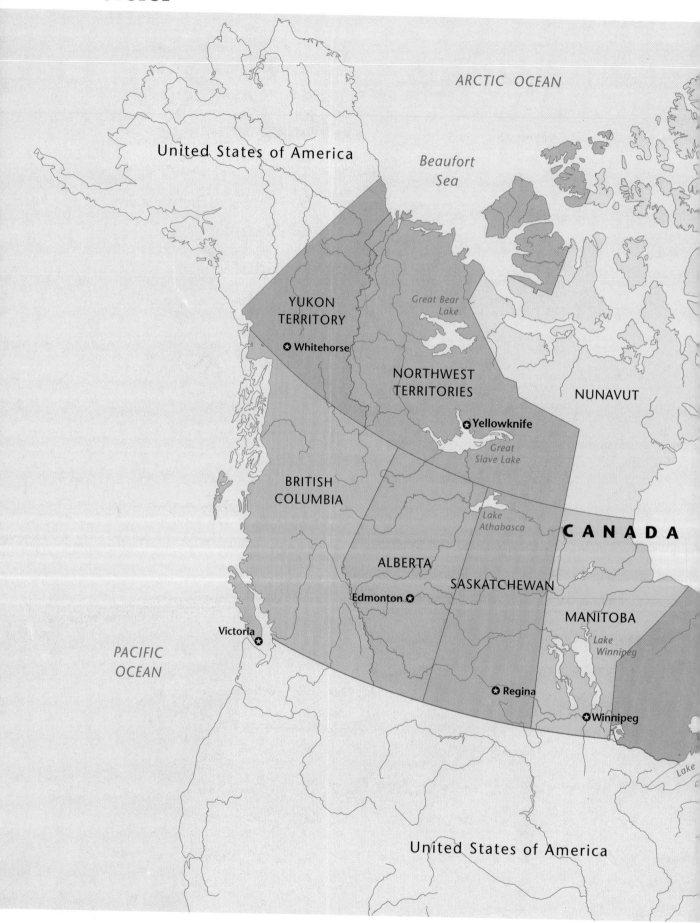

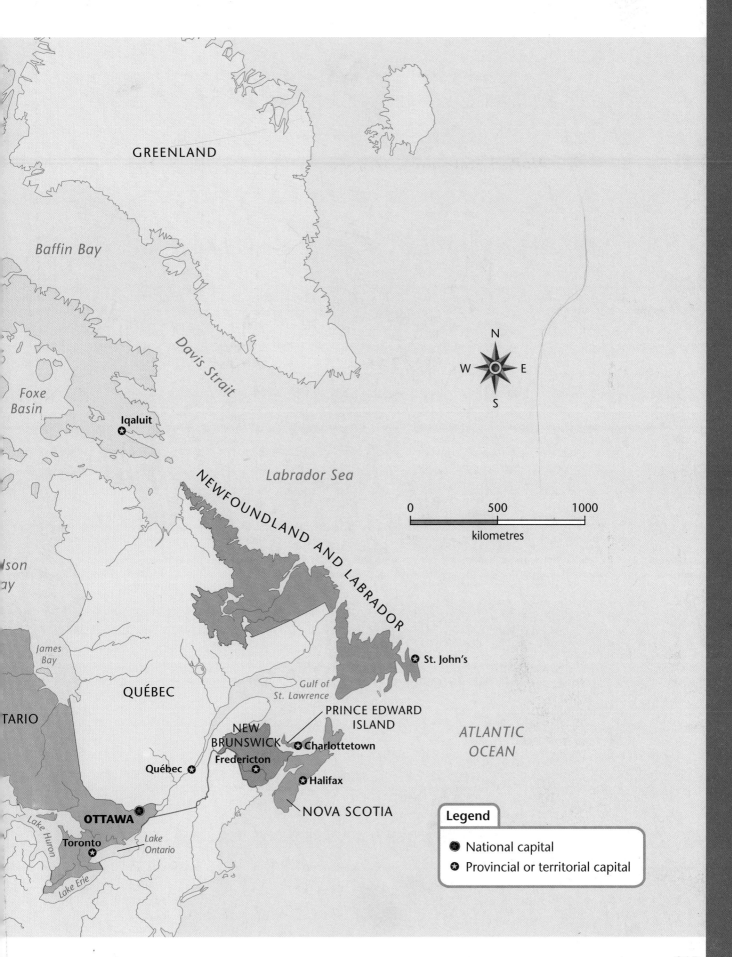

GREENLAND

Baffin Bay

Foxe
Basin

Davis Strait

Iqaluit

Labrador Sea

NEWFOUNDLAND AND LABRADOR

0   500   1000
kilometres

son
ay

James
Bay

QUÉBEC

St. John's

Gulf of
St. Lawrence

PRINCE EDWARD
ISLAND

NEW
BRUNSWICK

TARIO

ATLANTIC
OCEAN

Charlottetown

Fredericton

Québec

Halifax

OTTAWA

NOVA SCOTIA

Toronto

Lake
Ontario

Lake Huron

Lake Erie

Legend

● National capital

✪ Provincial or territorial capital

The World

ARCTIC OCEAN

GREENLAND
(DENMARK)

ICELAND

ALASKA
(USA)

CANADA

NORW

UNITED
KINGDOM

IRELAND

GI

FRANCE

NORTH
ATLANTIC
OCEAN

PORTUGAL   SPAIN

MOROCCO

ALGERIA

UNITED STATES
OF AMERICA

WESTERN
SAHARA

HAWAII
(USA)

CUBA   THE BAHAMAS

MEXICO

MAURITANIA

MALI

PACIFIC
OCEAN

JAMAICA

DOMINICAN
REPUBLIC

BELIZE

HONDURAS

SENEGAL

GAMBIA

GUINEA BISSAU

BURKINA

GUATEMALA

NICARAGUA

EL SALVADOR

GUINEA

SIERRA LEONE

GHANA

COSTA RICA

GUYANA

LIBERIA

BENIN

VENEZUELA

SURINAME

IVORY COAST

TOGO

PANAMA

FRENCH GUIANA

CAMEROON

COLOMBIA

Equator

EQUATORIAL GUINEA

ECUADOR

CONGO

PERU

BRAZIL

BOLIVIA

SOUTH
ATLANTIC
OCEAN

PARAGUAY

URUGUAY

N

ARGENTINA

W   E

CHILE

Falkland Islands
(UNITED KINGDOM)

S

South Georgia Island
(UNITED KINGDOM)

Prime Meridian

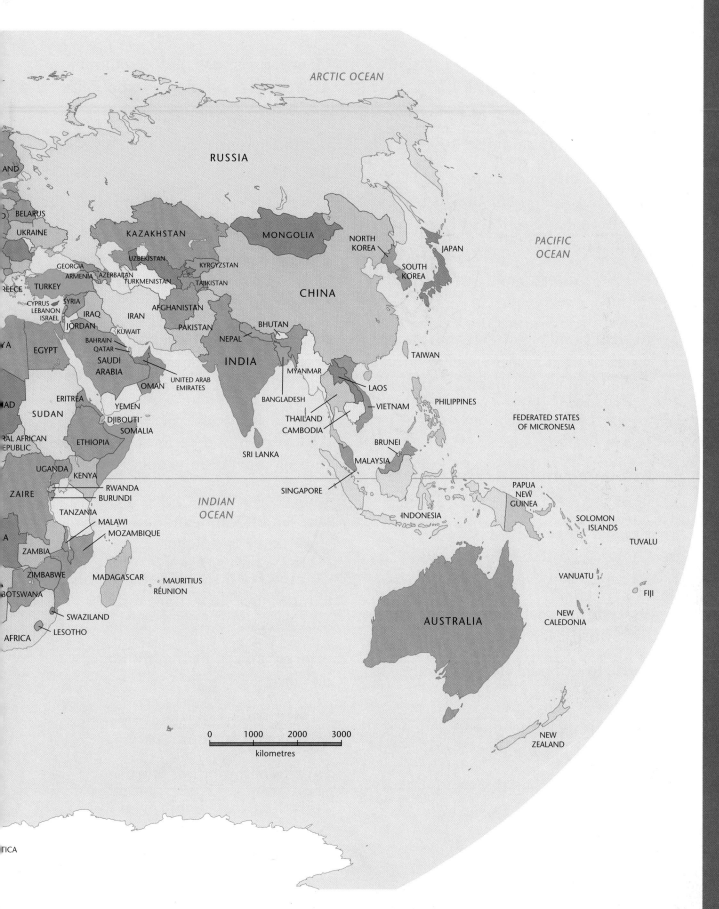

ARCTIC OCEAN

RUSSIA

BELARUS

UKRAINE

KAZAKHSTAN

MONGOLIA

NORTH
KOREA

JAPAN

PACIFIC
OCEAN

UZBEKISTAN

GEORGIA

KYRGYZSTAN

SOUTH
KOREA

ARMENIA AZERBAIJAN

TURKMENISTAN

TAJIKISTAN

GREECE

TURKEY

CHINA

CYPRUS
LEBANON
ISRAEL

SYRIA

IRAQ

IRAN

AFGHANISTAN

JORDAN

KUWAIT

PAKISTAN

BHUTAN

TAIWAN

BAHRAIN
QATAR

NEPAL

EGYPT

SAUDI
ARABIA

MYANMAR

INDIA

OMAN

UNITED ARAB
EMIRATES

BANGLADESH

LAOS

ERITREA

YEMEN

THAILAND

VIETNAM

PHILIPPINES

SUDAN

DJIBOUTI

CAMBODIA

FEDERATED STATES
OF MICRONESIA

SOMALIA

RAL AFRICAN
EPUBLIC

ETHIOPIA

BRUNEI

SRI LANKA

MALAYSIA

UGANDA

KENYA

SINGAPORE

ZAIRE

RWANDA

PAPUA
NEW
GUINEA

BURUNDI

INDIAN
OCEAN

INDONESIA

SOLOMON
ISLANDS

TANZANIA

TUVALU

MALAWI

A

MOZAMBIQUE

ZAMBIA

VANUATU

ZIMBABWE

MADAGASCAR

MAURITIUS

FIJI

BOTSWANA

RÉUNION

NEW
CALEDONIA

SWAZILAND

AUSTRALIA

AFRICA

LESOTHO

0   1000   2000   3000

kilometres

NEW
ZEALAND

TICA

317

Glossary

Aboriginal peoples First Nations, Inuit, and Métis peoples

agriculture the growing of crops and raising of animals

Alberta clipper a fierce, cold wind that starts near the Rocky Mountains and quickly blows out of the province

archeologists people who study buildings and objects from the past

artifacts include items that were made or used by people long ago. Some Aboriginal artifacts are known as historical cultural items.

bison buffalo

bitumen a thick, sticky tar made of oil

British Isles the countries of England, Scotland, Wales, and Ireland together

British the people who come from the British Isles

buffalo Canada's largest land mammal

Canadiens Francophones who were born in Canada

chinook a warm, dry wind that blows down from the Rocky Mountains

climate weather that is common in an area over a long period of time

conservation the careful use of natural resources, so that they will not run out

conserve to use something carefully so it will last longer

cultural heritage the beliefs, customs, knowledge, values, and history shared by a group of people

diverse population a population that is made up of people from many different cultures and backgrounds

drought a long period with far less rain or snow than usual

Elders people respected for their wisdom and understanding of traditional knowledge

electricity a form of energy that can produce heat, light, and movement

energy power, or the ability to do work

environment all the aspects of nature that surround us

fact something that is true

First Nations groups who were the first to live in North America

fort a building or set of buildings surrounded by a strong wall

fossil fuels fuels like oil, gas, and coal that come from the remains of ancient plants and animals

fossils the remains or shapes of ancient plants and animals that have turned into stone

Francophones people whose first and main language is French

Francophonie, la an organization of French-speaking countries around the world

fur trade the exchange of goods for fur between European traders and First Nations people, lasting from about the 1750s to the 1830s

geologists scientists who study land and rocks, and how they are formed

glaciers very thick sheets of ice and snow that move slowly across the land

governor general the representative of the British king or queen in Canada

habitat the place where an animal makes its home in nature

heritage rangelands protected areas that preserve the prairie grasslands

historical cultural items a respectful term used to define artifacts that are still used by Aboriginal people today

homestead the quarter section of land that the government granted to settlers who were willing to live on the land and farm it

homesteaders the people who lived on the homestead

iinisskimm special stones with great spiritual importance

immigrants people who move to a different country to live

immigrate to move to a different country to live

inquiry an investigation into a topic, especially by asking questions

irrigation supplying the land with water, using dams, ditches, and sprinklers

landforms the different features of the land, such as mountains, hills, or plains

landscape the natural scenery of a very large area

legislative assembly leaders who represent the people and make decisions about running a territory or province

logging cutting down trees and taking logs to the mills

lumber wood that has been cut into boards

Métis people descended from British or Canadiens traders and First Nations

missionary someone who travels to teach his or her religion to a group of people

national parks parks managed by the government of Canada to preserve the natural beauty or places of historical importance

natural heritage natural areas, animals, plants, landforms, and landscapes that are important to a country or region because of their beauty or history

natural region an area with its own natural vegetation, climate, and landforms

natural resources things found in nature that are useful to us, including air, water, soil, oil and gas, minerals, forests, and animals

natural vegetation the plants that grow naturally in an area

non-renewable resources resources that cannot be replaced or renewed

nun a member of a religious community of women who spends her life in prayer and service to others

oil sands a mixture of sand, clay, rock, and bitumen

opinion what someone thinks or believes

oral teaching a way of remembering the past through stories and spoken explanation, rather than in writing

paleontologists scientists who study fossils to learn about very old forms of life

parks areas of land where people can enjoy protected landscapes, plants, and wildlife

pemmican buffalo meat that has been dried, pounded, and mixed with hot buffalo grease and dried berries

perspective the point of view of a group of people; a way of seeing and understanding the world

population the number of people who live in an area

portage to carry a canoe and supplies over the land

protected areas areas of land governments have set aside to protect special features such as plants, animals, and landforms

provincial parks parks managed by provincial governments to preserve places of natural or historical importance

quality of life a person's or a community's sense of safety, comfort, security, health, and happiness

renewable resources resources that can be replaced, if they are used carefully

roots deep connections to a place where we belong

scrip a coupon that can be exchanged for land or money

seam of coal a long layer of coal below the Earth's surface

sustainable resource a resource that is used only as much as it can be replaced, so that it lasts for the future

technology any of the tools or ways of doing things that people use to get tasks done or to make their lives easier

tourism travelling and touring to see and enjoy places away from home

travois a frame, pulled by a horse or a dog, used for moving a teepee and for carrying belongings

treaty an agreement between two nations

urban areas towns and cities

voyageur a person who travelled by canoe, working for fur-trading companies

weather conditions such as temperature, rain, and sunshine on a single day

wetlands areas covered by water, including ponds, sloughs, and marshy areas, that provide a habitat for wildlife

wilderness areas large protected areas with strict limits on how the land is used; vehicles and many recreational activities are not allowed

wildland provincial parks large protected areas in a province where little development takes place; some activities like hiking and camping are allowed

Index

Credits

The publisher would like to thank the following people and institutions for permission to use their © materials. Every reasonable effort has been made to find copyright holders of the material in this text. The publisher would be pleased to know of any errors or omissions.

PHOTO CREDITS

CP:	Canadian Press Photo
LAC:	Library and Archives Canada
bg/i:	background/inset
t/c/b/l/r:	top/centre/bottom/left/right

Cover t Thomas Kitchin & Victoria Hurst/Firstlight; **c** Firstlight (boy), Daniel Bosler/Getty (bus), **b** Larry Macdougal/Firstlight; **1** Daryl Benson/Masterfile; **2** Alberta 2005 Centennial Initiative; **3 t** Gunter Marx Photography/CORBIS; **3 b (also on 5 tl, 18 b, 89, 147 t, 169 r, 180 l, 204, 217 t, 241 tr, 279 t)** FogStock LLC/Index Stock; **4 t (also on 19 b, 33 t, 52 t, 106, 141 t, 146 t, 167 t, 179 b, 215 t, 278 t)** Mel Curtis/Photodisc/Getty; **6 c (also on 17 c, 20 b, 58 t, 170 t, 194 t, 263 b)** Jerome Tisne/Getty; **6 b (also on 21 b, 37, 49 r, 130 t, 153 b, 230 l, 256)** CORBIS; **5 tc (also on 6, 47 b, 86 t, 112 t, 162 t, 221 tr, 291 t)** PhotoObjects.net; **5 tr (also on 7, 9, 10 l, r, 11 t, b, 22 b, 32, 99, 109 t, 165, 207 b, 272 tl)** Ray Boudreau; **5 cl (also on 17 r, 62 l, 75 t, 97 b, 124 t, 143 t, 156 t, 210 t, 276 t, 290 t)** Rob Lewine/zefa/CORBIS; **5 cr (also on 17 l, 76 cl, 94, 123 b, 175 r, 244, 268 tl)** Bananastock/Firstlight; **5 bl (also on 23 b, 42, 61 t, 67, 127 t, 198 b, 252, 257 t, 266 t, 286)** MF; **5 bc (also on 24 l, 69 t, 173 t, 188 tl, 237 b, 270 t)** Simon Watson/Stone/Getty; **11 c** Wolfgang Kaehler/CORBIS; **14 t** CORBIS; **bl** Larry Fisher/Masterfile; **br** Daryl Benson/Masterfile; **16** Gary Herbert; **18 bg** Government of Alberta; **il** AirPhoto/Jim Wark; **ir** Winston Fraser/Alamy; **19 bg** Darwin Wiggett/Firstlight; **it** J. A. Kraulis/Masterfile; **ic** Robert Holmberg and Bio-DiTRL, http://bio-ditrl.sunsite.ualberta.ca/; **20 bg** Troy and Mary Parlee/Alamy; **it** Town of Whitecourt; **ib** Raymond Gehman/CORBIS; **21 bg** Daryl Benson/Masterfile; **it** Alex Pytlowany/Masterfile; **ib** Alberto Biscaro/Masterfile; **22 bg** Paul A. Souders/CORBIS; **it** Gunter Marx Photography/CORBIS; **ic** Darwin Wiggett/Firstlight; **23 bg, it** Daryl Benson/Masterfile; **ic** Darrell Lecorre/Masterfile; **24** Troy and Mary Parlee/Alamy; **25** Stuart Petzinger; **26** Phil Schermeister/CORBIS; **27 l** Glenbow Archives, ND-3-2051a; **r** Darwin Wiggett/Firstlight; **28 t** David Nunuk/Firstlight; **c** Raymond Gehman/CORBIS; **b** Wally Bauman/Alamy; **29 head (also on 60, 71, 116, 131, 172, 190, 222, 249, 271)** Art Wolfe/Getty; **r** Phil Schermeister/CORBIS; **b** Rubberball/JupiterImages; **31 t** Government of Alberta; **(2nd)** Greg Stott/Masterfile; **(3rd)** Darwin Wiggett/Firstlight; **(4th)** Paul A. Souders/CORBIS; **(5th)** Daryl Benson/Masterfile; **b** Alan Sirulnikoff/Firstlight; **33 c** franzfoto.com/Alamy; **b** Darrell Gulin/CORBIS; **34 tl** Shirley Bray, Courtesy of Alberta Wilderness Association; **b** CP/Jeff McIntosh; **34–35c** Tony Krygier, Epyx Mountainboards Inc.; **35 tr** Ariel Skelley/CORBIS; **row 2** Nancy Brown/Photographer's Choice/Getty; **(row 3 l)** Lawrence Migdale/www.migdale.com; **(row 3 r)** Bananastock/JupiterImages; **bl** Ron Chapple/Taxi/Getty; **38** Larry Macdougal/Firstlight; **39** Paul A. Souders/CORBIS; **40 t** CP/Darryl Dyck; **c** Miles Ertman/Masterfile; **b** Air Mikisew/www.airmikisew.com; **41 t** CP/Ray Giguere; **b** CP/Olivier Asselin; **43 t** CP/Tim Smith; **(2nd)** Noel Hendrickson/Masterfile; **(3rd)** Bill Brooks/Alamy; **b** Kenneth Meisner/

Alamy; **46** CP/Jeff McIntosh; **47 t** CP/Jeff McIntosh; **48 tl** Paleobotanical Collection, Department of Biological Sciences, University of Alberta; **tr** Francois Gohier/Photo Researchers, Inc.; **bl** Super Stock/MaXx Images; **br** Larry Macdougal/Firstlight; **49 b** "Dawn at the Rookery," Mark Hallett Paleoart; **50 t** CP/Phill Snel; **b** CP/Richard T. Nowitz; **52 b** David McIntyre; **53 tl** Michael S. Yamashita/CORBIS; **tr** Kevin Schafer/CORBIS; **cl** Scenics & Science/Alamy; **cr** John T. Fowler/Alamy; **bl** Lawrence Lawry/Photo Researchers, Inc.; **br** Louie Psihoyos/CORBIS; **54c** Royal Ontario Museum; **l** Buddy Mays/CORBIS; **55 b** Glenbow Archives NA-937-10; **56** Mike Drew/Canadian Press; **57 l, c, r** Korite International www.korite.com; **58 b** CP/David Rossiter; **59 t** Paul A. Souders/CORBIS; **b** Darwin Wiggett/Firstlight; **60 t** Yellow Dog Productions/Getty; **c** Dave G. Houser/Post-Houserstock/CORBIS; **b** David McIntyre; **61 b** Gunter Marx Photography/CORBIS; **62 b** Alberta Energy and Utilities Board/Alberta Geological Survey; **66** CP; **292 tr** CP; **68** Glenbow Archives NA-5470-3; **69 b** Daryl Benson/Masterfile; **70** Sarah Leen/National Geographic/Getty; **71 t** Stockdisc Classic/Getty; **cl, br** Greg Halinda, Oil Sands Discovery Centre, www.oilsandsdiscovery.com; **bl** Andrew Hempstead; **72 t, b** Wally Bauman/Alamy; **73 l** Ian Jackson/EPIC Photography; **r** Syncrude Canada Ltd.; **74 t** Dave Pattinson/Alamy; **b** Mach 2 Stock Photography Ltd/Ron Kelly; **75b** Don Smetzer/Stone/Getty; **76 r** CP/Jeff McIntosh; **b** Digital Vision/Getty; **77 t** CP/*Lethbridge Herald*/David Rossiter; **78** Clarence Norris/Lone Pine Photos; **79** CP/Mike Stur; **80** Roy Ooms/Masterfile; **81 t** Izzy Schwartz/Photodisc/Getty; **r** Peter Beck/CORBIS; **82** Blood Tribe Agricultural Project; **84** Dave Schiefelbein/Photographer's Choice/Getty; **85** Mach 2 Stock Photography Ltd./Ron Kelly; **86 b** Ivy Images; **87 l** Ivy Images; **c** Alberta Sustainable Resource Development; **r** Government of Alberta; **90 t** City of Medicine Hat; **c** City of Red Deer; **b** Town of Bonnyville, Nathaniel Ostashewski, Osta Productions; **91 t** Troy and Mary Parlee/Alamy; **b** Lara Solt/Dallas Morning News/CORBIS; **96** Robert Postma/Firstlight; **97 t** Norm Sacuta; **100 bg** David Hosking/A.G.E. Foto Stock/Firstlight; **it** Greg Stott/Masterfile; **ib** Daryl Benson/Masterfile; **101** Glenbow Archives NA-1700-141; **104 t** CP/Ian Martens; **b** Glenbow Archives NA-250-2; **105 b** LAC C-114467; **107 t** Mike Anich/A.G.E. Foto Stock/Firstlight; **bl** Glenbow Archives NA-2770-4; **br** Fort McKay; **109 b** © "Morning Star," Janvier Gallery, www.alexjanvier.com; **110 tl** Robert McGouey/Alamy; **tr** Mark Tomalty/Masterfile; **bl** Daryl Benson/Masterfile; **br** Robert McGouey/RBMImages; **111** Norm Sacuta; **112 b** Norm Sacuta and Canadian Native Friendship Centre; **113 t** Royal Alberta Museum; **b** AF 1397 Storyrobe drawn by Percy Creighton, mid 20th century, Kainai L: 65.94 in x W: 62.99 in.: bison hide and oil paint, Collection of Glenbow Archives, Calgary, Canada; **114** Royal Alberta Museum; **115** Lorraine Good Striker; **116 r** Larry Macdougal/Firstlight; **b** Stock Connection Blue/Alamy; **118 t** AP 2642, saddle, Cree, early 20th century, commercial leather, glass beads, wool fringe, metal rings, Collection of Glenbow Archives, Calgary, Canada; **b** Glenbow Museum; **119 t** Glenbow Museum; **b** Royal Alberta Museum; **122** Glenbow Archives NA-3694-1; **123 t** J.A. Kraulis/Masterfile; **124 c** Canada Post Corporation (1851); **126** LAC, C-002773; **127 b** LAC, C-002774; **128 l** Private Collection/Archives Charmet/The Bridgeman Art Library; **r** Mary Evans Picture Library/Alamy; **129** Copyright & Trademarks of Hudson's Bay Company; **130 b** Royal Alberta Museum, Archaeological Survey of Alberta, Manuscript Series No. 6, 1985; **131 bl** Parks Canada/K. Dahlin/2004; **br** Darrell Lecorre/Alamy; **134** Glenbow Archives NA-3473-1; **135**

Glenbow Archives NA-973-7; **136** Glenbow Archives PA-377-20; **137** Glenbow Archives NA-879-5; **138** Manitoba Archives; **140 t** Northern News Services; **b** CP/David Bloom; **141 b** Glenbow Archives NA-2294-29; **142 r** Jason Kasumovic, www.photoalberta.ca; **143 b** CP; **144 b** Glenbow Archives NA-3981-11; **145 t, (2), (3), b** Jason Kasumovic, www.photoalberta.ca; **146** Glenbow Archives NA-51-2; **147 b** OB.205 Missionary Oblates, Grandin Collection (Provincial Archives of Alberta); **148** Jeffry W. Myers/CORBIS; **152** Glenbow Archives NA-967-11; **153 t** Daryl Benson/Masterfile; **155 l** Glenbow Archives NA-456-3; **r** Gunter Marx Photography/CORBIS; **156 c** Glenbow Archives NA-1365-5; **157** Glenbow Archives NA-3876-74; **158 t, b** Glenbow Archives NA-550-11; **c** James A. Janke; **159 l** Glenbow Archives NA-2206-1; **r** Robert Fried/Alamy; **160** Sandra Crazy Bull, Museum Interpreter, First Nations; **162 b** CP; **163** Glenbow Archives ND-8-390; **164 t** LAC C-144184; **b** Glenbow Archives NA-949-16; **166 l** Glenbow Archives M-1837-22a; **r** Glenbow Archives NA-1296-4; **167 b** Glenbow Archives NA-949-29; **168** George Littlechild; **169 l** CP/Phill Snell; **170 b** Glenbow Archives NA-2627-2; **171 t** Glenbow Archives NA-387-27; **b** William James Topley/ LAC C-004670; **172 l** Bob Daemmrich/Photo Edit; **r** Alberta Central Railway; **173 b** Glenbow Archives NA-695-5; **174** Glenbow Archives NA-3697-1; **175 b** Studio Six Photography Ltd., Lloydminster, SK; **178** Ukrainian Cultural Heritage Village; **179 t** LOOK Die Bildagentur der Fotografen GmbH/Alamy; **180 r** Glenbow Archives NA-125-2; **181** Glenbow Archives NA-2497-18; **182** LAC C-085854; **183** Glenbow Archives NA-649-14; **184 l** Glenbow Archives NA-1709-26; **r** Glenbow Archives NA-544-143; **185** LAC PA-066530; **186** Glenbow Archives NA-4210-1; **187 t** Glenbow Archives NA-949-97; **b** J. A. Kraulis/Masterfile; **188 c** Glenbow Archives NC-37-43; **b** Glenbow Archives NA-1334-2; **189** Glenbow Archives NC-5-6; **190 t** Photodisc/Firstlight; **b** CP/Preston Brownschlaigle; **191 t** Glenbow Archives NA-3903-79; **b** Glenbow Archives NA-474-4; **192 t** Glenbow Archives NC-43-173; **b** Glenbow Archives NC-54-4198; **193 t** Glenbow Archives NA-1406-29; **r** Millet and District Archives, Image MDHS190.01.99, Millet 1911; **194 c** Glenbow Archives NA-334-9; **b** Glenbow Archives NA-4334-23; **195 t** Brian Sytnyk/Masterfile; **c** Glenbow Archives ND-8-190; **b** Glenbow Archives NA-2835-9; **196** CP/Jeff McIntosh; **197 r** CP/Larry MacDougal; **l** CP/Marianne Helm; **198 t** Daryl Benson/Masterfile; **199 t** The Descendants of Louis Chevigny De La Chevrotière and Josephine Arcand. Emilie and George Chevigny, Plamondon, AB; **b** Provincial Archives of Alberta B4153; **200** School Board Photographer; **201** CP/Robert Taylor; **206** CP; **207 t** David Tanaka; **208** Glenbow Archives NA-1088-11; **209 t** Glenbow Archives NA-5339-19; **b** Tom MacDougall/ Stettler Independent; **210 b** Legal Archives Society of Alberta/LASA 47-G-11; **212** Provincial Archives of Alberta A6277; **213 t** Provincial Archives of Alberta PA3670; **b** Gregory Horne; **214 l** Provincial Archives of Alberta B3394; **r** Paul A. Souders/CORBIS; **215 c** Glenbow Archives NA-4429; **216 t** Glenbow Archives NA-1114-1; **b** CP/Larry MacDougal; **217 cl** Glenbow Archives NC-6-231; **cr** Andrew Hempstead; **b** City of Edmonton Archives EA-10-294; **219 t** Glenbow Archives NA-559-27; **b** Missionary Oblates, Grandin Archives at the Provincial Archives of Alberta OB1659; **220 l** Galt Museum and Archives P19800040000-GP; **r** Glenbow Archives NA-1840-4; **221 r** Glenbow Archives NA-2197-1; **l** Glenbow Archives NC-32-3; **222 t** Philip Nealey/Photodisc/Getty; **bl** Darby Sawchuk/Alamy; **br** Atlas Coal Mine National Historic Site, Coulee, AB www.atlascoalmine.ab.ca; **223** Glenbow Archives NA-2051-4; **224 t** Frank Greenaway, Dorling Kindersley; **b** Glenbow Archives NA-1308-20; **225** Richard A. Stein; **226 t** William James Topley/LAC PA-009739; **b** CSTMC/CN Collection CN000446; **227 t** Archives of Ontario F-1075-9-0-11; **c** LAC PA-117736; **b** South Peace Regional Archives/Isabel M. Campbell fonds/1998.27.425; **228 t** Glenbow Archives NA-5671-4a; **b** The City of Calgary, Corporate Records, Archives, CalA OCO #55-18LF57-12#32; **229 t** Town of Falher; **c** Joseph Plamondon, 1910. Emilie and George Chevigny, Plamondon, AB; **bl** Provincial Archives of Alberta A6669; **br** Provincial Archives of Alberta A6503; **230 r** Mrs. Theresa C. Wildcat, Hobbema, AB; **231 r** Office of Public Affairs, Government of Alberta; **b** Andrews-Newton Photographers Ltd. #84-0169/102; **232** EPCOR; **236** Alec Pytlowany/Masterfile; **237 t** Randy Lincks/Masterfile; **238 tl** SuperStock/MaXx Images; **tr** Raymond Gehman/National Geographic Image Collection; **bl** Royal Alberta Museum; **br** Rick Rudnicki/Lonely Planet; **239** J.A. Kraulis/Masterfile; **240** Willy Mmatheisl/Alamy; **241 cl, bl** Darrell Gulin/CORBIS; **cr** Raymond Gehman/CORBIS; **br** Paul Souders/CORBIS; **242 t, b** Parks & Protected Areas, Alberta Community Development; **243** Lloyd Sutton/Masterfile; **245 tl** Raymond Gehman/ CORBIS; **tr, cl** Daryl Benson/Masterfile; **cr** D. Wiggett/ Firstlight; **b** Ron Watts/CORBIS; **246 tl, cl** Raymond Gehman/CORBIS; **cr** Daryl Benson/Masterfile; **247 tl** Ron Watts/Firstlight; **tr** D. Wiggett/Firstlight; **b** Raymond Gehman/CORBIS; **248 tl** Roy Ooms/Masterfile; **tr** Raymond Gehman/CORBIS; **bl** Alec Pytlowany/Masterfile; **br** Larry Fisher/Masterfile; **249 t** imagesource/Firstlight; **b** Rick Rudnicki/Lonely Planet; **250 t** D. Wiggett/Firstlight; **c** Gordon Fisher/MaXx Images; **b** John Foster/Masterfile; **251 l** Ron Watts/Firstlight; **c** Janice Smith; **r** Tim Fitzharris/Masterfile; **253 t** Daryl Benson/Masterfile; **b** Jerzyworks/Masterfile; **254 t** Daryl Benson/Masterfile; **b** CP/Jeff McIntosh; **255 t** Gunter Marx Photography/CORBIS; **c** Gail Mooney/Masterfile; **b** Ron Watts/Firstlight; **257 b** Gloria H. Chomica/Masterfile; **258 r** Ron Watts/Firstlight; **262** Dynamic Graphics Group/i2i/Alamy; **263 t** Calgary Board of Education; **264 l** Lawrence Migdale/Firstlight; **r** Photodisc/Getty; **265 b** Dynamic Graphics Group/IT Stock Free/Alamy; **c** CORBIS; **b** Photodisc/Getty; **266 c** CP/Edmonton Sun/Preston Brownschlaigle; **b** ACFA/Association canadienne-française de l'Alberta; **267 t** Douglas Williams/Firstlight; **c** Daryl Benson/Masterfile; **bl** Richard Cummins/Lonely Planet; **br** Jeannie Charrois, Syzygy Research and Technology; **268 cl** Aboriginal Multi-Media Society (AMMSA); **cr** Provincial Archives of Alberta A3555; **b** Alberta Order of Excellence; **269 t** Old Man River Community Centre. Reg Crow Shoe; **c** Léo Piquette, Plamondon, AB; **bl** Glenbow Archives NA-3521-1; **br** Shimbashi Family; **270** Royal Alberta Museum; **271 t** Augustus Butera/Stone/Getty; **c** Bar U Ranch; **b** Darby Sawchuk/Alamy; **272 cl** Morgan Baillargeon/Canadian Museum of Civilization K94-1254; **r** Ron Fraess, Superintendent of Public Works Town of Elk Point; **bl** Paul Pivert/ South Peace Regional Archives; **273 t** Andrew Hempstead; **c** Stephansson House, Alberta Community Development; **b** Guy Lamoureux, Andrew, AB; **274 t** Michael T. Sedam/CORBIS; **b** CP/Larry MacDougal; **275** Jennifer George, Galileo Educational Network, University of Calgary; **276 t** © Jim Cupido; **b** © Nona Foster, Saamis Tepee Association and the City of Medicine Hat; **277 t** © 2006 Yalenka Enterprises Inc.; **b** © 2006 Peter Etril Snyder Gallery; **278 b** Murale "Co-op"/"Co-op" Mural, 1999. Artiste/artist: Rémi Genest. ACFA Centralta; **279 c** CP/Lethbridge Herald/Ian Martens; **281** Dr. E.W. Coffin Elementary School; **282** Andreanna Seymore/ Stone/Getty; **288 t** J. A. Kraulis/Masterfile; **bl** Design Pics; **br** Daryl Benson/Masterfile; **289 tl** Ron Stroud/Masterfile; **tr** CP/Winnipeg Free Press/Joe Bryksa; **cr** CORBIS; **b** Stockdisc Premium/Getty; **290 b** Roth & Ramberg Photography Inc., Edmonton, AB; **291 b** Lori Adamski Peek/Stone/Getty; **292 tl** Gary Herbert 2005; **tc** CP/Jeff McIntosh; **tr** CP; **bl** Robert Postma/Firstlight; **b2** Glenbow Archives NA-3694-1; **b3** Glenbow Archives NA-967-11; **br** Ukrainian Cultural Heritage Village; **293 t** CP; **r** Alec Pytlowany/Masterfile; **b** Calgary Board of Education; **307** Alberto Biscaro/Masterfile; **308** Royal

Alberta Museum; **309** J.A. Kraulis/Masterfile; **310 t** Corey Hochachka/MaXxImages; **c** Government of Alberta; **bl** Wolfgang Kaehler/CORBIS; **bc** Jeff Vanuga/CORBIS; **br** Lorne Fitch, Prairie Conservation Forum; **311 tl** blickwinkel/Alamy; **tr** Richard Herrmann/Getty; **c** David McIntyre.

LITERARY CREDITS

1 Sharon Stewart; **25** Glenbow Museum; **25** Pat Shultz; **26** Laura Hohn; **37** Darrell Willier; **46** Wendy Sloboda; **58** Blood Tribe Administration; **68** Linda Goyette, *Kidmonton: True Stories of River City Kids*, Edmonton Public Library/Brindle and Glass, 2004, pp. 74-75; **77** Nicole Mills; **78** Canadian Education Association and Gina Lorinda Yagos, Lee Lake, AB; **80–81** Tammy Marks, Elisabeth's mother, Hanna, AB; **82** Campbell Eagle Child; **87** Rita Loonskin; **96** Marge Friedel; **101** Chief John Snow, *These Mountains Are Our Sacred Places: The Story of the Stoney People*, with a new epilogue by Dr. Snow and intro by Ian Getty. (1977). Reprinted in 2005 by Fifth House Publishing; **102** Sandra Crazy Bull; **103** Lorraine Good Striker; **104** Frank Weasel Head; **106** Billy Joe Laboucan; **107** Myrtle Calahaisn; **108** Roy Fabian, Hay River, Northwest Territories, *Report of the Royal Commission on Aboriginal Peoples*; **110** Michael Merrier; **111** Members of the Golden Elders' Beading Circle; **112** Myrtle Calahaisn; **113** Dr. James Dempsey; **115** Lorraine Good Striker; **118** Gerry Conaty; **119** Frank Weasel Head; **135** Sharon Morin, Michif Institute; **136** Historical Society of Alberta; **139** Composed by Don Freed, © Scratchatune Publishing, SOCAN, www.donfreed.com; **140** Mark McCallum, Fort McMurray, AB; **143** James G. MacGregor, *Father Lacombe*. Edmonton: Hurtig Publishers, 1975, p. 112; **147** Emilie Chevigny; **147** Laura Vinson; **155** Dianne Meili, *Those Who Know, Profiles of Alberta's Native Elders*, NeWest Publishers, 310-10359-82 Ave, Edmonton T6E 1Z9; p. 191; **159** Alexander Morris (1826-1889), *The Treaties of Canada with the Indians of Manitoba and the North-West Territories* (Belfords, Clarke, Toronto: 1880) October 20, 1876; **160, 163, 164** Sandra Crazy Bull; **166** Saskatchewan Archives Board, Regina, Clippings file *Indians of North America—Biography of Chiefs, from Indians of the West*, by Father Hugnard, pg. 3; **169** Adapted from Caitlin Crawshaw, "Linguistics student helps preserve aboriginal language," *ExpressNews*, June 24, 2004; **170** Morley Roberts, *The Western Avenues or Toil and Travel in Further North America*. London: Smith, Elder & Co., 1887, p. 88; **173** Francophone Voices in

Alberta, Glenbow-Alberta Institute, St. Ann Ranch Trading Company fonds, M 8769-1; **178** Peter Svarish, *Memoirs 1877–1904*, tr. Wm. Kostash. Ukrainian Pioneers' Association of Alberta and Huculak Chair for Ukrainian Culture and Ethnographer. Edmonton, 1999; **184** *Of Us and the Oxen* by Sarah Ellen Roberts, Modern Press, 1968, p. 12; **185, 187** Adapted from: *Polish Settlers in Alberta: Reminiscences and Biographies*. Ed. Joanne Matejko. Printed by Polish Alliance Press Ltd., Toronto, 1979, and p. 33; **188** Quoted in Helen Evans Reid, *All Silent All Damned: The Search for Isaac Barr* (Toronto: Ryerson Press, 1969), p. 85; **189** Adapted from *Indian Tribes of Alberta*, Hugh A. Dempsey (Calgary, AB: Glenbow Museum, 1979), p. 19; **189** Dianne Meili, *Those Who Know, Profiles of Alberta's Native Elders*, NeWest Publishers, 310-10359-82 Ave, Edmonton T6E 1Z9; p. 29; **192** Margaret Rasmussen; **192** White Pine Pictures; **193** G.A. Cooper; **193** Richard A. Stein; **193** *Of Us and the Oxen* by Sarah Ellen Roberts, Modern Press, 1968, p. 29; **193** Bill McNeil, *Voice of the Pioneer*, Volume Two, Macmillan of Canada, 1984, p. 62; **198** Adapted from "Eagle Valley School—100 years in 2005," Marie Sihlis; **200** Jeannine de Moissac; **201** Shelley Jackson; **201** Marge Friedel; **209** Letters of Marcel Durieux, 1908. *Ordinary Heroes: The Journal of a French Pioneer in Alberta*, Edmonton: U of Alberta Press, 1980, p. 93; **214** *Alberta: 100 Years a Home—the People, Issues and Events That Built a Province*, Ch. 2, quoted from the *Calgary Herald*, September 2, 1905; **215** The Blackfoot Gallery Committee, *Nitsitapiisinni: The Story of the Blackfoot People*, Key Porter Books, pp. 72–73, © 2001 Glenbow Museum; **216** Bill McNeil. *Voice of the Pioneer*, Volume 2. Macmillan of Canada, p. 129; **220** Eileen Skinner; **223** *Ten Lost Years 1929–1939: Memories of Canadians Who Survived the Depression*, Barry Broadfoot, Doubleday Canada 1997, p. 42; **225** Richard A. Stein; **230** *kwayask ê-kî-pê-kiskinowâpahtihicik/Their Example Showed Me the Way: A Cree Woman's Life Shaped by Two Cultures*. Told by Emma Minde. Ed., tr., glossary by F. Ahenakew & H.C. Wolfart. Edmonton, University of Alberta Press, 1997, pg. 19; **231** From *Alberta: A State of Mind*, edited by Sydney Sharpe, Roger Gibbins, James H. Marsh, and Heather Bala Edwards. Key Porter Books © 2005, p. 84, Colleen Klein; **239** R.V. Rasmussen, http://raysweb.net; **241** The Honourable Dr. Lois E. Hole, CM, AOE, 2003; **257** Derek Tilson, Waterton Lakes National Park; **281** Dr. W.E. Coffin Elementary School; **288–289** ℗ © 2004 Mary Kieftenbeld/SOCAN. All rights reserved. Used with permission. www.marykief.com